EXPLAINING HUMAN ORIGINS
MYTH, IMAGINATION AND CONJECTURE

In this revised version of the French original, Wiktor Stoczkowski, an anthropologist, argues that the theories of human origins developed by naturalists, archaeologists and physical anthropologists from the early nineteenth century to the present day are structurally similar to modern popular theories, and to the speculations of earlier philosophers. Reviewing a remarkable range of thinkers writing in a variety of European languages, he makes a convincing argument for this case. Even though the book highlights the paucity of development in scientific explanations of human origins, it ends with an optimistic conclusion about the power of the scientific approach to deliver more reliable theories – but only if it is conscious of the baggage it carries over from popular discourse.

WIKTOR STOCZKOWSKI trained as a prehistoric archaeologist and ethnologist, and, later, as a historian of science. He is lecturer in anthropology at the Ecole des Hautes Etudes en Sciences Sociales (EHESS) in Paris, director of Groupe de Recherches sur les Savoirs and research member of Laboratoire d'Anthropologie Sociale. His publications include *Anthropologie naïve, anthropologie savante* (1994), *Aux origines de l'humanité: anthologie* (1996), *Des hommes, des dieux et des extraterrestres* (1999) and numerous articles.

EXPLAINING HUMAN ORIGINS

Myth, Imagination and Conjecture

WIKTOR STOCZKOWSKI

Translated by Mary Turton

PUBLISHED BY THE PRESS SYNDICATE OF THE UNIVERSITY OF CAMBRIDGE
The Pitt Building, Trumpington Street, Cambridge, United Kingdom

CAMBRIDGE UNIVERSITY PRESS
The Edinburgh Building, Cambridge CB2 2RU, UK
40 West 20th Street, New York, NY 10011-4211, USA
477 Williamstown Road, Port Melbourne, VIC 3207, Australia
Ruiz de Alarcón 13, 28014 Madrid, Spain
Dock House, The Waterfront, Cape Town 8001, South Africa

http://www.cambridge.org

Originally published in French as *Anthropologie naïve, anthropologie savante* by CNRS Editions and © 1994 by CNRS Editions. First published in English in 2002 by Cambridge University Press as *Explaining Human Origins: Myth, Imagination and Conjecture*. English translation © Cambridge University Press 2002.

This book is in copyright. Subject to statutory exception and to the provisions of relevant collective licensing agreements, no reproduction of any part may take place without the written permission of Cambridge University Press.

First published 2002

Printed in the United Kingdom at the University Press, Cambridge

Typeface Baskerville Monotype 11/12.5 pt.   *System* LATEX 2$_\varepsilon$ [TB]

A catalogue record for this book is available from the British Library.

Library of Congress Cataloguing in Publication data
Stoczkowski, Wiktor.
[Anthropologie naïve, anthropologie savante. English]
Explaining human origins: myth, imagination, and conjecture / by Wiktor Stoczkowski; translated by Mary Turton.
p.   cm.
Includes bibliographical references and index.
ISBN 0 521 65134 4 – ISBN 0 521 65730 X (pbk.)
1. Human beings–origin.   2. Anthropology, prehistoric.   3. Anthropology–philosophy.
GN281 .S85813   2001
599.93′8 – dc21   2001035900

ISBN 0 521 65134 4 hardback
ISBN 0 521 65730 X paperback

Contents

List of tables		*page* vii
Acknowledgements		ix
Introduction: in which the author briefly explains his aims		1
1	Prehistory and the conditioned imagination	3
2	Anthropogenesis and science	29
3	In search of causes	68
4	Evolutionary mechanisms: the constraints of nature or of imagination?	131
5	A double game	168
Bibliography		199
Index		225

Tables

1	Attributes of primitive hunter-gatherers and of industrial civilisation	page 24
2	The hominisation scenarios analysed	33
3	The distinctive characteristics either of humans in general, or of primitive humanity in particular, as described in our sample of hominisation scenarios	36
4	Different representations of the natural environment of the early hominids in the hominisation scenarios	56
5	First mentions of the 'causal' relations most frequent in our sample of the scenarios of hominisation	124
6	The first mentions in European literature of distinctive characteristics either of humans in general, or of primitive humanity in particular	125
7	Explanatory sequences extracted from our sample of hominisation scenarios and classified according to the mechanism of evolutionary change they presuppose	133

Acknowledgements

This book owes much to Jean-Claude Gardin: over the years his aid and indulgence have made my research possible. My gratitude goes also to those whose assistance has been precious to me: Catherine Perlès, Yves Coppens, Jacques Perriault, Henri-Paul Francfort, Jean Chavaillon, Arnold Lebeuf. Tim Murray, Suzan Murray and Nathan Schlanger kindly agreed to read through the manuscript and help to improve its final version.

The research presented here has been carried out with the financial assistance of the Foundation Fyssen and the Foundation Singer-Polignac.

Introduction: in which the author briefly explains his aims

> On a coutume de s'étonner que l'esprit humain soit si infini dans ses combinaisons et ses portées; j'avouerais bien bas que je m'étonne qu'il le soit si peu.
>
> C. A. Sainte-Beuve, *Portraits littéraires*[1]

Custom requires famous scholars to be depicted alongside their preferred instruments of observation: Copernicus with an astrolabe in his hand, Galileo looking through a telescope, Pasteur bending intently over a microscope. In the common-sense imaginary, the scientist is first and foremost an observer of the world, and all his knowledge can proceed only from observation.

The history and sociology of science have importantly rectified this naïve picture, by demonstrating that scientific thought is subject not only to the force of the empirical[2] but also, and sometimes even more so, to social constraints. However, are empirical and social elements sufficient to explain the content of scientific theories? Can scholarly knowledge be reduced to the results of a more or less complicated interplay between 'facts' and various 'social' factors, such as fashionable theories, paradigms, ideologies and power relations within the scientific community? It seems the answer must be negative, for although the empirical and the social may explain why the scientist favours a particular conception to the detriment of some other, this does not tell us how the ideas, whether accepted or rejected, are formed, and why they are as they are. Imagination is the true source of scientific theories.

But what kind of imagination? One deemed appropriate for modern art: free, indomitable, allied to pure fantasy? Or one described by Emile Zola: disciplined, exploring the territory conquered by science,

---

[1] Sainte-Beuve 1951/1852, II: 466.
[2] The term empirical has two main meanings today: in everyday language it means knowledge that remains on the spontaneous or common-sense level; in philosophy, it is applied to knowledge founded on experience or on factual data. It will be used here systematically in the second sense.

and resorting to intuition only when faced with the unknown, clearing the way for science? The answer is neither of these types of imagination, both invented, illusory, mere creations of a third type of imagination, the only one that really exists. This imagination, familiar to ethnologists, is not a faculty that enables us to step outside the conceptual box in which we are confined; on the contrary, it actually creates the box itself, and it is inside its enclosed space that – as Paul Veyne says[3] – religions and literatures are moulded, as are politics, behaviours and theories. The sides of this conceptual box, while not eternal and unchanging, can nevertheless remain fixed over long periods of time and often seem so transparent that we are not even aware of their existence, just like a fly that keeps coming up against a glass pane and remains oblivious of the obstacle.

We have already learnt to study the boxes of others, those distant from us in space or time: this is done very skilfully by ethnologists and by historians. But would the fly itself be able to study the invisible pane which impedes its own flight? In taking up such a challenge, the author, an anthropologist by training, has been quite naturally concerned with the conditioning undergone by the imagination of the academic tribe of which he is part. The problem of origins of humanity and culture, constantly pondered over millennia, provides a convenient opportunity for reconstructing a naïve anthropology widely accepted in western culture. This may enable us to retrace the influence exerted by this shadowy knowledge on present-day scholarly thought.

But let there be no mistake. My intention is not to disparage anthropological thinking, but rather to understand it and to explain some of its mechanisms. In such a task, a critical approach is often as useful as it is natural and inevitable; we must not forget that the methodical exercise of doubt is the very essence of scientific thought. To the reader who may find too much scepticism here, I dedicate the ironic recollection which Giovanni Giacomo Casanova (who was also a witty man of letters) had of his first tutor: 'He said that nothing was more uncomfortable than uncertainty, and for that reason he condemned thought because it engendered doubt.'[4]

---

[3] Veyne 1983: 12.   [4] Casanova 1986/1826–38: 43.

CHAPTER I

Prehistory and the conditioned imagination

THE INVENTION OF PREHISTORY

> On n'ouvre pas un livre de voyages où l'on ne trouve des descriptions de caractères et de mœurs: mais on est tout étonné d'y voir que ces gens qui ont tant décrit de choses, n'ont dit que ce que chacun savoit déjà.
>
> J.-J. Rousseau, 'Discourse sur l'origine de l'inégalité'[1]

What is conventionally known as the 'discovery' of America presented Europeans with a world they rapidly christened New. The first descriptions of this world were in no way new however, so much so that today they provide us with one of the most astonishing testimonies of the power by which a conceptual tradition conditions the observation of new phenomena. Throughout the century following Columbus' first expedition, the conquistadors and colonisers remained strongly attached to everything that had previously been imagined concerning the existence of some possible other world; the first representations of America were therefore inspired by images that preceded its discovery.[2] The River Amazon was so called by Carvajal because, he asserted, women similar to those described by Homer had fought heroically against Orellana's soldiers at the mouth of the Rio Negro. The freakish Ewaipanomas, depicted by Raleigh as having eyes on their shoulders and mouths between their breasts, came straight out of Pliny's *Natural History*, having adorned many of the fanciful geographies of 'Ethiopia', Asia and the Far East. Towns and exploits that had figured in the tales of chivalry, Old Testament prophecies, Greco-Roman myths – such as that of Atlantis and of the Hesperides – catalogues of fantastic bestiaries, medieval legends like the kingdom of Prester John, all were in turn transplanted to American soil, thus colouring these ancient reveries with a semblance of reality. No

---

[1] Rousseau 1973/1755: 416–17, note 10.   [2] Ainsa 1989: 111.

conventional attribute of the wonderful or the remote was to be missing from the accounts of these men when they penetrated further and further into the interior of the new continent in search of the mythical El Dorado.[3] 'That other world', comments Claude Kappler, 'is new only in the sense that it had never been visited before. For it had in fact existed for centuries in Tradition: Columbus evokes the Greeks and Romans. What was sought for was something "known" that had never been seen.'[4] In this respect, the discoverers of the New World remind us of the first explorers who, a few centuries later, would set off in search of prehistory.

'The unknown surrounds the scientist who ventures into the ocean of prehistoric ages': Emile Cartailhac's remark, written in 1889, is redolent of adventure, with all the romance and the unpredictability that it conjures.[5] The science of prehistory had only just been born, but already the unknown evoked by Cartailhac was thoroughly relative: the traditional view of the human past projected from the very outset a curious light on everything that met the pioneers' eyes. The most eloquent examples of this – because of their simplicity – date from the eighteenth century. When John Bagford in 1715 reported the discovery in London of a biface tool beside the molar of a mastodon, it seemed obvious to him that this could only be the spearhead of an Ancient Briton, lying with the remains of an elephant brought to the Island by the legions of the Emperor Claudius.[6] In a similar vein, the mammoth tusks uncovered in Siberia at the same period were often interpreted as the remains of elephants that had reached north either with an invading Greek or Roman army, or carried there by the biblical Flood.[7] In both cases, enigmatic fossils have been easily fitted into the framework of a pre-established view of the past; a past considered as known, familiar and domesticated, made up of biblical themes and references to ancient history.[8]

The tendency to explain new phenomena in terms of traditional concepts can be seen with the same clarity in the discovery of prehistory as in that of America, but an important difference precludes pushing this analogy too far. Voyages across the Atlantic were preceded by countless 'dream peregrinations' which made of America a confused reflection of imaginary prefigurations of the 'Antipodes'. The New World was thus invented before it was discovered, whereas prehistory seems at first sight to have emerged out of nothing: at the time of the first discoveries, all

---

[3] Eliade 1973: 569; Mahn-Lot 1970: 90; Greenblatt 1991. [4] Kappler 1980: 54.
[5] Cartailhac 1889: iii. [6] J. Bagford's text, published in 1715, is reproduced in Capitan 1901.
[7] E.g. Breyne 1741. See also Cohen 1994: chapter 4.
[8] A study of cases illustrating this mechanism can be found in Stoczkowski 1993.

that existed was the scene on which biblical and ancient events were played out. Interpreters of the tradition asserted that the world and humanity were created but a few millennia ago, and that History was fully accounted for in the Bible and in the texts of classical Antiquity. It seems that there was apparently no room in the western imagination for a dreamed prehistory, which preceded the discovery of traces of the real prehistory. The first non-mythical conception of human existence before History would be that put forward by archaeologists and geologists, arising from a void to replace the religious dogmas. 'Attempts to explain human origins', certain palaeoanthropologists say today, 'go back at least several thousand years, but only in the past hundred years or so have scientific methods begun to make headway against mythical and theological versions of creation.'[9]

According to this point of view, scientists set out to conquer a prehistoric past that had been recently rediscovered. Having as their only enemy the errors of religious beliefs, all they had to do was to choose: either they could reject the biblical Genesis, which might ultimately be transformed into an allegory of obscure significance, or they could adopt a hostile stance towards the naturalist view, in defence of the Christian doctrine.

Many pages have been written on the role of prehistory and palaeontology in the conflict between science and religion. We are not going to linger here over that question, although it deserves a much more thorough analysis than it usually receives. This is to emphasise that the biblical narrative still frequently passes for the only imaginary prefiguration of the origins of man produced by western culture before science seized the issue. For many, the burgeoning naturalist view, which collided head on with that of the book of Genesis, was developed in a kind of conceptual vacuum, and the imagination of the scientists had been thus free of the kind of conditioning that had influenced the first explorers of America.

The habit of reducing scientists' statements on the subject of prehistory to mere inferences from archaeological data seems to be one of the considerable consequences of this view of the beginning of prehistoric research: since all knowledge derives from the empirical, the empirical should explain everything. It is easy to accept that in order to understand conquistadors' accounts of men with their mouths between their breasts, even the most profound knowledge of sixteenth-century

---

[9] Zihlman and Lowenstein 1983: 677.

Amazonian peoples is insufficient. On the other hand, the knowledge of archaeological and palaeontological remains is deemed sufficient to explain what scholars say about the origins of man, and these vestiges are constantly invoked whenever differences and controversies arise in the numerous debates of prehistorians and palaeontologists.

But the naturalist conception of the origins of humankind and culture did not emerge like a *deus ex machina* thanks to the first discoveries of the material remains of the prehistoric past. It is true that the scientific view of anthropogenesis is, up to a point, the fruit of those discoveries, but it is not satisfactorily explained by them in its totality. In order to understand its distinctive features and its peculiar logic, we have to reconstruct an 'imaginary' prehistory that preceded the blossoming of scientific prehistory and yet did not belong in the domain of religious thought. To grasp the anthropological interest of this recourse to history, we could start with a detour that compels us first of all to go 'back to school'.

WHAT EVERY SCHOOLCHILD KNOWS

In primary school, we learn that 'only archaeological excavations... enable us to know about the life of prehistoric people'.[10] Oddly enough, schoolbooks promptly make the explanation suspect by putting forward a host of conjectures and explanations which can hardly be derived from the modest material remains spared by time and discovered by the archaeologist through excavations.

Not surprising, you may say: the distortions that schoolbooks purvey are well known. Historians, ethnologists and sociologists have already shown that history as taught in school is often swayed by the demands of ideologies, fashions and local intellectual traditions.[11] But what is true of the teaching of historical periods is not necessarily true of prehistory. It is surprising to find that conceptions of prehistory in school manuals display a remarkable uniformity from one country to another, even though views of historical periods may differ widely. It might perhaps be tempting to conclude that ancient and little-known times are not a fertile ground for ideological didacticism, and therefore that prehistory is spared, presenting the same objective image everywhere. But to assume that an image is objective merely because it is shared seems to jump to unwarranted conclusions. And such is indeed the case: prehistorians recognised long ago

---

[10] Milza *et al.* 1970: 12; also Korovkin 1974: 8; Bazylevic *et al.* 1954: 5; Ourman *et al.* 1986: 6; Gralhon 1975: 7; Chambon and Pouliqueu 1986: 7.

[11] E.g. Ferro 1981; Stomma 1988.

that schoolbooks deviate from scientific knowledge.[12] The striking convergences between the views of prehistory presented in Spain, France, Germany, Great Britain and Eastern Europe are thereby rendered more interesting: everything leads us to think that this widely shared representation is a pervasive social fact. Its analysis offers us therefore a priceless opportunity to reconstitute the knowledge that we have been innocently imbibing from very early childhood. The view of the Palaeolithic, the period considered to be that of human and cultural origins, will be the main subject of my analysis.[13] I shall restrict it to schoolbooks from France and the former Soviet Union, chosen to represent two poles of European tradition.

Genesis according to schoolbooks

Palaeolithic people are presented to children as the embodiment of our first ancestors. Starting with a description of the natural environment, all the schoolbooks paint the same picture of prehistoric life. Soviet children learn, as do French children, that it was very cold then and that nature was hostile, teeming with savage animals: 'The mountains and caves sheltered the most fearsome enemies of men – lions, bears and hyena.'[14] Our earliest ancestors roamed the sinister 'icy desert'[15] inhabited by wild beasts actively seeking human flesh, or at the very least threatening, if only because of their huge size.

It is easy to guess the unenviable fate of people living in such a terrifying world. Indeed, schoolbooks provide a spectacle full of dread. Our ancestors led a difficult existence, exposed to the constant dangers of cold and hunger. Fear was their daily companion, death stalked them: 'Some perished under the claws of predators, others – from disease and cold.'[16] So they were all doomed to atrocious suffering and their lives were necessarily reduced to the most basic needs: 'People had one concern only – the search for food.'[17] Hence the descriptions of desperate, starving bands roaming about in a wearisome quest for prey.

The schoolbooks are unanimous in stressing that the Palaeolithic was the period of human origins. It was then that humankind 'learnt', 'began',

---

[12] E.g. Perlès 1984.
[13] Given the strong resemblances between the first chapters of history books in every country, we can restrict our analysis to a few French and Soviet schoolbooks, representing two traditions fairly remote from each other: USSR: Korovkin 1974; Nieckina and Lejbengrub 1984; Bazylevic *et al.* 1952; France: Milza, Bernstein and Gauthier 1970; Ourman *et al.* 1986; Vincent *et al.* 1986; Gralhon 1986.
[14] Bazylevic *et al.* 1954: 4.   [15] Nieckina and Lejbengrub 1984: 8.   [16] Korovkin 1974: 14.
[17] Gralhon 1975: 10; see also Ourman *et al.* 1986: 12.

'discovered', 'noticed', 'invented' – these are the verbs that punctuate their narratives. In particular, humankind 'learnt' to make tools, to master fire, to live in groups and to build shelters. Occasionally added to this list are clothmaking and the invention of religion and magic. So the list comprises technology, social organisation and religion – in short, culture. It is the origin of culture that the schoolbooks set out to explain. Let us then examine the 'causal' relations put forward to elucidate the origin of tools, of the use of fire, of social organisation and of religion, not just in order to criticise their assuredly frequent inaccuracies or to poke fun at their very flagrant naïveté: these inaccuracies and naïvetés are interesting in so far as they reveal the tacit principles that govern the commonsense view of prehistory and give it great coherence.

We shall start with the origin of tools, explanations for which are highly consistent. Here are a few examples:

Men did not have powerful paws, or claws and teeth as strong as those of the big ferocious animals. But a tool was harder than teeth and claws, and a blow with a club more fearsome than a blow from a bear's paw.[18]

In order to defend themselves more effectively, men made weapons and tools.[19]

The axe ... increased their strength tenfold.[20]

So our forebears would have started making tools simply because they were exposed to attacks from powerful animals and because nature had denied them the weapons with which other creatures were endowed. To confront an animal in the struggle for survival, our ancestor was obliged to 'increase his strength tenfold'; the tool became an extension of his body, a substitute for claws and teeth.

The origin of the mastery of fire is explained along similar lines:

However, people noticed that this awesome fire could also be a loyal friend: it gave warmth in bad weather and protection against carnivorous animals ... At night, ferocious beasts dared not attack people sitting round a fire.[21]

Fire – was of major importance. Without fire men risked dying of cold ... The use of fire made the life of men easier. They could warm themselves at the hearth and protect themselves from the cold; with the help of fire they could ward off wild animals.[22]

Fire was in demand because it lighted the cave, putting the bears to flight.[23]

---

[18] Korovkin 1974: 12. [19] Ourman et al. 1986: 12. [20] Milza et al. 1970: 13.
[21] Korovkin 1974: 13. [22] Nieckina and Lejbengrub 1984: 8–9. [23] Milza et al. 1970: 13.

Prehistory and the conditioned imagination

This amazing discovery would bring them warmth and light, but also a means of defence against wild beasts who are in fear of fire.[24]

Protection against cold or fierce beasts is the common point of all these rationalisations. As in the case of tools, the use of fire is explained by the postulated conditions of the natural environment: cold and the menace of animals.

Schoolbooks devote a lot of space to explaining the origins of social life. Here too we find highly repetitive formulae:

> The first men could not live a solitary existence: they wouldn't have been able to get food or preserve fire. They would have died of hunger or become the prey of ferocious beasts.[25]

> People lived and worked in groups. This was very important. They would have perished if they had lived alone. They wouldn't have been able either to defend themselves against wild beasts or to find food.[26]

> Having only a club, a hunting spear and rudimentary tools at their disposal, men couldn't struggle alone against a hostile nature and carnivorous beasts. Danger lurked at every step. It was only by cooperation that men were able to defend themselves against attacks by animals and acquire essential food.[27]

> To protect themselves against cold, these people lived in groups.[28]

> Men grouped together for hunting.[29]

Living in groups, according to the schoolbooks, was thus a necessity imposed by the constraints of the environment and the weakness of our ancestors, unable to survive without the constant assistance of their fellows.

The emergence of religion is commented on at length in the Soviet schoolbooks:

> Man... experienced fear in the face of nature... Unable to understand the causes of natural phenomena, he explained them by the intervention of mysterious, supernatural forces... Religious beliefs prevented him from seeking the true explanation of natural phenomena.[30]

> More than once man had found himself powerless in the struggle against nature, on which he was totally dependent. Fear of the menacing and incomprehensible forces of nature gave rise to a belief in the supernatural power of the spirits of nature and then a belief in gods. Religion was unable to provide a correct

---

[24] Vincent et al. 1986: 13. [25] Korovkin 1974: 14. [26] Nieckina and Lejbengrub 1984: 7–8.
[27] Bazylevic et al. 1952: 4–5. [28] Milza et al. 1970: 13. [29] Gralhon 1986: 8.
[30] Korovkin 1974: 12.

explanation of the phenomena of nature and of human life. It impeded the search for truth, leading man along a path where he could find neither instruction nor knowledge.[31]

French schoolbooks do not comment directly on the origin of religion but they devote some attention to the function of Palaeolithic art which, in their view, would have constituted one of the chief manifestations of Palaeolithic religion, frequently associated with magic:

What, in fact, is the significance of the paintings of animals on the walls of the caves at Niaux, at Lascaux and at Altamira (Spain)? It was to ensure the success of the hunt: the animal to be killed was represented in as lifelike a way as possible, then it was killed with three arrows in the drawing. This cast a 'spell' which should ensure a fruitful hunt.[32]

On the walls of their caves, 20,000 years ago, the men of Niaux and Pech-Merle drew the animals they hunted, perhaps in order to secure a more fruitful hunt.[33]

To explain the birth of religion, Soviet schoolbooks claim that 'feeble humans' invented religion as a solace, searching in the creations of their imagination for an escape from the fears inspired by a 'hostile nature'. Represented as primitive and unsound science, Palaeolithic religion assumes a utilitarian character. In France also, the emphasis put on the utilitarian function reduces art and magic to problems of subsistence. Art would thus have been so close to the elementary needs of Palaeolithic people that its principles seem to prefigure social realism: 'Man endeavoured to represent what he saw around him. Usually he depicted hunting which supplied food.'[34] So, in both France and Russia magic and religion are presented to pupils as a creation of hungry hunters trying to satisfy needs far removed from any cultural dimension.

Whatever the area of culture may be, its origins are accounted for by one rationalisation and one only: our ancestors created culture because they were cold, hungry and frightened. Moreover, the verb 'to create', suggesting inventiveness and a spirit of enterprise, does not appear. One should rather say: the first humans 'began' and 'learnt'. That being so, it was because they were constrained to 'begin' and 'learn'; otherwise they could not have survived.

The schoolbooks are not alone in propagating this view. Comic strips offer a similar picture of the life of our Palaeolithic forebears. In France this can be seen in a popular series narrating the fortunes of the young hunter Rahan. This 'son of the savage ages', a brawny blond, spends his

---

[31] Nieckina and Lejbengrub 1984: 12. [32] Milza *et al.* 1970: 14.
[33] Gralhon 1986: 8; see also Chambon and Pouliqueu 1986: 15. [34] Korovkin 1974: 18.

time fighting not only against wild beasts but also against the superstitions of the other inhabitants of the Earth, for the most part disagreeable individuals, dark and bloodthirsty. Scenes of primitive fighting abound, too, in the 'prehistoric novels' of H. G. Wells (1921),[35] E. Haraucourt (1914)[36] or J.-H. Rosny Aîné, whose best-known book *La guerre du feu* (1909),[37] is recommended as optional reading in both French and Soviet schools. Rosny Aîné's *romans préhistoriques* have recently benefited from the success of a movie version of *La guerre du feu*, by Jean-Jacques Annaud, who has not omitted a single one of the classic attributes of our pitiful origins.

This view is so widespread and so popular that we are tempted to consider it credible and vouched for by science. Although the authors of schoolbooks assure us that their picture of prehistory is the outcome of meticulous work by archaeologists, it is difficult to accept that prehistoric vestiges can justify such statements about a diabolically menacing nature, the feebleness of the first humans and the resulting origins of culture. The true sources of this vision must undoubtedly be sought outside archaeology.

THE PREHISTORY OF THE PHILOSOPHERS

In order to understand the roots of this view, we must consider a prehistory that predates the prehistorians, and go back to times when nobody yet suspected the wealth of material vestiges of the human past lying buried in geological strata. The second half of the eighteenth century, before the emergence of prehistory as an academic discipline, seems to be the ideal period for such a study, because a host of thinkers were then pondering on the life of the first humans and the origin of culture. This subject was of special interest to French and Scottish philosophers and it is to their writings that we shall turn our attention.

It is often thought that the 'noble savage' was one of the main characters in the anthropological conjectures of the Enlightenment. Indeed 'noble savages' then peopled the pages of travellers' narratives and philosophical treatises, in which descriptions of the virtues of 'primitives' jostle with criticism of those who are 'civilised'. However, even if the educated European of the day indulged in stern self-examination, he remained an optimist, often believed in progress and would have felt no great enthusiasm for a return to an original state of 'pure nature'. We must not

[35] Wells 1958/1929. [36] Haraucourt 1988/1914. [37] Rosny Aîné 1985.

confuse the view of Antipodean space with that of the times of our beginnings: Enlightenment's 'noble savages' are largely missing from theories of human origins – only Rousseau's *Second discourse* and its derivatives, as particular as they are ambivalent, might prove an exception.[38] In general, eighteenth-century philosophers and naturalists imagined human ancestors as devoid of culture and reduced to an animal life, in a way that is more redolent of the Enlightenment view of the orang-utan than of the supposedly happy peoples of the Antipodes.

In works of the eighteenth-century thinkers, the origin of culture usually opens up the history of humanity,[39] although this epoch of origin may be preceded by a more perfect,[40] even paradisal[41] kind of existence that ends in a cataclysm, reducing our species to the precultural state. So the history of culture starts, or restarts, from scratch. Let us stay with this view of the beginning, in order to study the attributes commonly ascribed then to the natural environment and to early human existence.

Buffon provides this image of our ancestors' environment: they 'were witnesses of the convulsive motions of the earth, which were then frequent and terrible. For a refuge against inundation they had nothing but the mountains, which they were often forced to abandon by the fire of volcanoes. They trembled on the ground which shook under their feet. Naked in mind as well as in body, exposed to the injuries of every element, victims to the rapacity of ferocious animals.'[42]

Similarly, Nicolas-Antoine Boulanger sketches a frightening picture of the nature in which the few survivors of the Flood lived: 'So it was a time when the wretched inhabitants of the earth had to look with disgust on their dwelling place, which was the scene of the most terrible catastrophes' and when man had 'so many legitimate reasons to hate a nature that denied him everything, that destroyed even his hut, that constantly alarmed him and satisfied hardly any of his needs'.[43] Voltaire, in his *Essai sur les mœurs*, says that in the beginning, 'carnivorous beasts... must have covered the earth and devoured a portion of the human species',[44] an opinion shared by James Burnet, who speaks of 'a time when the wild beasts disputed with us the empire of the earth'.[45]

---

[38] See Lovejoy 1948.
[39] Condorcet 1971/1793; Ferguson 1767; Holbach 1822/1773; Home 1774; Millar 1979/1771; Rousseau 1973/1755; Voltaire 1963/1756.
[40] Boulanger 1766.
[41] E.g. Burnet 1774–92; Court de Gébelin 1773–82; Goguet 1758; Turgot 1973/1750.
[42] Buffon 1778, trans. W. Smellie 1791, IX: 381.   [43] Boulanger 1766, I: 367, 388.
[44] Voltaire 1963/1756, I: 10.   [45] Burnet 1774–92, II: 385.

For the philosophers, original nature is as hostile as that imagined in the schoolbooks: inhospitable, menacing and full of fierce beasts with a taste for human flesh. The view our philosophers had of the way our ancestors lived also reminds us of the school image. Buffon presents the first humans 'penetrated with the common sentiment of terror and pressed by necessity'.[46] Boulanger conjures up 'a life of wretchedness and terror', 'the harsh and unbearable existence', 'the uncertain, anxious, wandering life' which plunges humankind into 'a profound melancholy'.[47] Holbach depicts primordial man as 'a child without resources, experience, reason or industry, continually suffering hunger and destitution, who finds himself constantly obliged to fight against wild animals'.[48] In *L'esprit des lois*, Montesquieu assumes that our ancestors experienced first and foremost 'a sense of their own weakness', which must inevitably have been allied with the distressing 'sense of their needs'.[49]

In this sad state, 'men were chiefly concerned with obtaining the means of survival and with going about the tasks directly essential to their existence'.[50] To satisfy those needs, they had to create culture. That is in a nutshell how the Enlightenment philosophers explain the origin of tools, of social life and of religion.

According to Voltaire, 'men could defend themselves against fierce animals only by hurling stones and arming themselves with great branches of trees'.[51] Stones and clubs would have been their first weapons, and primitive combat against a fierce animal is sufficient to explain their origin.[52] Helvétius settled for a similar argument when he tried to throw light on the origin of social life: 'men joined forces against the animals, their common enemies'.[53] James Burnet takes the same line: 'Another motive which I mentioned as inducing men to enter into society, was self-defence; the necessity of which will appear the greater if we consider two things: first, that man is by nature weaker and not so well armed as many of the beasts of prey, and secondly that he is the natural prey of all those beasts.'[54]

Broad justifications for the genesis of religion are particularly worthy of attention. This is what Holbach, a well-known atheist, wrote: 'understanding nothing of the forces of nature, they believed it to be animated by

---

[46] Buffon 1778, trans. W. Smellie 1791, IX: 381. [47] Boulanger 1766, I: 367, 388, 390.
[48] Holbach 1822/1773: 275. [49] Montesquieu 1979/1748: 126.
[50] *Ibid.*; see also Buffon 1825b/1778: 308; Boulanger, 1776, I: 378; Goguet 1758, I: 67; Millar 1979/1771: 224; Voltaire 1963/1756, I: 9, 11.
[51] Voltaire 1963/1756, I: 10. [52] See also Burnet 1774–92, I: 401.
[53] Quoted in Duchet 1971: 386.
[54] Burnet 1774–92, I: 384; see also Goguet 1758, I: 9; Rousseau 1973/1755: 72; Virey 1801, I: 113.

some great spirit. Men filled nature with spirits because they were almost always ignorant of the true causes.'[55] Voltaire appealed to introspection to support the same argument:

> In order to know how all these cults or superstitions became established, it seems to me that we must follow the march of the human spirit left to itself. A settlement of virtual savages sees the fruits that feed it die; a flood destroys some huts; others are burned by thunder. Who has done them this evil? It cannot be one of their fellow beings, because all have suffered equally: it must therefore be some secret power that has harmed them, so it must be appeased.[56]

This way of reasoning would be followed later by the authors of schoolbooks. The oppression of the first humans helps to explain the birth of religion, but religion's very existence is already seen as proof of our ancestors' misfortunes. Nicolas-Antoine Boulanger was convinced of this when he wrote: 'If men had been happy, they would have had no motive for thus plunging into sadness, their worship would have been made up of joy, of praise, of gratitude for the blessings of nature and admiration for the works of the Creator; they would not have invented thousands of devices to cast down the soul, to poison their days with perpetual weeping, and to make their existence miserable.'[57]

Thus, the philosophical vision of the 'earliest times' corresponds almost exactly to prehistory as taught in schools. Without embarking on research that would demand a thorough historical investigation into the possible influences of Enlightenment philosophy on today's schools programmes, we need only observe that both of these, separated by two centuries, mobilise the same stock of images to reconstruct the life of our first ancestors and the origin of culture.

It is possible, though more difficult, to retrace the history of this imagery by going further back in time. In Lucretius' poem *De rerum natura* (first century BC) we find a conception whose principal lines are curiously similar. Here is how the philosopher-poet imagined the existence of the earliest humans:

> But what gave them trouble was rather the races of wild beasts which would often render repose fatal to the poor wretches. And, driven from their home, they would flee from their rocky shelters on the approach of a foaming boar or a strong lion... They would... shelter in the brushwood their squalid limbs when driven to shun the buffetings of the winds and rains.[58]

So humans led a miserable existence, 'wandering terror stricken'.[59] 'It was a necessity that mortal men... should have been able to denote

---

[55] Holbach 1821/1770: 123. [56] Voltaire 1963/1756, I: 13. [57] Boulanger 1766, I: 367.
[58] Lucretius, trans. Munro 1900: 140. [59] *Ibid.*: 139.

dissimilar things by many different words';[60] it was necessity too that drove people to live in society, 'or else the race of man would have been wholly cut off'.[61]

These few quotations are enough to testify to a striking resemblance between the ancient poem, the conjectures of the Enlightenment and today's schoolbooks: a hostile nature with its share of aggressive animals, the pitiful condition of the earliest humans, and the pragmatic genesis of culture created by elementary need. The opinions of Lucretius on religion and its origins also resemble those that would mark the Enlightenment philosophy and modern common sense: 'And now what cause has ... implanted in mortals a shuddering awe which raises new temples of the gods?'[62] Lucretius explained it by the action of imagination which presented people with images of perfect beings, but, chiefly, by ignorance: 'They would see the system of heaven and the different seasons of the year come round in regular succession and could not find out by what causes this was done; therefore they would seek a refuge in handing over all things to the gods.'[63] That, he says, is how religion was born, 'subjugating' people by a kind of 'superstitious terror'. And the Roman poet exclaims pathetically: 'O hapless race of men, when that they charged the gods with such acts and coupled with them bitter wrath! What groaning did they beget for themselves, what wounds for us, what tears for our children's children!'[64]

We are often reminded that Lucretius' poem was favourite reading of Enlightenment philosophers. A study of the relations – rich in borrowings, reworkings and transformations – interwoven between Antiquity and the eighteenth century would require a separate and more far-reaching survey than the limited ambitions of my undertaking. Suffice it to say that Lucretius, still republished in large printruns in our own day, was not the only ancient author whose texts, in the eighteenth century, provided ideas useful to feed the conjectural reconstructions of miserable human origins. We can find different ingredients of this vision in the second century BC in Polybius,[65] in the first century BC in Diodorus Siculus,[66] Vitruvius[67] and Cicero.[68] Later, in the fourth century, they would re-emerge in the writings of Gregory of Nyssa[69] and Nemesius;[70] a belated medieval trace appears in the eleventh century with the Byzantine monk Tzetzes.[71] Fierce beasts threatening the first humans is, moreover, a widespread motif in ancient literature from the fifth century

---

[60] *Ibid.*: 142. [61] *Ibid.*: 141. [62] *Ibid.*: 144. [63] *Ibid.*: 145. [64] *Ibid.*: 145.
[65] Polybius 1921, book VI. [66] Diodorus Siculus 1737: 18. [67] Vitruvius 1834, book II.1.
[68] *De republica*, reproduced in Lovejoy and Boas 1965/1935: 246.
[69] Gregory of Nyssa 1944: 103–13. [70] Nemesius 1844: 13–14. [71] Cole 1967: 10.

BC on, as is the theme of the physical inferiority of humans in relation to animals.[72] So the ideas concerning human weakness and the hostility of nature are ancient ('*natura non mater, sed noverca*', wrote Cicero).[73] They were often used as commonplaces, together or singly, to construct varied theories, sometimes far removed from the view of miserable origins. They would later be found on different occasions in theological conceptions, despite the fact that the Christian doctrine places the earliest humans, strong and perfect, in the welcoming environment of Eden; the same *topoi* can be used as stereotypical raw material in discourses whose principal theses might be strongly original and oppose one another on philosophical or theological planes.

Despite its fluctuating popularity over the centuries, the components of what would become in the eighteenth century the view of the miserable origins has persisted in European culture for more than two millennia. These basic images of conjectural prehistory, recurring in naturalist thought from the middle of the eighteenth century, triumphed in the following century and became the very kernel of evolutionist theory; they are easy to find in the works of Herbert Spencer, Charles Darwin, Alfred R. Wallace, Lewis H. Morgan, John F. McLennan, John Lubbock and Edward B. Tylor, to mention only the names of the most eminent and well-known scholars. In the twentieth century, as we have seen, traces of the same conceptions are still present in Western culture.

CONJECTURAL HISTORY: A METHOD

Although the vision of prehistory held by the Enlightenment philosophers seems dubious today, it nevertheless remains coherent, the end result of reasoning that follows sufficiently well-defined rules to lead its users, in different social and historical contexts, to similar conclusions. The image of feeble man and hostile nature remains its starting point, from which it is inferred that the life of the first human beings was devoted entirely to the struggle for survival; the emergence of culture, an instrument in that fight, would simply be a consequence of it. Such a deduction implies a few complementary assumptions, almost always passed over in silence as if they were self-evident. Here are the most important:

1. *Environmental determinism*. The behaviour of primitive humans would stem principally from stimuli in their environment. This principle

---

[72] Anaxagoras, *Fragments* 21b, reproduced in Lovejoy and Boas 1965/1935: 206; Plato 1967a: 52–3.
[73] See also Stoczkowski 1996; Blundell 1986.

allows no room for conduct imposed by the arbitrary character of cultural conventions, at times running counter to natural constraints.

2. *Materialism.* An assumption closely linked to the previous axiom: it is not just a moderate materialism that is postulated, according to which human existence is not entirely determined by culture, but a very extreme materialism, asserting that material existence fully defines culture and cognition. Our ancestors would have spent their entire time in the search for food,[74] and it was only rarely, when fortune had smiled on them and the hunting was good, that they had time to think.[75] These brief moments aside, it is assumed that people did not really think, so cognition could play no part in the genesis of culture.[76]

3. *Utilitarianism.* Everything which humans did would have been an expression of basic needs and would always have been directed towards practical ends. Tools were nothing more than substitutes for claws and fangs, society was the result of economic cooperation, and religion a means, however imperfect, of combating fear and uncertainty in the face of a mysterious and menacing nature.

4. *Individualism.* The origin of culture would be explained by reference to individual needs alone. It was the individual who was cold, hungry, frightened; he it was who was a prey to terror. The social dimension of culture is thus neatly obliterated.

The assumptions of environmental determinism and materialism allow human cognition – believed to be indeterminate and unpredictable – to be eliminated from the anthropological vision, while the assumptions of utilitarianism and individualism banish the equally awkward role of social conventions, the arbitrary and local character of which would get in the way of huge generalisations and historical retrospect. So, what remains active is an ecological and biological determinism which provides apparently solid foundations for a deductive reasoning. What could be more simple than reconstructing prehistory! Since it is obvious that in the beginning was the individual, that the individual was weak, determined by nature, and that nature was hostile, nothing could be easier than to foresee, or rather to 'retrospect', the behaviour of the first humans and the way culture must have come into being.

---

[74] See, for example, Korovkin 1974: 16; Gralhon 1986: 7.   [75] Gralhon 1975: 13.
[76] See, for example, Burnet 1774–92, I: 159; Boulanger 1766, II: 388; Condorcet 1971/1793: 78; Home 1774: 88; Millar 1979/1771: 12; Goguet 1758, I: 179; Voltaire 1963/1756, I: 12; Virey, 1801, I: 95–7.

This deductive procedure enjoyed a great success in the eighteenth century: 'when we cannot trace the process by which an event has been produced', explained Dugald Stewart in 1793, 'it is often of importance to be able to know how it may have been produced by natural causes'.[77] Stewart was one of the first to give a name to this method:

> To this species of philosophical investigation, which has no appropriated name in our language, I shall take the liberty of giving the title Theoretical or Conjectural History; an expression which coincides pretty nearly in its meaning with that of Natural History as employed by Mr. Hume and with what some French writers have called *Histoire Raisonnée*.[78]

The ambitions and rules of the method are very clear. Its aim is to determine the causes of genesis, and the data base on which the explanations must rest are the following:

1. A list of elements whose origin calls for explanation (tools, religion, society, etc.).
2. The principles of plausible explanations: in accordance with our four axioms, the genesis of a character should be the result of its usefulness for the basic needs of the individual, those needs being determined by stimuli from the natural environment.
3. The attributes of the period of human origins: hostile nature, natural cataclysms, attacks by wild animals, human weakness in the absence of culture.

TRANSFORMATIONS OF A MYTH

> Say not thou, What is the cause that the former days were better than these? for thou dost not inquire wisely concerning this.
>
> Ecclesiastes VII.10

Let us return to those conceptions which served as a starting point for the arguments of those philosophers who conjectured about the origin of culture. Neither the principles of *histoire raisonnée* nor determinist views of human nature are able to clarify the source of the ideas of a 'hostile nature' and a 'weak and suffering primordial man'. These two fundamental premises of the 'prehistory' of the philosophers seem to lead an autonomous existence.

The time has come to resort to the term myth, even though its excessive use these days has made it a masker word, lacking any precise meaning.

---

[77] Stewart 1795/1793: xlii.
[78] *Ibid.* A historical and methodological analysis of *histoire raisonnée* can be found in Leffler 1976.

Indeed, it has become customary to say that everything is myth and that myth is omnipresent, or else the term simply becomes synonymous with any erroneous or fallacious opinion. While having no sympathy for the fashion that requires us to introduce the word at every turn, I must nevertheless acknowledge that the philosophical and school texts we have just been scanning have some features in common with those traditional myths that are summarily consigned to the category of myths of origin. These myths, when narrating how things came into being, used to answer indirectly another question: why did things come into being?[79] The same goes for *histoire raisonnée*. As Helvétius said, it tells us what happened in 'the first days of the world' and attempts to imagine how culture came into being, while trying simultaneously to explain why it did so.

However, we must also take into account divergences – no less interesting – that separate conjectural 'prehistory' from myths of origin. In our culture, a substantial number of traditional narratives situate the beginnings of humankind in a paradisal world of perfect harmony, free from all the conflicts and heartbreaks that later ages would have to endure. In this primordial period, myths tell us, nature was kind to humans, no seasons interrupted everlasting spring,[80] the Earth spontaneously provided all creatures with food in such abundance[81] that neither humans nor animals needed to kill in order to eat; the wolf cropped grass beside the lamb and both were equally mild and obedient to humans, whose hands were unstained not only by the blood of animals but also by that of their fellows.[82] Mankind lived, shielded from disease and unhappiness, with hearts free from sorrow and full of love.[83]

A comparison between those attributes that a significant part of our cultural tradition associates with a paradisal existence and those attributes claimed by naturalist thought for the period of origins is very instructive. The original existence as conceived by the majority of

---

[79] Lévi-Strauss and Eribon 1988: 195; Boas 1940/1914: 455.
[80] 'It was a season of everlasting spring, when peaceful Zephyrs, with their warm breath, caressed the flowers that sprang up without having been planted' (Ovid, *Metamorphoses*, trans. Innes 1955: 32).
[81] 'The earth itself, without compulsion, untouched by the hoe, unfurrowed by any share, produced all things spontaneously ... Then there flowed rivers of milk and rivers of nectar, and golden honey dripped from the green holm oak' (Ovid, *Metamorphoses*, trans. Innes 1955: 31–2).
[82] 'All were gentle and obedient to man, both animals and birds, and they glowed with kindly affection towards one another' (Empedocles, *Fragments*, quoted in Lovejoy and Boas 1965/1935: 33).
[83] 'Like gods they lived, with hearts free from sorrow and remote from toil and grief' (Hesiod, quoted in Lovejoy and Boas 1965/1935: 27); cf. also Genesis I–II; Greco-Roman texts can be found in Lovejoy and Boas 1965/1935; medieval texts in Boas 1948; Renaissance texts in Levin 1969.

Enlightenment philosophers and by the authors of modern schoolbooks is manifestly the mirror image which, by a process of inversion, depicts a Golden Age in reverse, where the paradisal features are replaced by their opposites: here food in plenty, there famine; here happiness, there misery; here a kind nature and a friendship with the animals, there a pitiless nature and perpetual warfare with fierce beasts; here a powerful humanity, controlling nature, there a weak man in fear of nature.

Until the eighteenth century, the Bible preserved its status as a fundamental historical work and Moses, the presumed author of the first five books, including Genesis, was called 'the most ancient of historians, the most sublime of philosophers'.[84] It was through the Bible, together with Greek and Latin texts, that the myth of original bliss became, in post-classical Europe, the main source of the representations of earliest times. J.-B. Bossuet, who, in his position as tutor to the Dauphin in the years 1670 to 1680, developed his *Discours sur l'histoire universelle*, painted this picture of the origins: '[Moses] shows us ... the Perfection and Power of Man, how much he bore of the Image of God in his entirety; his Empire over all Creatures; his innocence, together with his Felicity in the Garden of Eden, whose memory is conserv'd in the Golden Age of the Poets'.[85]

The myth of primordial felicity, rooted as much in the biblical tradition as in parts of the Greco-Roman legacy, steered people's dreams towards the earliest times, towards an original perfection that subsequent periods have debased, leaving them little to be proud of in what has been accomplished on Earth; they would have to wait for this world to be destroyed in an apocalypse that would restore a new paradise.

It is true that theologians have never been prone to condemn terrestrial toil or practical knowledge. However, the latter, '*scientia*', was in their teaching merely an 'inferior part of the reason by which humans manage their earthly affairs and profane occupations and try to live correctly in this depraved world'.[86] No Christian should forget the question in Ecclesiastes 1.3: 'What profit hath a man of all his labour which he taketh under the sun?'

The classical mind, inspired by the Bible and the Greco-Roman tradition, seems enamoured of immutability, while the rebellious spirit of the Enlightenment, in complete contrast, desires change: change that claims to be development and progress. Condorcet was not the only one to paint 'an image of humanity marching with a firm, sure step

---

[84] Bossuet 1966/1681: 47.   [85] *Ibid.*
[86] The Venerable Hildebert, *1st Sermon on Palm Sunday*, quoted in Boas 1948: 127.

along the road to truth and happiness', towards a future free of 'the crimes and injustices that still stain the earth'.[87] The Enlightenment philosophers, even if they dreamed of a 'noble savage' and criticised the barbarity of civilised peoples, never abandoned hope that humans and their society have a 'natural tendency to improve their lot'.[88] How could they at the same time believe that the original state represented absolute perfection?

Authors who insisted on respecting the authority of the Bible and the Ancients were circumspect in their references to the age of Eden,[89] but free thinkers could not refrain from bitterness when describing the supposed original happiness of humanity. For Holbach, 'the savage life or the natural state, to which disgruntled speculators have wanted to return humanity, the Golden Age so praised by the poets are, in truth, nothing but states of wretchedness, imbecility, irrationality. To invite us to return to them is to tell us to return to infancy, to forget all we know, to relinquish the enlightenment our minds have succeeded in acquiring.'[90]

For the generation that was fascinated by the creative power of the human spirit, for the century that would see the goddess of Reason set up on the altar of Notre Dame in Paris, the myth of the Golden Age could easily become an insult. And so Buffon, at the end of his ironic sketch of the comforts of the Golden Age, asked sarcastically: 'To be happy, what is needed, other than to desire nothing?' And he continued passionately: 'If that is so, let us say at the same time that it is sweeter to vegetate than to live, to crave nothing than to satisfy our craving, to lie in apathetic sleep than to open our eyes to see and to feel; let us consent to leave our soul in torpor, our mind in darkness and never to use either, to place ourselves below the animals, in the end to be nothing but masses of crude matter attached to the earth.'[91]

The picture of paradise is presented as a mere eulogy to passivity and inertia. Against this, the Enlightenment set the apotheosis of the active life that must be led down here by humans, as pilgrims seeking truth and happiness by building a civilisation based on reason. The path of progress leads from the state of primitive savagery towards the pinnacle of civilisation; only Rousseau vigorously contested this view, while Helvétius

---

[87] Condorcet 1971/1793: 284.
[88] Holbach 1822/1773: 273; also Burnet 1774–92, I: 147–9; Rousseau 1973/1755: 343; Voltaire, quoted in Duchet 1971: 285.
[89] E.g. Burnet 1774–92, I: 367; Turgot 1973/1750: 65.   [90] Holbach 1822/1773: 276.
[91] Buffon 1825e/1758: 164; see also Boulanger 1766, I: 388.

and Diderot, who are occasionally suspected of sharing his opinion, seem rather to have believed that the moral depravity of their contemporaries was the fruit of bad legislation, and that happiness would be possible in a reformed civilisation.[92] According to a conception very popular in the second half of the eighteenth century, successive stages of technical progress would be marked by transformations in the arts of subsistence, starting from the age of hunting and moving on to the age of trade by way of periods of herding and agriculture.[93] The stage of development at which certain philosophers believed themselves to have arrived allowed them to contemplate the image of achievement that is best depicted by Buffon:

Flowers, fruits, and grains matured to perfection, and multiplied to infinity; the useful species of animals transported, propagated and increased without number; the noxious kinds diminished and banished from the abodes of men; gold, and iron, a more useful metal, extracted from the bowels of the earth; torrents restrained, and rivers directed and confined within their banks; even the ocean itself subdued, investigated, and traversed from the one hemisphere to the other; the earth everywhere accessible, and rendered active and fertile; the valleys and plains converted into smiling meadows, rich pastures, and cultivated fields; the hills loaded with vines and fruits, and their summits crowned with useful trees; the deserts turned into populous cities, whose inhabitants spread from its centre to its utmost extremities; open and frequented roads and communications everywhere established, as so many evidences of the union and strength of society. A thousand other monuments of power and of glory sufficiently demonstrate that man is the lord of the earth; that he has entirely changed and renewed its surface; and that from the remotest periods of time, he alone has divided the empire of the world between him and Nature.[94]

So, human beings succeeded, by dint of hard work, in planting with their own hands the Garden of Paradise. For the landscape Buffon paints for us has all of its attributes: 'Uncultivated nature is hideous and languishing' and only man can 'render her agreeable and vivacious.' Thus will 'Nature acquire redoubled strength and splendour from the skill and industry of man.'[95] It is certainly paradise, but transferred from the beginning of History to its end. Did not Saint-Simon assert later: 'The Golden Age, that blind tradition placed in the past, lies ahead of us'?[96]

The history of humanity thus became a Genesis, in which the civilised world represented a new creation, with Humankind, instead of God, as

---

[92] Diderot 1972/1773–4: 177–8, see Duchet 1971: 393, 436–8. [93] Meek 1976.
[94] Buffon, trans. Smellie 1791, VI: 261. [95] *Ibid.*: 259–60. [96] Quoted in Cioran 1960: 133.

the Creator.[97] It is useful (though not essential) to the structure of this vision that the Golden Age – or its equivalents – should lie at the end of the time axis. At the other extreme, the Golden Age then finds itself replaced by its reverse image. This is how, in the eighteenth century, conceptions were formed that served as the starting point for the deductive reasoning of *histoire raisonnée*.

The idea of redemption by civilisation is modelled on the well-known pattern of Christian thought. The hope that progress will bring to the people their longed-for bliss revives periodically in the western tradition. Already present among the Epicureans, this hope grew stronger in the eighteenth century and saw its greatest triumph in the century that followed. Charles Fournier, to cite just one example among others, prophesied the construction of the boreal corona that would supply warmth and light to the arctic regions; the formation of liquid citric acid which, combined with salt, would make the sea taste of lemonade; the destruction of monsters and the 7.5 degree shift in the axis of the earth so that everlasting spring should reign everywhere.[98]

This kind of technical (or social) utopia is often very hostile to the myth of paradisal origins and displays a marked leaning towards the conception of humble origins; in order to be convinced of this we have only to read the critique of the vision of the Golden Age by Lenin,[99] or the flamboyant discourse on our pitiful origins included in the programme of the Communist Party of the Soviet Union.[100] It seems that hopes for the future are proportional to pride in the achievements of the past: 'If it is true that we had brutes for ancestors', wrote Clémence Royer in 1870, 'the progress already achieved by our race gives us the measure of what we may still achieve, and our humble past shall serve only to give us more magnificent hopes for the future.'[101]

Every time doubt starts gnawing at these hopes, the notion of our miserable origins is immediately affected and its popularity rapidly declines. It was in the momentous year of 1968 that Marshall Sahlins, in his famous article 'The original affluent society',[102] proposed to reject the traditional conception of our ancestors' miserable existence in order to demonstrate that primitive hunters lived in a state of well-being, highly contrasted with the discomforts of decadent industrial civilisation (Table 1).

[97] Duchet 1971: 277.   [98] Fournier 1841, I: 66.
[99] Lenin, 'The agrarian question and the "critique" of Marx', quoted from Boriskovski 1979: 166.
[100] Extracts quoted in Mongait 1962: 3.   [101] Royer 1870: 150.   [102] Sahlins 1968a.

Table 1. *Attributes of primitive hunter-gatherers and of industrial civilisation, after Sahlins (1968a, 1968b, 1972)*

Hunter-gatherers	Industrial civilisation
Abundance 'an affluent society' 'all the people's material wants are easily satisfied' 'an unparalleled material plenty' 'kind of material plenty'	**Penury** 'to exist in a market economy is to live double tragedy, beginning in inadequacy and ending in deprivation' 'the market-industrial system institutes scarcity' 'one-third to one-half of humanity are said to go to bed hungry every night' 'this is the era of hunger unprecedented' 'starvation is an institution'
Limited needs 'wants are restricted' 'want not, lack not'	**Infinite needs** 'much produced, much desired' 'infinite need' 'wants are great, not to say infinite'
'Not much labour' 'hunters often work much less than we do' 'the food quest is episodic and discontinuous' 'getting food was not strenuous or exhausting' 'the people do not work hard' 'hunters keep bankers' hours, notably less than modern industrial workers'	**Hard labour** 'we are sentenced to life at hard labour'
Leisure 'plenty of time to spare' 'leisure is abundant' 'there is more sleep in the daytime per capita than in any other conditions of society' 'the food quest is so successful that half the time people seem not to know what to do with themselves' 'their existence is ... fixed singularly on eating with gusto and digesting at leisure'	**Absence of leisure**

Table 1. (cont.)

Hunter-gatherers	Industrial civilisation
Confidence 'they are not worried' 'the hunters have a confidence-born human means' 'they are never in a hurry' 'their wanderings, rather than anxious, take on all the qualities of a picnic outing on the Thames' 'they can look to the morrow without anxiety'	**Anxiety** 'despair at the inadequacy of affluence' '[we] can never do anything without hurry and worry'
Equality 'all the people can usually participate in the going prosperity' 'democratic character of property'	**Inequality** 'odious class distinction' 'a relationship of exploitation'
Freedom 'the hunter is comparatively free of material pressures'	**Enslavement** 'our humiliating enslavement to the material'
Happiness 'happy condition' '[the hunters] enjoy life'	**Unhappiness**

Happiness, claimed Sahlins, depends on the complete satisfaction of our needs, and this becomes impossible when we are too demanding. And we, of industrial civilisation, want too many things. We produce a lot and want to possess more than we make; this thirst accelerates the senseless rhythm of production, and its demands sentence us to 'life at hard labour'. So we founder in frustration because consumption begins in inadequacy and ends in deprivation.[103] To this are added inequalities, exploitation and famine, the latter being, in the author's eyes, the very symbol of the twentieth century. Only primitive hunters are seen as safe from these scourges, and for a very simple reason: they are content with little. So it is easy for them to satisfy all their needs without effort and then to enjoy unrestricted leisure in a free and egalitarian society. Sahlins speaks with conviction of an original existence in which people enjoyed their food and gave themselves over to carefree digestion.

[103] *Ibid.*: 644–5.

So, alongside a pessimistic view of contemporary civilisation, an idyllic vision of the life of primitive hunters reappears. This juxtaposition is based on binary contrasts that bring the classic attributes of paradisal existence and their reverse images into play: material abundance/penury, limited needs/infinite needs, not much work/hard labour, leisure/absence of leisure, confidence/anxiety, equality/inequality, freedom/enslavement. Towards the end of the 1960s, a decade that saw the flowering of the counter-culture, no one wanted to reproach Sahlins for the naïveté of his critique of contemporary civilisation. On the other hand, his idealised picture of hunter-gatherers' life was immediately attacked by ethnologists.[104] Sahlins had based his bucolic view of primitive existence almost exclusively on highly unrepresentative data furnished by three weeks' observation of a !Kung group and by three weeks' observation of two Aboriginal groups in Arnhem Land; the generalisation of those data to all hunter-gatherers, including those of prehistory, is a product of the usual procedures of conjectural history, traditionally rich in fragile extrapolations and unconcerned with providing a sufficient empirical basis for its assertions.

This weakness deserves to be emphasised, but it seems of greater interest to observe that Sahlins' argument, unsatisfactory as it is from an epistemological standpoint, at the same time conforms perfectly well to the rules of transformation of conjectural theories. His description of hunter-gatherers' way of life corresponds to the vision of the Golden Age, and contemporary civilisation becomes a new avatar of the state of savagery. There is nothing original in that. In particular, the main idea that excessive needs are the chief source of our torments is hardly recent. '*Multa potentibus, desunt multa*', as Horace had written (*Odes* III.16). Besides, it was a central tenet of the Cynics, who maintained that to achieve happiness we must reject artificial desires and confine ourselves to a very few natural needs. And it is precisely those Cynics who have left the first testimony of the revolt of the civilised against civilisation. We might say that they were the first exponents of the counter-culture ethos.[105] Similar ideas have been formulated again and again, for example at the beginning of the nineteenth century in Romantic literature. The end of the decade of the sixties saw a new flowering of this tradition which does not believe in 'redemption' by technical means and dreams of a paradise supposedly destroyed by civilisation.

---

[104] See 'Does hunting bring happiness?' in Lee and DeVore 1968: 89–92.
[105] Lovejoy and Boas 1965/1935: 118.

Sahlins' article enjoyed a huge success and created a considerable echo, the range of which can notably be measured by the number of its translations. A recent French schoolbook refers to it explicitly, and a subheading in one of its chapters takes the form of this question, long absent from such manuals: 'The Palaeolithic: a paradise lost?'[106] There is, of course, no question of the Palaeolithic here, but of ourselves, of the anxieties and hopes inspired by our times. The transformations of conjectural prehistories follow our collective moods, and the image of the primordial period slides towards either the positive or the negative pole of the conventional system of binary oppositions.

Yet it would be trivial to conclude that 'ideology' or *Zeitgeist* alone determines visions of our origins. That is true to some extent, in so far as the popularity of different versions of prehistory matches the rhythm of change in social representations. But it is more important to note that these various versions of the conjectural theory of human origins are constructed by permutations of the same generative scheme, limited to a list of Eden-like attributes, twinned with their opposites in binary contrasts. Spontaneous speculation about our origins is a hotchpotch of prefabricated elements that provide the basic data for deductive reasonings whose course thus becomes determined, in large measure, by the nature of this conceptual material, which is always the same. Although each of the visions of earliest times – and the causal explanations flowing from it – has a more or less local character, subject to the moving constraints that are of interest to the historian, their underlying matrix has been unchanging for more than two millennia, serving equally as a foundation for ancient philosophical conjectures and for modern common-sense representations. Through these divergences, there emerges a genuine *longue durée* structure of western anthropological imagination, partly independent of changing social and historical circumstances. When pondering on our origins, we have a tendency to move in a limited field of possibilities, where innovations are most often restricted to combinations of conventional elements, that can also be arranged into broader compositions; for example, the 'positive' and 'negative' periods can be multiplied at will and linked together in complex historico-philosophical constructions – decadence, fall and redemption, progress, perverted progress, cycles of progress and decadence, etc. – like letters in an alphabet, whose limited number enables countless words to be formed, or like words, the

---

[106] Wytteman 1986: 20; see the image of Eden in a schoolbook of the second half of the nineteenth century, Bachelet 1885/1868: 13–14.

raw material of possible sentences infinitely more numerous than the words.

So far, I have touched on a vision of our beginnings which was apparently formed without the support of material vestiges of the past. But, from the nineteenth century onward, imaginary prehistory has found itself confronted with traces of 'real' prehistory. Henceforth, the vision of our origins could be constructed not only in line within the constraints of a conceptual matrix, but, equally, on the basis of factual data. The nature of this encounter between the imaginary and the factual is much more obscure than might be thought.

CHAPTER 2

Anthropogenesis and science

THE IMAGINARY ENCOUNTERS THE FACTUAL

L'évolution ne tire pas ses nouveautés du néant. Elle travaille sur ce qui existe déjà, soit qu'elle transforme un système ancien pour lui donner une fonction nouvelle, soit qu'elle combine plusieurs systèmes pour en échafauder un autre plus complexe.

F. Jacob, *Bricolage de l'évolution*[1]

In American colleges, one student out of two still recently believed that 'cavemen' had to defend themselves against marauding dinosaurs.[2] Prehistorians often deplore the ignorance of the public, and express their surprise that even those who seem interested in the past are prone to accept the most unsound ideas. Yet the struggle of humans against dinosaurs, a very popular image in Europe as well, could be considered not simply as the manifestation of ignorance, but also as a kind of knowledge – one that is erroneous. An erroneous idea does not become less absurd merely for being shared by half the population; it becomes nevertheless interesting as a social phenomenon. In fact, the image of the caveman fighting dinosaurs is not entirely devoid of factual elements: nobody will deny that the dinosaurs really existed, just as prehistoric humans did. On the other hand, the origin of the deep-seated conviction that our ancestors shared the Earth with the dinosaurs remains obscure, because human remains have never been found in the same geological formations as dinosaur bones, and no scholar has risked suggesting that our forebears lived alongside these giant reptiles. It was laypeople, rather than scientists, who forged this idea, thus bequeathing us an excellent illustration of ordinary thinking at work.

---

[1] Jacob 1981: 64.
[2] From the results of a survey conducted between 1974 and 1983, Almquist and Cronin 1988: Table 2.

We should remember that already Buffon was imagining the world of the first humans as 'a vast desert peopled with monsters' of which our ancestors 'often became the prey'; it was only with time that they 'made the wild beasts gradually retire ... purged the earth of those gigantic animals, whose enormous bones are still to be found'.[3] This passage is very instructive, for it enables us to grasp one of the earliest moments of the encounter between conjectural prehistory and prehistoric vestiges: on one side, the 'wild beasts' which have peopled the imagination for millennia; on the other, the 'enormous bones', recently discovered in ancient geological strata. The spontaneous linking of the two as synonymous, for which Buffon is not responsible, led later to an inevitable identification. Traditional imagery required the rivals of primitive humans to be 'huge, fierce and menacing'.[4] The size of some of the bones would have been enough in itself to cast animal fossils in that role. When, in the first half of the nineteenth century, palaeontology described the first dinosaurs as enormous, their jaws equipped with long teeth, they became ready-made candidates for completion of the prehistoric tableau. Their impressive dimensions and the terrifying appearance given them in popular literature fully measured up to the demands of naïve imagery, and embarrassing details were scrupulously avoided. What did it matter that the dinosaurs were often vegetarian, that their remains lay in deep strata where there were no traces of humans? Lay thinking chooses from the data only those facts which seem useful and familiar, and these become like actors cast in advance for the roles in a ready-made scenario.

The 'caveman' image, familiar to every reader because of the scientific backing it received from the first excavations in the nineteenth century, provides us with another illustration of the same propensity to seek in known data only facts which confirm preconceived ideas. It is commonly admitted that prehistorians were unanimous in thinking that the first humans lived mainly in caves, because they had started their excavations in caves, easier to locate than open-air sites. However, while discoveries of Palaeolithic remains were for a very long time more numerous in caves than in the open air, the idea of a 'caveman' was not necessarily a conclusion drawn from the uneven distribution of archaeological finds.

Causality seems to have operated in reverse here: it was the idea of 'caveman' that induced the early prehistorians to explore caves in the first place. For we must remember that caves had already been designated

---

[3] Buffon, trans. Smellie 1791, III: 305.
[4] The schoolbooks constantly mention 'huge bears and fierce lions' or 'enormous animals', Korovkin 1974: 16; Bazylevic et al. 1954: 4.

Anthropogenesis and science

as the dwelling place of the first humans by Latin authors like Cicero, Lucretius, Prudentius and Vitruvius,[5] for whom life in caves was synonymous with a savage, animal existence; and before that, Homer had chosen to make subterranean caverns the dwelling of the Cyclops, those lawless giants who lived in the state of nature and whose savagery was cruelly experienced by Ulysses and his companions.[6] In the eighteenth century, cave dwelling continued to be considered as one of the chief characteristics of animals,[7] with which the earliest humans – depicted as semi-bestial creatures – were readily compared. Even in 1817, a few years before the first French excavations began in caves, the geologist A. Brongniart had no doubt that 'these cavities so profuse on the surface of the globe, and hollowed out by nature, served as a refuge for wild animals, as dwellings for early humans'.[8] It was then believed that caves had existed ever since the creation of the world and formed vast galleries plunging into the very centre of the Earth, in which could be found traces of its most remote antiquity.[9] According to W. Buckland, one of the British pioneers of geological excavations, caves were the only places where vestiges of the antediluvian period could have been spared from the ravages of the Flood.[10] So excavators often directed their steps first towards caves, thought to be unique archives of prehistory and the sole dwelling place of our ancestors.

The idea of the caveman is therefore more ancient than the excavations of caves; we must suspect that it is not their result, but rather their cause, or at least one of them. The bones and stone artefacts brought to light by excavations merely confirmed what was believed about early humans.[11] Nowadays we can judge the extent to which these researches were incomplete and how many sites outside caves passed unnoticed.

It is not unusual to read that archaeology simply confirmed the brilliant intuitions of some of the ancient philosophers.[12] There are even some authors who assume, in line with the tendency to explain all knowledge by empirical data, that precise information about early humans could have been available to Lucretius or Pausanias, because Neanderthal man had survived until classical times in the forests of Europe.[13] But this disturbing resemblance between statements by Lucretius and certain recent archaeological data may have another, more simple explanation:

---

[5] Cicero, *De republica*, I.xxv.40, quoted in Lovejoy and Boas 1965/1935: 246; Aeschylus 1976: 177, vv.450–5; Lucretius 1964: 85, v. 955; Prudentius 1948, II.28–9; Vitruvius 1834: 41, II.1.
[6] Homer 1965: 130, IX: 110–20.   [7] E.g. Voltaire 1879/1764, XIX: 389.
[8] Brongniart 1817: 298.   [9] Rupke 1983: 391–5.   [10] Buckland 1823.   [11] Stoczkowski 1993.
[12] E.g. Lenoble 1968: 117.   [13] Bayanov and Bourtsev 1976.

far from confirming ancient intuitions, archaeology may have become their victim. Had Lucretius been right? In truth, there are few ideas so unsound that there cannot be at least a few facts to confirm them. Hence the need to look for disconfirmatory evidence, if one really wants to subject an idea to critical examination.

The idea of the caveman, to take just one example, was put to the test not by excavations in caves, which could bring only confirmation of it, but by counter-evidence found outside caves. However, ordinary thinking demonstrates a strong tendency to seek confirmation; this is indicated by numerous experiments on the common-sense validation of hypotheses.[14] When people persist in looking for confirmation without bothering about counter-evidence, empirical data are left with the role of mere illustration: this is a typical procedure of layperson thinking.[15]

A science which takes the same approach runs the risk of remaining confined to the universe of naïve imagery, where novelty finds a place only if it fits in with traditional opinions, and where scholarly hypotheses, conditioned by old ideas, evolve like living species, whose forms are restricted by a morphological heritage resulting from their long history.

SCIENTIFIC SCENARIOS

Does the traditional speculative method of *histoire raisonnée* with its traditional imagery still influence the scientific view of the origins of humanity? Has scholarly anthropology found a sure means of shedding its heritage so as to construct knowledge that rises above the conjectures deriving from a 'naturalisation' of the old mythical themes? In order to attempt to answer these questions, I have analysed twenty-four scenarios of hominisation, of which the first was published in 1820 and the last in 1986 (Table 2).[16] These two dates mark a period of a century and a half, starting at the moment when the period of purely philosophical speculation came to an end.

This century and a half has seen the spectacular development of the natural and human sciences which, from the outset, displayed a particular interest in the problems of anthropogenesis. In choosing my sample of scenarios, I have tried to take account of the great diversity of theories put forward by most eminent and well-known authors. The first

---

[14] Klahr and Dunbar 1988; Klayman and Ha 1987; Oakhill and Johnson-Laird 1985; Watson 1977.
[15] Stoczkowski 1992a.   [16] Several of these texts are assembled in Stoczkowski 1996.

Table 2. *The hominisation scenarios analysed*

I	Lamarck, J.-B., 1820, *Système analytique des connaissances positives de l'homme*. Paris, A. Belin.
II	Royer, C., 1870, *Origine de l'homme et des sociétés*. Paris, Masson.
III	Darwin, C., 1871, *The descent of man, and selection in relation to sex*, 2 vols. London, John Murray.
IV	Engels, F., 1971 (1st edn 1896), 'Le rôle du travail dans la transformation du singe en homme', in J.-L. Calvet, ed., *Marxisme et linguistique*. Paris, Payot, pp. 55-75.
V	Coon, C. S., 1955 (1st edn 1954), *The history of man from the first human to primitive culture and beyond*. London, Jonathan Cape.
VI	Oakley, K., 1957, 'Tools makyth man', *Antiquity* 31: 199-209; Oakley, K., 1968, 'The earliest toolmaker', in K. Gottfried, ed., *Evolution und hominisation*. Stuttgart, Gustav Fisher Verlag, pp. 257-72.
VII	Niestourkh, M. F., 1958, *Proiskhozdienie tscheloveka* [*The origin of man*]. Moscow, Izdatelstvo Akademii Nauk SSSR.
VIII	Washburn, S. L., 1960, 'Tools and human evolution', *Scientific American* 239: 63-75.
IX	Ardrey, R., 1961, *African genesis: a personal investigation into the animal origins and nature of man*. New York, Atheneum Press.
X	Leroi-Gourhan, A., 1964, *Le geste et la parole: technique et langage*. Paris, Albin Michel.
XI	Hockett, C. F. and Ascher, R., 1964, 'The human revolution', *Current Anthropology* 5: 135-68.
XII	Laughlin, W. S., 1968, 'Hunting: an integrating behaviour system and its revolutionary importance', in R. B. Lee and I. DeVore, eds., *Man the hunter*. Chicago, Aldine, pp. 304-20.
XIII	Jolly, C., 1970, 'The seed-eaters: a new model of hominid differentiation based on baboon analogy', *Man* 5: 5-26.
XIV	Wolpoff, M. H., 1971, 'Competitive exclusion', *Man* 6: 601-14.
XV	Ruyle, E. E., 1977, 'Labour, people and culture: a labour theory of human origins', *Yearbook of Physical Anthropology* 20: 136-63.
XVI	Tanner, N. and Zihlman, A. L., 1976, 'Women in evolution. Innovation and selection in human origins', *Signs* 1: 585-608; Zihlman, A. L., 1978, 'Subsistence and social organisation among early hominids', *Signs* 4: 4-20.
XVII	Isaac, G., 1978, 'The food-sharing behaviour of proto-human hominids', *Scientific American* 238: 90-108; Isaac, G., 1978, 'Food-sharing and human evolution: archaeological evidence from the Plio-Pleistocene of East Africa', *Journal of Anthropological Research* 34: 311-25.

Table 2. (cont.)

XVIII	Boriskovski, P. I., 1979, *Drevneiseie proshloie tschelovetschestva [Ancient Past of Man]*. Leningrad, Nauka.
XIX	Lovejoy, C. O., 1981, 'The origin of man', *Science* 211: 341–50.
XX	Hill, K., 1982, 'Hunting and human evolution', *Journal of Human Evolution* 11: 521–44.
XXI	Lumdsen, C. and Wilson, O. E., 1983, *Promethean fire: reflections on the origin of mind*. Cambridge, MA, Harvard University Press.
XXII	Kurland, J. A. and Beckerman, S. J., 1985, 'Optimal foraging and hominid evolution: labour and reciprocity', *American Anthropologist* 87: 73–93.
XXIII	Kelso, J. and Quiatt, D., 1985, 'Household economics and hominid origins', *Current Anthropology* 26: 207–22.
XXIV	Shipman, P., 1986, 'Scavenging or hunting in early hominids: theoretical framework and tests', *American Anthropologist* 88: 27–43.

four texts date from the nineteenth century[17] and will serve to establish a bridge between the *histoire raisonnée* of the eighteenth century and the anthropology of the second half of the twentieth century, as represented by work published between 1957 and 1986.

The criterion for selection, in the latter case, has been the frequency of citations in the specialised literature, the accepted indication of a text that is recognised by the scholarly community. This principle led me to give a place to Robert Ardrey's controversial best seller *African genesis*,[18] the work of a playwright turned populariser of the work and theories of the palaeoanthropologist Raymond A. Dart.[19] The popularity of Ardrey's books soon outstripped that of his learned model – a phenomenon not difficult to understand – and nowadays even specialists quote his work, if only to criticise it. So in my sample I have kept this book as an exception to the academic status of the whole, and for a very precise reason: it is interesting to compare the architecture of a non-scientific scenario that is recognised as such, with that of constructions whose scientific character is not contested.[20]

---

[17] Lamarck 1820; Royer 1870; Darwin 1871; Engels 1971/1896.   [18] Ardrey 1973/1961.
[19] E.g. Dart 1953.
[20] The inclusion of Ardrey's book among the analysed texts might lead to the suspicion that the aim was to increase the share of 'naïveté' in my sample of scholarly publications; in other words, that I wanted to set up a straw man, the better to destroy it. So it is worth stressing that the impact of the presence of this book on the overall image of the works selected is quite slight. For example:

The authors of the chosen scenarios belong to several disciplines: apart from Ardrey and the nineteenth-century scholars (two philosophers and two naturalists) they consist of six cultural anthropologists, nine physical anthropologists, two primatologists, a biologist, six prehistorians, a linguist and even a nuclear physicist, who appears as the co-author of a book. They represent the research traditions of different disciplines and different countries: the United States, Great Britain, France and the former Soviet Union. The American publications are the most numerous: this can be seen either as proof of the important contribution made by American researchers to studies on human origins or else as a sign of their predilection for this particular kind of anthropological literature – the hominisation scenario.

In order to have a complete spectrum of diversity, I have included different methodological and even ideological options in the sample: Lamarckism, classic Darwinism, neo-Darwinism, classic Marxism, orthodox Soviet Marxism, the western version of Marxism, the ecological approach inspired by optimisation models, economic determinism, technical determinism, and demographic, sociobiological and feminist approaches. The pre-Darwinian, Darwinian and neo-Darwinian conceptions are thus represented; as are works belonging to the period preceding the crucial discoveries in East Africa and the period that followed them. However, it is worth stressing that although the various hypotheses testify to a great abundance of ideas, the scenarios I have selected do not reflect the entire state of palaeoanthropological knowledge. It must not be forgotten that I shall be examining just one type of anthropological literature here, and not the discipline in general.

(a) Ardrey is only one of the eighteen authors who identify the characteristics of the human ancestor with those of apes;
(b) the logical structure of Ardrey's scenario differs in no way from those of the other texts analysed;
(c) Ardrey is one out of some twenty authors who hold ecological change to be the first cause of hominisation and one of fourteen who opt for the classic view of a hostile nature;
(d) no fewer than a third of the eighteen most widespread causal relationships in all the texts are found in Ardrey; the explanations in his scenario are most common in the scholarly works;
(e) the presence of Ardrey's scenario does not appreciably change the ratio between the different types of explanation in our sample as a whole (cf. chapter 4):

Type of explanation	Including Ardrey	Excluding Ardrey
'Traditional'	74.9%	74.9%
'Lamarckian'	5.9%	5.2%
'Darwinian'	19.2%	19.9%

So it is clear that the inclusion of Ardrey's book does not significantly change the image of my sample as a whole; on the other hand, it provides an opportunity to demonstrate that this book, universally disparaged, offers explanations which are in fact entirely analogous with those found in undeniably scholarly works.

Table 3. *The distinctive characteristics either of humans in general, or of primitive humanity in particular, as described in our sample of hominisation scenarios (the Roman numerals refer to the numbering of the texts in Table 2)*

SCENARIOS CHARACTER	I	II	III	IV	V	VI	VII	VIII	IX	X	XI	XII	XIII	XIV	XV	XVI	XVII	XVIII	XIX	XX	XXI	XXII	XXIII	XXIV
Tools	X	X	X	X	X	X	X	X	X	X	X	X	X	X	X	X	X	X	X	X	X	X		X
Bipedalism	X	X	X	X	X	X	X	X	X	X	X	X		X	X	X	X	X	X	X	X			X
Free hands	X	X	X	X	X		X	X		X	X					X	X	X	X		X			
Language	X	X	X	X	X	X		X	X	X	X		X		X		X	X			X			
Social life	X	X			X		X				X	X	X			X	X			X	X	X		X
Voluminous brain			X	X	X	X		X	X	X	X	X			X	X		X		X	X			
Superior mental faculties	X	X	X	X	X			X	X	X	X				X	X		X		X				
Reduced canines			X					X	X	X			X	X	X	X			X	X				
Cooperation			X	X		X					X	X	X		X	X	X	X		X				
Sexual division of labour					X			X	X			X	X				X		X	X	X		X	
Food-sharing									X		X	X				X		X	X	X	X	X		
Hunting			X	X	X			X	X	X	X	X		X				X	X	X	X			
Perfectibility			X	X	X			X	X	X	X	X												
Family organisation															X		X		X		X		X	
Reproductive success	X										X							X	X				X	
Prolonged childhood								X							X					X				
Absence of oestrus															X				X	X	X			
Carnivorous diet				X	X	X				X										X				

Table 3. (cont.)

SCENARIOS / CHARACTER	I	II	III	IV	V	VI	VII	VIII	IX	X	XI	XII	XIII	XIV	XV	XVI	XVII	XVIII	XIX	XX	XXI	XXII	XXIII	XXIV
Large cranium								X		X	X													
Sociability				X											X									
Cranium and jaws modified				X				X		X														
Sexual dimorphism				X															X	X				X
Scavenging						X																		
Omnivorous diet						X										X								
Protection of elders											X													
Menopause																				X				
Reduced incisors								X																
Strong incisors																				X				
Large molars																				X				
Sexual dimorphism reduced																X								
Burial of dead											X													
Religion															X									
Magic															X									
Longevity																				X				
Fire			X	X																				
Culture						X								X										
Moral sense		X																						
Labour			X																					

My sample is none the less broad enough to reflect the majority of the intellectual modes and tendencies that have marked reflections on human origins. To what extent has this proliferation of ideas, in which palaeoanthropology has faithfully played its part for a century and a half, enriched the vision of the genesis of humankind and culture? Has scientific thought succeeded in going beyond the limits of naïve anthropology? Finally, how should we understand the disconcerting variety of modern accounts of hominisation, which often claim to be based on the very same empirical data?

However disparate these questions may appear at first sight, their assemblage here has its reasons, the significance of which will become clearer in the following chapters. We shall look first of all at the definition of the human being, at the principles of the combinatory game at work in our texts, and at ideas concerning the 'first cause' of the hominisation process.

HOW DO WE DEFINE HUMAN SPECIES?

How did humans appear? It would be difficult to understand the methods and structures of the scenarios that attempt to answer this question without first explaining what their authors understand by 'humans'.

'Humans' are defined by a conglomeration of characteristics that are given the status of distinguishing features of our biological family. Consequently, to explain anthropogenesis means to explain the origins of these human characteristics. These are considered to be mutually dependent, and the links between them acquire a particular quality in our scenarios, namely that of the relation of cause to effect; the appearance of one 'human' characteristic is deemed to lead to the emergence of another, which gives rise to the next one, and so on, until this etiological sequence reaches the 'end' of the hominisation process.

If we standardise the terminology which designates 'human' characteristics in our twenty-four texts, their profusion can be reduced to a list of thirty-eight properties (Table 3). Among them we find, alongside features supposed to distinguish humans, a few characteristics (carnivorous or omnivorous diet, scavenging) attributed only to the earliest hominids in comparison with their ancestors, and playing, we are told, a major role in anthropogenesis. So the human condition in general, or that of the first hominids in particular, is defined by eleven anatomical and five reproductive characteristics, by the use and manufacture of tools, the type of subsistence (four properties) and social life (six properties), articulate language, the level of mental capacities, spiritual life (three properties), the faculty of perfectibility, mastery of fire and, in general, moral sense and culture.

It is striking that the core of this list, consisting of the most frequently mentioned characteristics, has changed very little over 150 years. The leading roles are constantly played by attributes such as tools, bipedalism, free hands, language, social life and cooperation. The pair 'sexual division of labour' and 'food-sharing' makes its appearance in 1957,[21] becomes fashionable in the seventies and afterwards is one of the recurring elements in the conceptions of hominisation. From 1960, the list is augmented by other acquisitions: 'large cranium' and 'prolonged infancy', then, in 1976, 'disappearance of oestrus'. However, the impression of the novelty of these additions derives only from the limited number of works analysed. All these characteristics had already been brought into play in speculation on anthropogenesis: the pair 'sexual division of labour' and 'food-sharing' is found in Rousseau;[22] similarly 'large cranium' and 'prolonged infancy' in Virey in 1801.[23] Prolonged infancy is mentioned as a typically human characteristic as early as the eighteenth century;[24] Aristotle himself,[25] followed by the whole tradition of naturalist thought, was already stressing the absence of oestrus in the human species.

On the other hand, scavenging is indisputably an innovation on this list. As far as I have been able to establish, our ancestors were first represented as scavengers in 1953, by G. A. Bartholomew and J. Birdsell.[26] Taken up by K. Oakley[27] and J. D. Clark,[28] the idea became very popular in the eighties. One curious fact: traditional speculation never envisaged that the first humans could have been scavengers. It is worth noting that in the western tradition carrion and scavenging have long carried extremely negative connotations; the medieval penitentials, for example, counted carrion (*morticina*) among the particularly impure substances, and the penance imposed for consuming it was as long as it was severe.[29] Right down to the present, carrion has remained unclean for westerners, so it is possible that its symbolic charge may long have helped to keep the scavenging hypothesis systematically on the sidelines: the accursed food was unworthy of our ancestors.

Other new attributes, added to the list of 'human characteristics' in recent decades, are chiefly concerned with dentition (reduced incisors,

---

[21] Oakley 1957.   [22] Rousseau 1973/1755: 351.   [23] Virey 1801, I: 1.
[24] E.g. Buffon 1825f/1766: 80; Robertson 1777: 317.   [25] Aristotle 1968: v.8.
[26] Bartholomew and Birdsell 1953.   [27] Oakley 1957.   [28] Clark 1959.
[29] Bonnassie 1989: 1039.

strong incisors, large molars); their appearance in the scenarios is the result of palaeontological discoveries which have enabled scientists to trace changes in dental morphology of fossil hominids. The influence of new empirical data, however, remains limited: despite progress in comparative studies, which are no longer restricted to looking for clear distinctions between human beings and living animals, the view of 'human' characteristics, found in the majority of the scenarios, has undergone no significant transformation. It remains to this day the prolongation of a deep-rooted tradition.

It is a curious tradition. The characteristics it attributes to humans are deemed to distinguish them from the animal world. And yet we have only to take this statement literally for a good many inconsistencies to emerge. Bipeds, humans? Yes, but penguins and ostriches, not to mention chickens, are also bipeds. Demosthenes dodged this difficulty by calling humans 'featherless bipeds', but our situation is more complicated because we know that some dinosaurs – also featherless – walked on their two hind feet. In the nineteenth century, such objections were already being labelled 'frivolous'.[30] Yet it would be unfair to consider them out of place and gratuitous, for they have the merit of highlighting the need to define the unique human mode of locomotion not by the vague term of bipedalism but by the precise feature of our particular bipedalism (one bipedalism among others); physical anthropologists have long been capable of doing this, but our scenarios, curiously, neglect to do so.

The 'brain size' criterion is unsatisfactory too: should we be proud of the weight of our brains (1–2 kg) compared with those of elephants (5–6 kg) or whales (more than 7 kg)? Even if we resort to certain relative measurements, like the ratio of cerebral volume to body weight, the difficulty by no means disappears, for certain small mammals achieve more advantageous ratios than ours.[31] In order to mark out humans by the size of their brain, we would have to use very complex methods of measurement (for example, allometric analysis) and these results are not unambiguous either.[32] Nor is discrimination between humans and animals more firmly established by properties such as 'social life', 'sexual division of labour', 'food-sharing', 'family organisation', so long as they continue to be designated in non-quantitative terms so general that they could just as well apply to certain animal species.

In reply to such criticisms, it can be said that this list of characteristics does not define humans as opposed to animals but, more specifically,

---

[30] Virey 1824, I: 33.   [31] Cartmill 1990: 180.   [32] *Ibid*.: 180–1.

the contrast between humans and apes, and certain scenarios do state this. Indeed, the absolute volume of an ape's brain does not equal that of a human's; similarly, only humans, of all living primates, have fully mastered bipedal locomotion. To define the particularity of humans in contrast to apes seems a right and proper strategy, given that numerous studies emanating from molecular biology, cytogenetics, embryology, physiology and comparative anatomy have confirmed the idea of a very close kinship between the families of the pongids and the hominids, which means that they are close not only in their 'forms' but also in their history, which was formerly a common one. Nevertheless, when we examine the results of this definition strategy in our scenarios, certain inconsistencies persist: there exists among apes cooperation,[33] social life,[34] complex mental faculties;[35] apes use tools and even make simple ones,[36] they hunt[37] and share food.[38]

There is no question, as one may guess, of criticising the ancient definition of humans in the light of new data supplied by recent observations of primates in their natural environment. Primatological researches of the last thirty years have, indeed, changed the image we have of apes, so much so that we might be tempted to explain the traditional view of the differences between humans and apes, recurrent in our scenarios, by the limited character of former empirical knowledge. Yet we must recall that the view currently accepted by scholars – highly anthropomorphic, and so contrary to what we find in most of our scenarios – is not genuinely new and has existed in western thought since at least the seventeenth century. It has inspired countless travellers' narratives, which did not deny the great apes social life, use of tools, cooperation or food-sharing. The modern view of apes, undoubtedly fed by recent and more precise observations, bears such a strange resemblance to that of two centuries ago that we may wonder whether our way of conceptualising apes is not simply the outcome of the swing of a pendulum, that has been going on for a long time. Pierre-André Latreille remarked as early as the beginning of the nineteenth century: 'at first too much was given to the ape; then too much was taken away'.[39]

---

[33] E.g. Strum 1981; Teleki 1973.
[34] E.g. Dunbar 1988; Kummer 1971; Smuts *et al.* 1987.   [35] E.g. Beck 1982; Premack 1976.
[36] Beck 1980; Boesch and Boesch 1983; Galdikas 1982; Goodall 1964; Jones and Sabater 1969; Jordan 1982; Lethmate 1982; McGrew 1974, 1992; Nishida and Hiraiwa 1982.
[37] Harding 1975, 1981; Nishida *et al.* 1978; Strum 1981; Teleki 1973.
[38] Gilk 1978; Lefebure 1982; McGrew 1975, 1979; Strum 1981; Teleki 1981; de Waal 1989.
[39] Latreille 1800: 262; see also the authors quoted and criticised in Buffon 1825f/1766: 83, 1825g/1766: 90–7; also Bondt 1658: 50–86; Rousseau 1973/1755: 410–11, note 10; Burnet

But the question remains open: how are we to understand that all these characteristics, already attributed long ago to apes, and the majority of which are in fact found in apes, continue to figure in the list supposedly describing the features peculiar to human species? The contrast made by our scenarios between humans and apes does not correspond any better with reality than does the antinomy which some of them construct to contrast humans with animals in general. It is certainly permissible to seek to define what differentiates humans from animals in general, or humans from apes in particular, by a set of oppositions, but this approach can lead to simplistic conclusions, and will do so all the more easily if we adopt a distorted view of animality. This is the shortcoming of the majority of hominisation scenarios.[40] Such a flaw is not without interest, in so far as the distortions to which representations of the animal are subjected are not arbitrary or random. They stem from a very coherent process whose main lines we are now going to retrace.

The idea of the animal – we should rather say bestial – condition of our ancestors is part of the classic legacy of conjectural anthropology (this conception may be quite unconnected with the theory of species transformation; cf. chapter 4). The tendency to compare the earliest humans with animals has existed from Antiquity,[41] and it is easy, starting from a few texts chosen at random, to draw up a list of the main attributes ascribed by conjectural history to that 'bestial' state: absence of religion,[42] absence of government,[43] absence of laws,[44] absence of language,[45] absence of individual property,[46] absence of clothing.[47] Here we have a definition by negatives, in which every item expresses the non-existence of 'typical' manifestations of culture. So the bearers of those attributes find themselves again confined to the state of nature, represented in

---

1774–92, I: 268–9. On the evolution of the image of apes in western culture, see Barsanti 1990; Corbey and Theunissen 1995.

[40] Five of our scenarios make greater use of information about apes: Darwin 1871; Jolly 1970; Tanner and Zihlman 1976; Lovejoy 1980; Hill 1982.

[41] Stoczkowski 1992b.

[42] Acosta 1598: 316; Cicero *Rhetorica*, book I, quoted from Burnet 1774–92, I: 373; Garcilaso de la Vega 1982/1603: 110.

[43] Garcilaso de la Vega 1982/1603: 117; Leon Africanus, quoted from Burnet 1774–92, I: 246; Vico 1953/1744: 104.

[44] Acosta 1598: 316; Garcilaso de la Vega 1982/1603: 117; Horace 1932: 99; Lucretius 1964: 85, v. 558–9.

[45] Diodorus Siculus 1737: 18; Garcilaso de la Vega 1982/1603: 108; Horace 1932: 99; Lucretius 1964: 88, v. 1028–32; Vitruvius 1834: 41, II.1.

[46] Lucretius 1964: 91, v. 1108–16; Garcilaso de la Vega 1982/1603: 118; Virgil 1967: 100–1.

[47] Acosta 1598: 316; Garcilaso de la Vega 1982/1603: 109; Lucretius 1964: 85, v. 558–60.

the image of animals and, like them, lacking everything believed to be specific to humans.

Such a view of animality comes from a simple inversion of the image we have of humans, that is, of ourselves. So, for example, ethnologists of the nineteenth century defined animality as promiscuity, in contrast to the principle of monogamy, whose dictates they followed (or tried to follow). On the other hand, for the 'savage' Kandyaus, who were polygamous and 'quite scandalised at the idea of having only one wife',[48] monogamy was synonymous with bestiality. By bringing the figure of inversion into play, ethnological thought, as Lévi-Strauss emphasised,[49] can join the attitude of the 'savages', by adopting one of their typical practices. Reasoning by inversion ends up with a distorted view of animality which becomes a counter-image of humanity, as defined by the local norms of a particular culture.

The idea of the 'bestial' beginnings of humanity, in juxtaposition with the imaginary view of the animal, belongs among the enduring structures of anthropological thought. The end of the eighteenth century brought a major correction to that conception: man started as an animal, but it was a particular animal, comparable in form to the ape. The resemblances between our species and the great apes were so incontrovertibly obvious that they could not escape even the dullest observers. In 1735, when Linnaeus placed humans alongside apes in the same order of Anthropomorpha, he was merely continuing a long tradition going back to Antiquity. Aristotle was already maintaining that 'some animals share the properties of man and the quadrupeds'.[50] A better knowledge of morphological affinity, established through the first dissections by the seventeenth- and eighteenth-century anatomists, was easily able to stimulate speculation as to genealogical affinity. Although sceptical himself, Buffon felt obliged to formulate arguments against the idea of a simian ancestry for humans, disseminated in clandestine works from the seventeenth century on.[51] The literature of the following century abounds in anthropomorphic descriptions of the orang-utan which, in the eyes of certain authors like Burnet, Ferguson and Rousseau, could serve to illustrate the original state of humanity.[52] This line of thought

---

[48] Lubbock 1869/1865: 424.   [49] Lévi-Strauss 1973: 384.
[50] Aristotle, trans. Thompson 1967/1910, II: 8, p. 502a; see also the twelfth-century work of Hildegard of Bingen 1989: 221.
[51] Buffon 1825d/1753: 143; on the emergence in the eighteenth century of the idea of the simian ancestry of humans, see Stoczkowski 1995a.
[52] E.g. Burnet 1774–92, I: 270; Ferguson 1767: 7; Rousseau 1973/1755: 411–15; Delamétherie 1802: xxii; Virey 1801, I: 95; see also the chapter 'The philosophers and the apes' in the excellent book by Hastings (1936: 109–32).

led ultimately, at the beginning of the nineteenth century, to the clearly formulated idea of the simian descendance of humans.[53]

Henceforth the earliest humans, often previously depicted as beasts, began to be represented as apes. The ape replaced the 'beast' but inherited all its attributes. So this image, too, would be a counter-image of 'humanity', and humans would deny the ape what they wished to restrict for themselves: the use of tools, social life, food-sharing, division of labour, cooperation, hunting, family organisation, etc. Besides, the figure of the ape, as a negative portrait of man, especially of 'civilised' man, is a recurrent theme in European culture; it can equally be found in the imagery of the Middle Ages[54] as in products of modern mass culture (for example in the film *Planet of the apes*, based on a novel by Pierre Boulle).

These conceptions are not without consequences for the theories of hominisation, since, in most of the scenarios, the ape becomes an actual embodiment of our ancestor, an image of the primordial creature from whom we are descended. This concurs with the very popular idea, expressed in the terse formula attributed to Darwin, that 'man descends from the ape'. Darwin himself, in fact, never did accept this unseemly simplification and spoke only of the 'ape-like progenitors of man'.[55] The authors of our scenarios seem less cautious, or less precise: nineteen of the twenty-four texts analysed identify the original state of humans with that of simians and push the analogy very far indeed, not only with regards to anatomy and behaviour but also to social organisation and subsistence. Only five of our authors exercise more restraint, suggesting common ancestors for both the great apes and humans, a more appropriate but much less gratifying opinion since it imposes constraints on the deployment of analogies.[56]

It is easier now to understand why the list of 'human' characteristics has changed little despite the discoveries of fossil hominids: the ape – an imaginary ape – continues as before to serve as a model for the portrayal of our ancestor. The definition of humanity is constructed in such a way as to cast the differences between humans and apes in a system of binary oppositions of 'presence/absence'; so if the ape does not think or cooperate or hunt, it is simply because humans do think, cooperate and hunt. Thus most of the scenarios will try hard to explain how thought, cooperation, hunting, etc. have emerged from simian nothingness. Clearly, if the achievements of science over the last century and a half have

---

[53] Lamarck 1809, I: 349.   [54] Clébert 1971: 376.   [55] Darwin 1871, I: 136.
[56] Darwin 1871, I: 136; Leroi-Gourhan 1964: 108, 133; Hockett and Ascher 1964: 137; Hill 1982: 242; Lumsden and Wilson 1983: 89.

brought little enrichment to the list of human traits, it is because that list belongs less to the empirical order than to a tradition prone to contrast 'humanity' and 'bestiality' in antithetical terms, a tradition where animality is first defined as the absence of 'human' attributes, so that humanity may then be described in contrast to the imaginary 'animality'.

None the less, even philosophers who practised *histoire raisonnée* came to perceive the weaknesses of this type of argument; thus Adam Ferguson, the eighteenth-century Scottish philosopher, wrote: 'our method, notwithstanding, too frequently is to rest the whole on conjecture... to imagine that a mere negation of all our virtues is a sufficient description of man in his original state'.[57] This sagacious caution did not however preserve the learned Scot from the trap of which he was well aware. Incidentally, this trap does not belong to the chronicles of the history of science, as some would like to believe. To be convinced, one need only refer to some recent works in which the principle of reasoning by inversion has been raised to the status of a method. The Russian archaeologist B. F. Porsniev calls it the 'method of contrast' and has no doubt that the culture of the remote past was the opposite of that of today.[58] In a scenario published at the end of the 1970s, P. I. Boriskovski was unable to refrain from this eloquent declaration: 'The primitive horde I have just characterised proves in large part to be an amorphous negative, an absence.'[59] 'An amorphous negative', 'an absence' – these are the images that set the starting point for anthropogenesis as many scholars, and not only Russian ones, imagine it. The binary categories thus establish the very foundation of the simplistic view of hominisation and, consequently, it can only be a process leading from nothing to everything, from the negative of Nothingness to the positive of Being.

THE MORPHOLOGY OF HOMINISATION SCENARIOS

> Rule Three: the connections must not be original. They must have been made before, and the more often the better, by others. Only then do the crossings seem true, because they are obvious... They confirm one another; therefore they're true. Never trust originality.
> Umberto Eco, *Foucault's pendulum*[60]

Hominisation scenarios present a paradoxical ambiguity: although they all differ from each other, reading them leaves, curiously enough, an

---

[57] Ferguson 1767, I: 114. [58] Porsniev 1974: 54–5; trans. W.S.
[59] Boriskovski 1979: 167; trans. W.S. [60] Eco 1990: 283, 682.

impression of great monotony. If the diversity of ideas they put forward is disturbing at first, reading them all together soon produces the same feeling of tedium as we get from the stereotypical uniformity of the products of mass culture.

Take the movie genre of Westerns as an example. Each one presents its own story and uses a narrative style of its own, which prevents us confusing the Wild West adventures told by John Ford with those filmed by Sergio Leone. And yet, after watching no more than a dozen films of the genre, each new Western will leave us with a sense of *déjà vu* as far as the general framework of the scenario is concerned. This is because, as a narrative form, the Western always resorts to the same basic pattern, which, for all its invariability, leaves the field open to a host of permutations, within certain limits. The model is simple. First comes an agreed list of classic characters: the law upholder, his inexperienced auxiliary, the outlaw, the sheriff, the local despot corrupting the town, the citizens – respectable but frightened – a barman behind his counter and the inevitable saloon girl. Long as this list may be, it is still limited and imposes on the scriptwriters a group of characters who are 'obligatory' in the poetics of the genre, while limiting free choice to the minor roles. Precise rules govern also the relations that can unite the heroes of the Western or set them against each other, forcing them into alliance, now with the forces of Good, now with those of Evil. Such are the ingredients that can be used to concoct a story of the Wild West, in which invention and dramatic art are mere seasonings, pleasant but not absolutely necessary to make the dish palatable.

This comparison of hominisation scenarios with Westerns is not merely a jest. Underlying these two genres (and a host of others), we find a similar type of generative pattern. 'Human' characteristics are the ingredients of the hominisation scenario, just as the sheriff and the outlaw are of the Western, and we can bring them together in a list, in which stereotyped positions mark the 'principal roles', such as *bipedalism, tools* or *free hands*, and the place of the secondary characters, such as *prolonged infancy* or *disappearance of oestrus* (Table 3). The whole of these relations, which are frequently put to use and which establish the connections between these characteristics, is just as schematic (from now on I shall call them simply 'relations', but we must remember that these scenarios give them a causal status). I can give as examples here the inseparable pairings 'bipedalism → free and skilled hands', 'hunting → cooperation', or again 'tools → reduced canine teeth'.

Let us linger for a moment on the technical problems of analysing the scenarios. A study of the differences and similarities between the texts and between the ideas necessitates an appropriate method for representing their content. The traditional rhetoric of the human sciences, on which our scenarios draw, gives their content a rather blurred form of expression: scraps of facts merge with methodological statements, inferences lie beside a display of erudition, ideological confessions are mingled with statistical data. The texts, often unduly lengthy – as custom demands – form a coherent whole only from the standpoint of the constraints of the rhetoric. This presentation does not facilitate analysis of the logical structure of the texts. So the first task consisted in giving a clearer form to the content of the scenarios, so as to express their basic logical articulations. I have therefore subjected them to a rewriting in accordance with the principles of logicist analysis developed by Jean-Claude Gardin.[61]

The logicist analysis consists in envisaging the text as a construction, the skeleton of which is laid out between a starting point and an arrival point. The analyst tries, first of all, to identify in the text all the initial propositions, that is to say, those with no explicit antecedents in the author's argumentation, and an assemblage of terminal propositions, which themselves give rise to no subsequent inference in the construction. The next stage aims to reconstruct the chain of intermediary propositions which establish a bridge between the starting and arrival points, the intermediary propositions being linked together by operations of inference. Thus the logicist reconstruction allows a long text, full of rhetoric, to be transformed into a series of derivations in the form of operations of the type 'if a, then b'.

This form of representation is enormously helpful in studying the representations that lie at the basis of the explanations advanced in the hominisation scenarios. The long labour of analysis to which each of these scenarios and its results has been submitted will not be related in detail here.[62] I will rather concentrate my attention on the rules of inference that appear most frequently in these works, a recurrence of which indicates a widely shared confidence in their validity. Since each derivation can be considered, from a logical standpoint, as an autonomous operation, I shall try to study them outside their 'vertical' context in the arguments, stressing the comparisons of homologous propositions and their similar use in the hominisation scenarios. This distinctive feature

---

[61] E.g. Gardin 1980, 1985, 1992.   [62] These details can be found in Stoczkowski 1991.

of the analysis is worth emphasising, for it distinguishes my procedure from the way historians of science usually proceed; they are accustomed to comment on complex and heterogeneous conceptual constructs such as 'theories', 'paradigms', 'conceptions', etc. What may sometimes be true of these composite entities is not necessarily so of their elementary components.

All the explanatory relations observed in our twenty-four scenarios can be reduced to 144 simple binary sequences of the type 'if x then y'. Since these bring a total of forty-one elements into play, it is easy to calculate the number of possible binary permutations, equal to 1722 ($n(n-1)$) sequences, that is to say almost twelve times as many as the number which actually turn up in the analysed texts. The difference might be explained, at least in part, by the fact that our choice of scenarios is very limited; it is unlikely that twenty-four texts could exhaust all the possibilities for combinations that might be made from the underlying conceptual matrix. However, certain indications suggest that a portion of these relations has been deliberately discarded *a priori*, while others, for reasons that require an explanation, enjoy a considerable success. Certain elements are thus ascribed great explanatory power, which could be measured by the number of 'human' properties of which they are deemed to explain the origin: for example, tools play a part in generating some twenty characteristics, whereas disappearance of oestrus explains only one. We must emphasise that 'religion' and 'magic' are never found on the left-hand side in causal relations, the side of the explainers; this is tantamount to saying that 'religion' and 'magic' (whatever these terms mean) are treated as epiphenomena in the evolution of humankind and culture, appearing only when anatomical and cultural transformations are sufficiently advanced for all the other 'principal' manifestations of culture to be already present. We can see from this last example that the type and number of relations envisaged may be limited on grounds of a peculiar anthropological view: in the event, a conception of spiritual life as having a role that, rightly or wrongly, is arbitrarily restricted to a marginal status.

So we stress yet again that our object is to examine the most frequent relations in these hominisation scenarios: I have singled out for analysis the ones that appear at least three times and constitute the nucleus of the explanations offered in our texts. To avoid any misunderstanding, it must be stressed again that my aim is not to pronounce judgement either on palaeoanthropology as a whole or on the entire body of conjectures concerning the origins of humanity, but solely to analyse the foundations of the most current causal explanations in the hominisation scenarios. These explanations, of which there are twenty-one, drawn from all our texts, are interlinked and can be represented in the form of a synthetic scheme (Fig. 1), which defines the cardinal axes along which the hominisation scenarios can be generated.

For the majority of them, a change in the natural environment functions as the prime mover that triggers the process of hominisation (see the next chapter). From there, three main pathways mark the beginning of the divergences between the scenarios and lay the foundations of part of their variety (Table 4). Depending on the importance the authors attach to anatomy, technology and subsistence activities, change in the environment is thought to lead sometimes to the adoption of bipedalism, sometimes to the origin of tools, sometimes to the transition to a hunting subsistence. Then, each of these three initial characteristics (bipedalism, tools, hunting) serves to set a whole 'causal' chain in motion. If our ancestors adopted an upright posture, their hands were freed from locomotion; the free hand made it possible to produce and use tools; the tools replaced the canines in a great many functions and consequently the canines were reduced in size; learning to make tools required a complex means of communication, so language was created, and so on. When an author favours the view that it was hunting that played a decisive role in anthropogenesis, we see the explanations evolve in a different direction: hunting implies sexual division of labour which means the division of economic tasks between the two sexes; that establishes the custom of food-sharing and duties of reciprocity; thus the germ of social life is formed; a social existence gives rise to the need for communication, immediately generating language; the use of words enables the mental faculties to blossom; they, in turn, lead the early humans to perfect their culture, etc.

Whichever path is followed, the network of conventional relations allows some fifteen chief 'human' characteristics to be 'explained' at the end of the operation. One might ask, in passing, if all the sequences contained in this cumulative scheme have already been proposed in anthropological literature; it is possible to produce new 'artificial' scenarios mechanically, starting from the initial point (change in the natural environment) and progressing randomly through the graph following the branching system indicated by the arrows (Fig. 1).

The number of versions that can be constructed on the authority of this scheme is quite obviously very limited because it is so simple. The simplicity of this scheme enables us, on the one hand, to understand

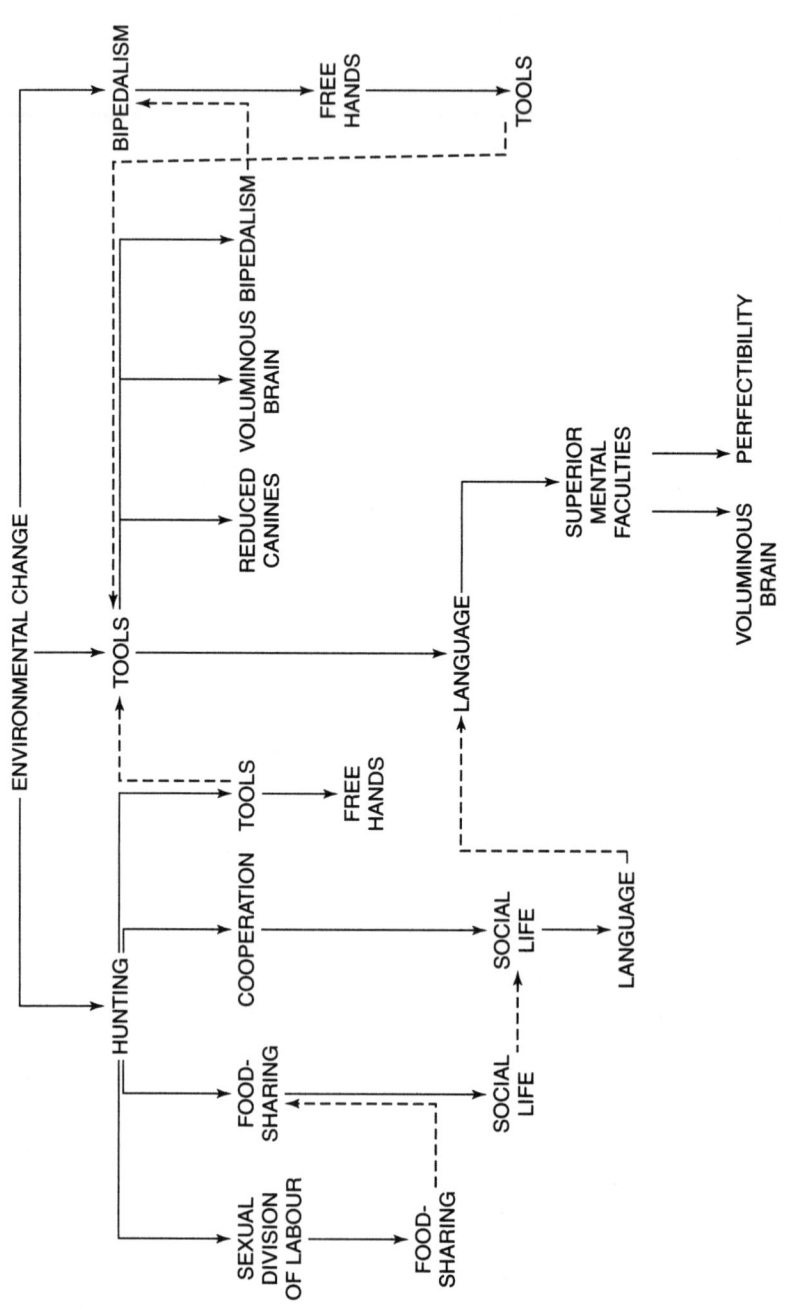

Figure 1. The most frequent explanatory sequences constituting the nucleus of the generative scheme in the hominisation scenarios.

the monotonous and uniform nature of the scenarios, most of which are developed from such a perfunctory matrix. On the other hand, even if the matrix is simple, this simplicity makes it possible to generate a certain number of permutations, which explains the diversity of the scenarios. This diversity may be increased if the original scheme is enlarged by complementary relations, which are used less frequently and are therefore left out of the analyses that will follow. For example, in Fig. 1, some of the strings that stop at 'large brain' could be prolonged in the sequence 'large brain → large cranium', then 'large cranium → premature childbirth', 'premature childbirth → prolonged infancy', etc. So we are dealing with an open-ended structure, capable of being expanded.

The notion of causality implies that of chronology, for the cause must necessarily precede the effect. But, curiously, time is not much in evidence in the hominisation scenarios and the events that follow on from each other remain suspended in an astonishingly vague chronological space, all consigned to a more or less ill-defined period, that is designated, in line with the knowledge or uncertainties of the hour, as 'the end of the Tertiary', the 'pivotal point between the Pliocene and the Pleistocene', the 'Plio-Pleistocene', the 'lower Palaeolithic', etc. The consecutive stages of hominisation are presented almost devoid of chronological indications and the only dates mentioned are intended to demarcate, still only approximately, the general outlines of this long period of origins, contained within the last 10 million years or so.

It is during that muddled period that humans came down from the trees and settled in the savannah, stood up on their back legs, freed their hands, grabbed a tool, killed an animal, shared the meat with their fellows, perhaps uttering the first word as they did so – these are just a few elements of the usual scenario. It is not without significance that the events thus portrayed could have been equally well spread over the vast expanse of millions of years or concentrated into a single day. The image of evolution proposed by our scenarios is sufficiently malleable to be easily adapted to chronological landmarks freely chosen in accordance with the available data, or the constraints of the vision it has been arbitrarily decided to construct. Alluded to more or less symbolically, precise dates play only a limited and minor role in our texts, which is to situate the entire process in a remote past whose prehistoric exoticism is conveyed by its approximate chronology. So the reader should not be surprised if exact dates are as rarely mentioned in my analyses as they are in the texts analysed: apart from a few rare exceptions, they have had no visible impact on the form of the causal explanations advanced in hominisation scenarios.

We will return now to the core of the generative scheme drawn up from twenty-one of the most repetitive causal relations. Since these causal relations are the subject of a certain consensus, it is worthwhile to analyse their foundations, in order to find out how far their popularity can be explained by their epistemological reliability, and how far it should rather be ascribed to their conformity with the schemes of naïve anthropology.

Since I shall frequently make use of texts from the past, samples of which stretch from Antiquity to our own times, the reader might suspect that the author's intention is to prove insidiously that in palaeoanthropology there is 'nothing new under the sun', and that the reflection of specialists on the origins of humanity have hardly evolved over centuries. Some readers may even try to accuse me of wanting to manipulate scraps of ancient texts unscrupulously, to take them out of their historical contexts and proclaim, each time a rough similarity is found between the past and the present, that the moderns have invented nothing.

To forestall this regrettable misunderstanding, I want to emphasise here and now that I have never been tempted to do anything so simplistic and sterile. In the first place, I am hardly proposing to analyse palaeoanthropological knowledge in its entirety, and nothing will be said, for example, about phylogenetic issues, cladistic methods or the application of molecular approaches in palaeoanthropology, fields in which this discipline has made enormous advances in recent decades. My purpose is in fact restricted to an examination only of those studies that aspire to explain the causes of hominisation, and these form just one category among many in the rich literature of palaeoanthropology. In the second place, the essence of my analyses will be centred not on all the hominisation scenarios available in the specialised literature, nor even on all the twenty-four scenarios selected, but chiefly on twenty-one causal explanations that occur most frequently in them. So it is a matter not of demonstrating that nothing has changed in palaeoanthropological scenarios but, on the contrary, of subjecting to detailed examination the explanations that have, in fact, persisted stubbornly for a century and a half in reflections on human origins. The observation that there are historical continuities in this domain is not a conclusion that would ensue from my analyses, but actually an empirical observation that gave rise to them, their starting point rather than their end result. And I must insist that this determined interest in ideas that change little or not at all over time is by no means equivalent to disputing the existence of those that do change.

But why pay this almost exclusive attention to recurrent ideas? Recurrent ideas, that survive changes in paradigms and whose existence straddles the boundaries of chronological, cultural, national and disciplinary contexts, seem to me interesting, for if we are to believe the historians of science and the sociologists of science, they ought not to exist. The conventional wisdom of the history of science is that ideas always take shape and subsist in their own 'social' or 'political' context, and that changes in that context unfailingly bring in their train modifications to scientific representations of the world. It may be, still according to the same view, that certain ideas pass from one context to another, but that would be possible only for ideas possessed of such firm empirical foundations that even a change of paradigm is incapable of casting doubt on them. Thus, only ideas that are indubitably 'sound', 'reliable' or 'self-evident' would be invariable, in time and beyond the vicissitudes of history, while all the others, that is to say the majority, would be condemned to be transformed by changing context, for they would simply be a 'cultural construct' and would therefore have to follow the rhythm of cultural metamorphoses.

It is precisely this assumption that only 'natural evidence' is invariable whereas 'cultural constructs' are always variable that I propose to subject to critical examination, by analysing the most widely accepted ideas that form the consensual nucleus discernible in the hominisation scenarios. How do I propose to go about it?

It is reasonable to assume that five causes, operating separately or together, could be responsible for the success of recurrent ideas in speculation on human origins. These ideas might be widely accepted over a long period because they:

1. are unanimously confirmed by empirical data amongst which there is nothing that might disconfirm them;
2. are the only ones that are thinkable, since no alternative conception can be envisaged that might challenge them;
3. are the only ones that satisfy fully the conceptual constraints of the theory of evolution;
4. are the only ones that conform to an ideology to which an author adheres;
5. enjoy the status of common-sense ideas which gives them credibility irrespective of the four preceding criteria.

So the success of the recurrent ideas could stem from empirical considerations, from logic, from theory, from ideology, from 'conceptual inertia'. We can discard the 'theoretical' and 'ideological' hypotheses straight away, in that our recurrent causal explanations come from the texts of authors belonging to different ideological and theoretical contexts (the question of the theoretical foundations of these explanations will be discussed at greater length in chapter 4; the ideological commitments of the authors of our texts will be analysed in the last section but one of chapter 5). All that remains, therefore, is to verify which of the three factors staying in the lists could be responsible for the lasting success of the twenty-one explanations I have selected, which have adorned anthropological literature for more than a century. Each of them will therefore be subjected to a threefold examination and considered from three standpoints:

1. Is it really confirmed by the empirical data?
2. Is it the only one thinkable?
3. Does it correspond to the common-sense anthropological premises that, in Western tradition, preceded the emergence of palaeoanthropology in particular and the human sciences in general?

Confronting recurrent ideas in palaeoanthropology with factual data is not conceived simply as a critique of established knowledge; my main purpose is to elucidate the reasons for the popularity of the widely accepted ideas. Just as the factual criticisms to which these ideas will be subjected do not aim to replace them with others, so reflection on alternative explanations to the widely accepted ideas is in no way a striving to throw a new light on the emergence of this or that human characteristic. The more modest role comes down to showing, whenever possible, that the credibility of certain palaeoanthropological explanations has nothing to do with the lack of plausible alternatives. Excursions into the past, and the setting in parallel of modern and ancient explanations (from Antiquity to the beginning of the nineteenth century) is not a matter of hunting for 'precursors' – so often stigmatised by historians of science – which would try to demonstrate that modern science has invented nothing or that recent ideas are identical on every point with ancient ideas; it is, more simply, a matter of verifying whether the popularity of the most 'successful' ideas can be explained by their conformity to thought patterns that belong to common-sense anthropology or whether it should be explained by their empirical reliability and logical obviousness. I shall not seek for perfect likenesses between ancient and modern knowledge, any more than I shall attempt to gloss over the differences that exist between chronologically disparate conceptions that have only fragmentary or superficial resemblances. My task is to measure the extent to which ancient and modern explanations match up to tacit premises underlying

Anthropogenesis and science 55

a spontaneous anthropology that has dominated Western tradition for at least two centuries. Reconstructing these premises, which seem to form a coherent system in our anthropological imagery, is one of the main objectives of this book, although it sets itself a more limited task in the first place: I shall attempt first and foremost to explain the success of a certain number of recurrent causal explanations in hominisation scenarios by examining possible justifications for them according to three alternative hypotheses (which may also be complementary): 'empirical', 'logical' and 'conventional'.

NATURE: MOTHER OR STEPMOTHER?

Of the twenty-four scenarios analysed, twenty state that the first impetus towards the process of hominisation was given by some climatic change.[63] Human history would therefore have started with a transformation in nature; the decisive role conferred on this ecological metamorphosis prompts a detailed analysis of how it is reconstructed.

Let us pause first at the most popular view, present in the majority of our scenarios, which places the first hominids in a hostile environment[64] (Table 4). That hostility, manifested principally by shortage of food and the menace of carnivores, is not considered to be an intrinsic property of nature, and we see it appear only following climatic change. At a period, the precise dating of which varies from one text to another depending on the data of the moment, a great drought ravaged East Africa, bringing in its train the replacement of tropical forest by open savannah, thereby

---

[63] The idea of environmental change is absent from Lamarck (1820), Engels (1971/1896) and Leroi-Gourhan (1964). Only Glynn Isaac (1978a, 1978b), of all the authors of the texts analysed, emphasised that an ecological crisis, although plausible, is not really necessary from a theoretical point of view in order to explain hominisation. Indeed, the theory of evolution, especially in its Darwinian version, allows the transformations of the species to be conceived as a process that may at times be independent of environmental change.

[64] Palaeoanthropological scenarios describe our ancestors' new environment as having a remarkably standardised assemblage of attributes. These can be divided into three groups:

(a) Negatives: drought, absence of vegetable food, shortage of water and food in general, attacks by predators, competition from carnivores, ecological factors inducing mortality.
(b) Positives: abundance of game, abundance of food, diversity and density of game species, absence of predators.
(c) Neutrals: savannah, open country, patchy environment, ecological change.

More than half the scenarios (14 out of 24) ascribe negative properties to the new environment of the Hominidae, two give it positive features (Hill 1982; Kelso and Quiatt 1976), one text uses both simultaneously (Tanner and Zihlman 1976), while only two mention only neutral attributes (Lumsden and Wilson 1983; Kurland and Beckerman 1985). See Table 4.

Table 4. *Different representations of the natural environment of the early hominids in the hominisation scenarios*

Attributes		Royer (1870)	Darwin (1871)	Coon (1954)	Oakley (1957)	Niestourkh (1958)	Washburn (1960)	Ardrey (1961)	Hockett and Ascher (1964)	Laughlin (1968)	Jolly (1970)	Wolpoff (1971)	Ruyle (1977)	Boriskovski (1979)	Lovejoy (1981)	Hill (1982)	Shipman (1986)	Quiatt and Kelso (1985)	Tanner and Zihlman (1976)	Lumsden and Wilson (1983)	Kurland and Beckerman (1985)
Negative	Drought				X			X	X	X											
	Lack of vegetable food		X	X	X			X		X	X		X								
	Food and water shortage	X		X					X												
	Competition from predators																X		X		
	Attacks by predators	X	X	X		X	X	X	X			X	X	X							
	Environmental factors inducing a rise in mortality rate							X	X					X	X						
Neutral	Savannah			X	X			X	X			X		X		X	X		X	X	X
	Open country				X	X	X	X	X				X			X			X	X	
	Environmental change		X																		
	Patchiness																				X
Positive	Abundance of food															X		X	X		
	Abundance of game															X		X			
	Diversity of game species															X					
	Absence of predators															X					
		Hostile nature														Benevolent nature		Ambivalent nature		Neutral nature	

causing the disappearance of the vegetable food on which our allegedly vegetarian ancestors had depended until then for subsistence. The forests, rich in plant resources (especially fruit), gave way – according to the majority of our scenarios – to an arid savannah teeming with carnivores, from which flight into the trees was impossible, since there were no more trees around. As a consequence, our forebears are believed to have entered on a difficult period of ecological crisis. In order to survive, they had to take up nature's challenge and abandon an ancient way of life that allowed them to satisfy their needs in the hospitable milieu of the forest, but that proved useless in the hostile savannah. Henceforth the hominids had to eat meat and learn to hunt; in the open country, obliged to adopt an upright posture, they began to cooperate and defend themselves against predators by using tools. This is how, in the struggle against a hostile environment, the first hominids would have laboriously moulded their nature.

Is this view the fruit of empirical data? Admittedly, climatic changes of the Plio-Pleistocene in East Africa, marked in the long term by an expansion of open environments at the expense of tree cover, seem to be well attested.[65] On the other hand, we cannot say the same for the vision of a sharp transition from forest to savannah, nor for the actual image of the savannah, painted in such dark terms. Indeed, the zones of covered environment (forests, savannah woodland) and the open zones (shrub savannah, grass savannah) had always coexisted in the landscape of the period, and it was only their proportions that were subject to changes. The climatic variations of the Plio-Pleistocene in East Africa consisted of cool periods, accompanied by a reduced rainfall and expansion of the open environments, alternating with periods of warm, dry climate, marked by an expansion of the tree cover.[66]

---

[65] E.g. texts assembled in Coppens 1985.
[66] E.g. Bonnefille and Vincens 1985: 272; Vrba 1985; cf. further texts assembled in Coppens 1985. Since the first French edition of this book in 1994, new data have strongly supported my doubts about the habitual view of climatic change in East Africa during the late Miocene, while weakening the climate-change theory of hominisation. First, analysis of carbon residues in ancient soils of the Rift Valley in Kenya have indicated that a heterogeneous environment, in which open savannahs existed alongside denser vegetation, had dominated in this region of Africa for 15 million years, with the first traces of drying out dating from 23 million years ago (Kingston, Marino and Hill 1994). Second, more exhaustive studies of climate change, as revealed in deep-sea cores, made it possible to demonstrate that these bear no correlation to the dates for the emergence of the successive taxons of Hominidae (Foley 1994). Third, it turns out that ancient hominid forms like *Australopithecus ramidus*, discovered in Ethiopia in 1993, lived probably in a forested habitat (White, Suwa and Asfaw 1994; Woldegabriel et al. 1994). Fourth, the recent discovery of remains of an Australopithecine in Chad, 2500 kilometres west of the Rift

As for the arid savannah, it is not, as some scenarios suggest, totally devoid of plant food suitable for primates. The Chacuna baboons (*Papio ursinum*), to take just one example, find seeds, tubers, fruits and other plant parts there, and only consume meat as a complement to an essentially vegetarian diet.[67] The average annual net primary productivity of the savannahs, lower in general than that of the equatorial and subequatorial forests on average, may sometimes equal or even exceed them. The index of net primary productivity gives us no direct information about the quantity of plants that could be utilised by primates, but ecological data suggest that the rain forest of Central Africa has 'an annual period of about five months during which wild plant food of calorific importance is essentially unavailable'.[68] This evidence, although imprecise, is enough to make us no longer so firmly convinced that savannahs are always and everywhere poorer in plant food than forests.

Likewise, it is not certain that the move from life in the forest to life on the savannah must systematically imply a greater threat from predators. Since the authors of the scenarios often claim to construct the image of the savannah on the basis of present-day ecological analogies, let us remember that, today, a leopard (*Panthera paradus*) in the forest can be just as dangerous as a lion in the savannah.[69] Moreover, in neither environment does this danger seem to be the main threat to primates. Chimpanzees living in the trees are not excessively worried by leopards;[70] in the event of a chance encounter on the same branch, a solitary chimpanzee is usually capable of intimidating the predator and seeing it off.[71] Nor does the threat from carnivores appear to be troublesome in an open environment: observations of chimpanzees for forty-four months in the national park of Niokolo Koba (Senegal), where forests constitute only 3 per cent of the plant cover, have revealed not a single case of aggression by carnivores like lions, leopards, hyenas or wild dogs, yet all these are present in the region.[72] Adrian Kortland, who took the trouble to review a considerable literature on the great apes of Africa in order to find confirmation of the ever-present threat to primates from predators, encountered only one case of the death of an ape at the claws of an attacker.[73] One can,

---

Valley, reminds us of the continuing uncertainty surrounding the designation of the cradle of the hominids, too hastily associated with a region where it is hoped to find traces of an appropriate climatic crisis which would have coincided with the key moment of anthropogenesis (Brunet et al. 1995).

[67] Hamilton and Curt 1982.　[68] Pianka 1974: table 3.1; Hart and Hart 1986.
[69] Brain 1981: 85–97; Clark 1964.　[70] Tutin, McGrew and Baldwin 1981.
[71] Bandini and Baldwin 1978.　[72] Tutin, McGrew and Baldwin 1981.
[73] Kortland 1980: 80; see also Goodall 1986: 556–7.

of course, reply that today's primates offer a very poor analogy with the situation of our ancestors, who lived in a somewhat different environment, where the carnivores known today were accompanied by extinct Felidae like *Dinofelis, Homoterium, Pantera speleus, Actionyx* and two species of *Hyenidae*.[74] Consequently, this greater diversity and concentration of carnivore population may have been reflected in greater predation pressure. But, yet again, we cannot be sure of that *a priori*. It is possible that this greater predation pressure was matched by a greater diversity of prey species, and by larger herds of herbivores.[75] In the latter case, hominids may have been no more subject to predation than recent primates. It must be added that certain fossil carnivores, *Megantereon* and *Dinofelis* for example, probably preferred the covered environment of the forest where they could hunt effectively in the trees[76] which, in common-sense imagery, remain a reassuring refuge for our ancestors. Even if some fossil traces of predation on hominids exist,[77] the hypotheses of a great threat from predators in the savannah, or the absence of such a threat in the forest, have no solid foundation and will remain mere conjecture as long as more precise data are not available about the interactions of predator populations and their preys in prehistoric environments. Besides, it is unlikely that these always very complex interactions can be reduced to the binary pattern (absence/omnipresence of predators) so frequent in our scenarios.

Two conclusions can be drawn from this analysis. First, the picture of a clear transition from forest to savannah is just an unwarranted simplification, difficult to confirm with palaeoecological data. It is quite certain that the ratio of covered to open zones changed in East Africa during the Plio-Pleistocene, but this process probably took place through long oscillations which led ultimately to a more or less mixed landscape.

Second, we should not look on the shortage of plant food and the threat of predators in the savannah as certainties. Reference knowledge of present environments allows us to imagine that the new environment of the hominids would equally be rather hostile and poor, or relatively hospitable and bountiful. Yet only the conception of a hostile nature with food shortage and the threat of predators has been judged convincing *a priori* by most of the authors. How are we to understand this success in view of the empirical fragility of the construct? It is striking that the weak empirical foundation of this conception goes hand in hand with a perfect conformity to the pre-empirical conjectures of philosophers.

[74] Petter and Howell 1985: 147.   [75] *Ibid.*   [76] Marean 1989.   [77] Brain 1981: 270–1.

Even before the discovery of the first human fossils, philosophers and naturalists demonstrated a marked predilection for seeing the key moment of anthropogenesis as the transition from a period of abundance to times of scarcity. In works published between the end of the seventeenth and the beginning of the nineteenth centuries,[78] the first step of anthropogenesis was associated with a transition from a period I shall call A to another I shall name B. Period A represents a static state with no changes, during which our ancestor led a peaceful existence. At the beginning of the nineteenth century, the naturalist Jean-Claude Delamétherie depicted it in these terms:

> This man of nature had a great mass of enjoyments. Dwelling in a fair land, he always enjoyed an agreeable temperature. The land supplied him with abundant food; he had neither toil nor fatigue. Boredom never afflicted him; he entertained himself with his fellows. His days passed in calm and serenity unmarred by any sickness. He reached his last hour unaware of its approach.[79]

Natural causes (we shall see later what they were) put an end to the harmony of period A, destroying its stability. Period B sees the emergence of the 'struggle for existence'.

The attributes of the two periods, as described by the philosophers and naturalists, form a system of pairings of opposites with which we are already familiar:

PERIOD A	PERIOD B
natural man	social man
vegetarian diet	carnivorous diet
abundance of food	shortage of food
'pleasant temperature'	cold
'neither toil nor fatigue'	labour
absence of predators	fight against animals
absence of disease	disease
love of nature	fear of nature
'natural mildness'	cruelty
peaceful life	war

The characteristics of period A correspond to those of the Golden Age or earthly paradise; moreover it is explicitly compared, even by militant materialists, with the Golden Age or with Eden.[80] Period B becomes a Golden Age in reverse.

---

[78] Delamétherie 1802: 11–19; Holbach 1786: 426–57; Locke 1947/1690: 17; Virey 1801, I: 98–100.
[79] Delamétherie 1802: 11.   [80] E.g. Virey 1801, I: 98.

Certain eighteenth-century naturalists and philosophers, while avoiding or even rejecting the biblical myth of human origins, proposed a conception that reproduced the scheme of the Original Fall. They placed the beginning of human history at a time of catastrophic transition from a nature endowed with paradisal features to a state where it was annihilated and negated. A good many of the scientific scenarios seem to accept this model. The earliest of those works, such as Clémence Royer's book, explicitly call period A 'the Edenic age' or the 'golden age'.[81] In the more recent scenarios, the tropical forest, with its amazing abundance, absence of predators and the vegetarian diet of its inhabitants, is endowed with paradisal attributes. The savannah, with its lack of sufficient food, which made it necessary to hunt and therefore to kill, with all the predators thirsty for human blood that teem in it, becomes a new avatar of the Cursed Ground. For Robert Ardrey, who believed (as the subtitle of his book indicates) that he was proposing a 'personal hypothesis', this dual identification becomes quite deliberate, and the author compares life in the Miocene forests with a paradisal existence ('every indication of science points to Miocene Kenya as the Eden of the human stock'), while speaking of the advent of 'the terrible Pliocene' as the expulsion from paradise.[82] The majority of anthropologists have refused to acknowledge any scientific value in Ardrey's speculations; but it is worth noting that his view of the ecological transformation seems 'personal' more for the excesses of his florid style than for its content. The conception of a radical transition from a bountiful forest to a hostile savannah is found in fourteen of our scenarios, and its great success coincides with its perfect conformity to traditional imagery.

This view, to which we have been accustomed for so long, provides a simple and 'convincing' answer to the question of the cause of the transformation of a simian creature into a human being. I have already stressed that a portion of our scenarios assimilates the characteristics of our ancestor to those of apes. This identification, in which we may suspect more than just simple rhetorical clumsiness, could pose an apparently awkward problem, frequently raised by the 'man in the street': if, long ago, an ape actually changed into a human being, why do apes no longer transform themselves into humans today? The answer might be, and certain scenarios pride themselves on anticipating it, that apes nowadays live in too hospitable an environment, lacking the stresses and difficulties that alone are capable of acting as a ferment and the wellspring

---

[81] Royer 1870: 151. [82] Ardrey 1973/1961: 246; cf. also Chapter 9.

of development. That is what the American anthropologist Eugene E. Ruyle thinks: 'We would expect that if contemporary chimpanzees were to be left free to occupy a plains niche, they would increasingly become dependent on social production and would, in the course of millions of years, transform themselves into human beings.'[83]

According to this argument, the chimpanzee would be some kind of potential human who had not been subjected to the ultimate sublimation induced by propitious ecological conditions. So it would be enough to place chimpanzee raw material in the open spaces of the savannahs in order to unleash, in an automatic and determinist manner, the essential phase of the hominisation process, which could thus be reproduced like the simplest experiments in physics or chemistry, the only drawback being the considerable duration needed for such a procedure: several million years. The 'humanogenic' power of the transition from the forest to the savannah would stem from the characteristics of the two environments: the ease of life in the forest would not encourage the changes, plunging all the creatures into the inertia peculiar, it is said, to the state of affluence, and only the challenges of existence in the hostile savannah could lead to some kind of transformation. Thus we bring wisdom closer to common sense, for which necessity alone is the mother of innovation. Although there is no lack of opportunities to be aware that innovation is often the mother of need, naïve anthropology still remains faithful to the first formula and, in its conjectures, the difficulties, the source of the need, constitute the indispensable condition for change. Malthus wrote:

> The savage would slumber for ever under his tree, unless he were roused from his torpor by the cravings of hunger, or the pinchings of cold... In those countries where nature is the most redundant in spontaneous produce, the inhabitants will not be found the most remarkable for acuteness of intellect. Necessity has been, with great truth, called the mother of invention. Some of the noblest exertions of the human mind have been set in motion by the necessity of satisfying the wants of the body.[84]

Herder was one of those who shared this opinion. He thought, as a consequence, that the cultural superiority of Europe could be explained by the magnitude of the obstacles its inhabitants had to overcome: 'Had Europe', he said, 'been as rich as India, flat as Tartary, hot as Africa, isolated as America, what has appeared in it would never have been produced.'[85]

In 1871, Darwin introduced an undeniable innovation into speculation on the causes of the development of culture. He assumed it to be

[83] Ruyle 1977: 155.   [84] Malthus 1798: 357–8.   [85] Herder 1962/1784–91: 507.

proportional to the rigour of natural selection, which in turn was induced by a huge growth in population. One cannot fail to note that this ingenious explanatory formula, in which natural selection is the consequence of the 'struggle for survival', comprises the superimposition of a new concept on an ancient imagery. While preserving its principal idea of the close relationship between the extent of human progress and the magnitude of the obstacles to be faced, Darwin's chief innovation on that point is to dissociate progress from the struggle against a hostile nature alone and associate it equally and above all with the struggle and competition against fellow creatures, in the process of natural selection.[86] The authors of most of the scenarios have not considered it necessary to make use of Darwin's innovation and preferred to remain faithful to the old idea of the hostility of original nature.

Development, for conjectural anthropology, is simply the outcome of afflictions, distresses and perils; thus the absence of cataclysms becomes synonymous with stagnation. The explanation of anthropogenesis proceeds from these two categories: first, the abundance and static harmony of the prehuman period; then a cataclysm that inaugurates the dynamic epoch of hominisation. The first humans can only be placed within a hostile nature, because otherwise they would be condemned to an everlasting animal existence, like the orang-utan, which Bory de Saint-Vincent said remains bestial because it lives too harmoniously in the native forests to think of improving its lot and cultivating its faculties.[87]

So any climatic change which destroys the original static harmony and which threatens our ancestor with annihilation is useful as a prime mover and forms a good substitute for the archangel with the flaming sword driving humanity over the Cursed Ground. We find a similar conception of the genesis in Virgil's *Georgics* where, this time, the transition from a friendly nature to a hostile nature takes place through the intervention of Jupiter:

> ... the Father himself
> Willed that the path of tillage be not smooth,
> And first ordained that skill should cultivate
> The land, by care sharpening the wits of mortals,

---

[86] 'When we see in many parts of the world enormous areas of the most fertile land peopled by a few wandering savages, but which are capable of supporting numerous happy homes, it might be argued that the struggle for existence had not been sufficiently severe to force man upwards to his highest standard... No doubt such advancement demands many favourable concurrent circumstances; but it may well be doubted whether the most favourable would have sufficed, had not the rate of increase been rapid, and the consequent struggle for existence severe to an extreme degree' (Darwin 1871, I: 180).

[87] Bory de Saint-Vincent 1827.

> Nor let his kingdom laze in torpid sloth.
> Before Jove's reign no tenant mastered holdings,
> Even to mark the land with private bounds
> Was wrong: men worked for the common store, and earth
> Herself, unbidden, yielded all more fully.
> He put fell poison in the serpent's fang,
> Bade wolves to prowl and made the sea to swell,
> Shook honey down from the leaves, hid fire away,
> And stopped the wine that freely flowed in streams,
> That step by step practice and taking thought
> Should hammer out the crafts...
> Toil mastered everything, relentless toil
> And the pressure of pinching poverty.[88]

The explanation of the origins of culture by transition from a mother nature to a stepmother nature forms a genuine *longue durée* structure of our anthropological imagery. This scheme, characteristic of European myths, has been taken up by philosophical speculation and finally given a place in scientific theories. It is odd to see this idea accompanying the first palaeoanthropological discoveries, with countless scholars stubbornly looking for *ad hoc* arguments in its favour. In the late nineteenth and early twentieth centuries, the cradle of humanity – as the Abbé Breuil remarked ironically – became a cradle on wheels, moving from one continent to another at staggering speed. The conception of an ecological cataclysm followed in its tracks; here are a few examples.

In 1900, Adrien and Gabriel de Mortillet claimed that human species originated in Europe, represented first by the semi-apelike 'Neanderthal race' and later replaced by modern humans of the 'Laugerie race'. The Mortillets gave the Neanderthal environment 'an unstimulating climate, so monotonous as to slow any individual development', and imagined the Laugerians within a hostile nature where the only things in abundance were difficulties, which spurred on development.[89] According to Léonce Manouvrier, who saw the direct ancestor of humanity in the *Pithecanthropus* discovered by Dubois in Java in 1893, the cradle of humanity must have been situated in that part of the world, and it was there that the original catastrophe should be envisaged: humanity would have been born following the disappearance of the forests in South East Asia, wiped out by increased volcanic activity.[90] The American palaeontologist Henry F. Osborn, who argued for human origins in Central Asia, supposed great orogenic processes in that part of the world in the

---

[88] Virgil 1982: 6, 1.121–46.   [89] Mortillet and Mortillet 1900: 345.   [90] Manouvrier 1897.

Tertiary, which would have pushed up a vast plateau, where abundant forest would have been rapidly transformed into an open environment, arid and full of menace.[91]

Nowadays, the cradle on wheels has stopped, probably for good reasons, in Africa, but the old habits persist. Andrew Hill reports significant changes in the interpretation of palynological data from the site of *Kenyapithecus* at Fort Ternan (14 million years ago). At the time when *Kenyapithecus* was seen as the first link in the hominid ancestral stock, it was claimed that the palynological data confirmed the hypothesis of a savannah, although there were also tree pollens present, owing, it was said, to the proximity of the Tinderet volcano, then covered with forest. But when *Kenyapithecus* had fallen from his function as the ancestor of humans, and when the key moment for hominisation had been fixed further down the time axis, the spread of the savannah in turn was pushed back in the same chronological direction and *Kenyapithecus* came to be considered as a forest dweller. The latest research, however, seems to indicate – according to Hill – that its environment was indeed an open savannah.[92]

We find an echo of this example in another one, concerning *Australopithecus africanus*. Nine of our scenarios still consider this species to be the direct ancestor of *Homo*[93] and invariably place it in the savannah. But since *Australopithecus africanus* has begun to be rejected from our direct ancestral line, more and more frequently reference is made to data indicating that at least some of the groups preferred the forest and its fringes.[94] So we see that the old habit is still there in the palaeoanthropological literature, even in highly technical discussions: candidates for the role of ancestor have the right to be in the savannah, while our collateral apelike relatives are banished to the forests.

So now we have a better understanding of how representations of the critical moment of anthropogenesis have become transformed over the centuries. The common denominator is the vision of a transition from a paradisal nature, often associated with the forest, where plentiful food went hand in hand with security, to the dynamic state of a hostile nature, associated with an open environment, where scarcity of resources led to a fierce struggle for survival. It is only opinions concerning the cause of the

---

[91] Osborn 1926.   [92] Hill 1987.
[93] Coon 1955/1954: 25; Washburn 1960: 3; Ardrey 1973/1961: 255; Hockett and Ascher 1964: 145; Jolly 1970: 23–4; Wolpoff 1974: 602; Ruyle 1977: 155; Tanner and Zihlman 1976: 587; Boriskovski 1979: 52–3.
[94] Cadman and Rayner 1988.

change from mother nature to stepmother nature that vary. In biblical myth, it is in order to expiate their original sin that humans are driven out to the Cursed Ground, where in the sweat of the face they eat bread (Genesis III.19). For Virgil, the Golden Age ends with the intervention of Jupiter, who orders humans to brave a hostile nature and create the 'crafts'. According to the conjectures of naturalists of the late eighteenth and early nineteenth centuries, culture appears when the proliferation of species destroys the harmony of original existence and obliges humans to mobilise their forces in a struggle for increasingly scarce resources. In a good many of our scenarios, it is climatic change that transforms a fertile and hospitable forest into a threatening savannah, where culture becomes indispensable for our forebears. Throughout these transformations, the 'two epochs' model keeps its habitual place, and the same goes for the attributes ascribed to it, based invariably on pairs of opposites such as: 'abundance of food/shortage of food', 'threat of predators/absence of predators', 'peaceful existence/struggle for survival', etc.

A few scenarios have shaken off this vision of the transition from friendly nature to hostile nature. Two of the texts analysed present the new savannah environment of the hominids as a habitat without threat from predators, and with an abundance of game and all kinds of food[95] (Table 4). The American anthropologist Kim Hill gives to this picture the status of a hypothesis, without trying to test it against data or at least imagining a possibility of some empirical verification.[96] J. Kelso and D. Quiatt assimilate the savannah to a type of 'ecotone' environment[97] and go on to assert – quoting a standard manual of ecology[98] – that any ecotone zone is characterised by great variety and an abundance of food resources. However, the validity of this argument by analogy has not been tested with palaeoecological data. What is more, the claim of no threat from predators is put in question by the traces of predation on certain fossil bones of Hominidae.[99] These inconsistencies should not be too surprising: this new image of the savannah is incoherent only from an empirical point of view, while its form matches up well to the rules of transformation typical of naïve anthropology. In Hill's scenario, the savannah is characterised by traditional attributes (resources, predators) which this time tend towards the positive pole (abundance, absence of menace) and metamorphose our ancestors' environment into a new avatar of the Garden of Eden.

---

[95] Hill 1982; Kelso and Quiatt 1985. [96] Hill 1982: 532. [97] Kelso and Quiatt 1985: 209.
[98] Odum 1971. [99] E.g. Brain 1981.

According to this new permutation, it is the state of affluence that provides the first impetus to the process of anthropogenesis. The mere inversion of periods A and B does not, even so, change the principle of the explanation. In the traditional version, it is the hostile environment that forces our ancestors into an activity that ends in the great transformation. The environment fashions the human being; it alone determines his behaviour. This role of the environment is preserved in the new version, which in fact corrects only the view of human nature. The latter is conceived in line with the premises of Optimal Foraging Theory, very fashionable with certain American anthropologists at the end of the 1970s and the beginning of the 1980s. In conformity with the axioms of this theory, the principle of human behaviour is first and foremost the optimisation (even maximisation) of economic yield. Our ancestor, placed suddenly in a new environment with plentiful resources, abides by this universal law and acts like a model capitalist, adopting a new strategy to ensure greater economic efficiency.[100] As a consequence, the process of hominisation is launched. It is paradoxical that, while attributing abundant resources to the hominids' milieu, K. Hill at the same time calls on Optimal Foraging Theory, the principles of which, by definition, apply only to situations where resources are scarce.[101] Thus the premises of an ecological theory with a restricted domain of application are misrepresented as 'universal laws' valid at all times and in all places.

Whatever the view of ecological change may be, our ancestor is still a creature with eternal characteristics that popular wisdom has no trouble in defining: sometimes 'need is the father of invention', sometimes 'every person goes for profit'. The first saying could accompany the view of nature transformed from a mother into a stepmother; the second could go with the reverse. Naïve anthropology purports to know the stimulus necessary to set anthropogenesis in motion, and its recipe for making a human being becomes quite simple: take an ape who could be incited to act only by necessity, remove it from the protective shell of environment A and put it on the grill of a hostile nature for a few million years (environment of period B). If your ape is more orientated towards optimisation of profit, surround it with a host of savoury ingredients of period A in order to obtain the same end result. The recipes are clear and easy for they demand only a premise concerning human nature and a stereotyped view of the ecological change.

---

[100] See the analysis of the assumptions of this theory in Stoczkowski 1990.
[101] See Cody 1974; MacArthur and Pianka 1966; Pyke 1974; Smith 1983; Stephens and Krebs 1986.

CHAPTER 3

In search of causes

We can recognise common sense 'fundamental truths' from the fact that their opposites are also believed to be 'fundamental truths'.

Niels Bohr

FROM CAUSE TO EFFECT

The notion that associates the first cause of hominisation with environmental change, together with a list of the characteristics attributed to humans, form a conceptual skeleton on which the causal explanations are constructed in paleoanthropological scenarios. We shall now attempt to analyse the nature and foundations of those explanations.

If, for example, our authors claim that a hunting economy necessarily implies sexual division of labour, we must ask the following question: why are specialists inclined to consider these two elements to be associated in a sequence in which one of them becomes the effect of the other? It is usual for a scenario to leave the question unanswered, and we must then assume that the author deemed the relation to be sufficiently obvious to need no comment. But it may also happen that the same relation is liberally justified in another text. Thanks to this, parallel analysis of the same sequences over the twenty-four scenarios gives a better understanding of the underlying assumptions which serve as the basis of these causal explanations, since what is tacit in some texts becomes explicit in others.

The justifications of causal relations, moreover, are as stereotyped as the relations themselves and most often take the form of extreme generalisations. To come back to our example, the thesis in which hunting always implies a sexual division of labour (hunting masculine and gathering feminine) is frequently founded on the following premises:

(a) Hunting requires great mobility and great strength.
(b) Women, encumbered with children, are not very mobile.
(c) Women are weak, whereas men are strong.

So we shall have to gather all these premises together and then, by means of logicist analysis, reconstruct their structured form. After that, any proposition mobilised in the most prevalent 'causal' relations will be the subject of a twofold examination, aimed at determining, on the one hand, how it fits in with empirical data (in cases where the comparison is possible) and, on the other, how it fits into the conceptual schemes of naïve anthropology.

When looking for the historical antecedents of propositions devoid of empirical foundations, I shall not operate like the historians, who are often concerned with retracing the vicissitudes of the ideas and then reconstructing their emergence, metamorphoses and 'social context'. This analysis of the scenarios of anthropogenesis will not be a scenario of the genesis of ideas. My task is quite different: it is to determine whether the success of persistent ideas in scholarly anthropology is better explained by their empirical and logical foundations, or rather by their conformity with the long-term structures of common-sense anthropology.

FROM ECOLOGICAL CHANGE TO HUNTING

The causal relation 'ecological change → hunting' occurs in eight scenarios.[1] In order to portray our ancestors' environment, seven of them resort to the vision of 'hostile nature' while only one[2] uses the image of 'edenic nature'. Logicist analysis enables us to determine the nature of the assumptions underpinning those explanations, starting with the most popular version which resorts to the image of hostile nature.

The reasoning in two of the scenarios[3] can be reduced to the following formula:

If human ancestors shifted from life in a tropical forest to life in the savannah,

and if life in the savannah necessitated hunting subsistence,

then following the transition from the tropical forest to the savannah, human ancestors started to hunt.

The reasons why life in the savannah would be a sufficient and necessary condition for the appearance of hunting are not indicated. Other

---

[1] Coon 1955/1954; Ardrey 1973/1961: 261–5; Hockett and Ascher 1964: 141; Laughlin 1968: 319; Jolly 1970: 21–2; Ruyle 1977: 144, 154; Boriskovski 1979: 49; Hill 1982: 532.
[2] Hill 1982.   [3] Ruyle 1977; Boriskovski 1979.

scenarios[4] offer more complete reasonings, which can be summed up thus:

If (a) the reduction of forests led to either the disappearance of fruits or a lack of plant food in general,
and if (b) before the change in their environment, human ancestors were either fruit-eaters or vegetarians,
then (c) by depriving our ancestors of plant food, the reduction of forest cover forced them to become carnivores and live by hunting.

These last three propositions give rise to some comments:
(a) the savannah, as I have already said, is not always lacking in plant food suitable for primates;
(b) observation of use-wear marks on teeth of fossil hominids, together with chemical analysis of bones, enables us today to reconstruct the diet of extinct species, but the argument that our ancestors were strict vegetarians is difficult to evaluate, inasmuch as the scenarios in question do not make clear which type of hominids they have in mind. The hypothesis of original vegetarianism had been based largely on analogies with modern primates, who were formerly believed not to eat flesh. Recent observations of primates in the wild have shown that they hunt[5] and that meat and eggs make up more than a third (37 per cent) of their food intake;[6]
(c) even if we accept that our ancestor metamorphosed from a vegetarian into a carnivore, we should not forget that hunting is not the only way of obtaining meat; scavenging is another.

It would be rash to deny that the hominisation process could have been accompanied by an increasing proportion of meat in the diet of our ancestors. It seems, however, that the notion of original strict vegetarianism, followed supposedly by meat eating and hunting, finds relatively little support in the empirical data. On the other hand, it is interesting to see how this hypothesis fits into the tradition of naïve anthropology. A similar view can be found in countless authors of the eighteenth century, and on into the next century,[7] and also in Antiquity where it appears in Diodorus

---

[4] Coon 1958: 26; Ardrey 1973/1961: 261–5; Hockett and Ascher 1964: 141; Laughlin 1968: 319.
[5] E.g. Harding 1975, 1981; Strum 1981; Teleki 1973.   [6] Harding 1981: 37.
[7] Burnet 1774–92, I: 452; Delamétherie 1802: 11; Du Pont 1775, quoted from Meek 1976: 182; Goguet 1758, I: 71–2; Home 1774: 44; Lacépède 1830: 188; Quesnay 1763, quoted from Meek 1976: 91; Virey 1801, I: 98–9.

Siculus,[8] Horace,[9] Lucretius,[10] Macrobius,[11] Ovid,[12] Pausanias[13] and Varro.[14]

The resemblance to old myth motifs is patently obvious: in the Golden Age or in paradise, first humans were always vegetarian or more specifically fruit-eaters.[15] The abundance with which paradisal nature favours not only humans, but all the animals as well, is infinite, so that no creature is obliged to kill in order to live, and friendship between humans and animals becomes an essential feature of the primordial existence, where universal love holds sway and no conflict pits either humans or beasts against each other. The end of the Golden Age destroys the harmony of this union: the bloodthirsty chase makes its appearance, at the same time as crime, antagonism and hate. In very many texts, hunting is likened to war[16] and murder.[17] Herder mentions war and hunting side by side so as to classify them as phenomena of degeneration, following on from the original state.[18] As Porphyry reports, Dicaearchus thought that the condition of bliss of the first humans was due in part to their meatless diet, which allowed them to avoid wars; wars appeared only when humans had stained their hands with blood, and it was animals that became the first victims of their murderous insanity.[19] 'Henceforth', Delamétherie would comment later, referring to the same imagery, 'they assumed the character of carnivores: their natural gentleness gave place to violence.'[20] Alexander Pope painted the resulting revolution in this manner:

> Ah! how unlike the man of times to come!
> Of half that live the butcher and the tomb;
> Who, foe to nature, hears the gen'ral groan,
> Murders their species and betrays his own.
> But just disease to luxury succeeds,
> And ev'ry death its own avenger breeds;
> The Fury-passions from that blood began,
> And turn'd on Man a fiercer savage, Man.[21]

---

[8] Diodorus Siculus 1737: 18.   [9] Horace 1932: 99, I.iii.   [10] Lucretius 1964: 84–5, v. 936–44.
[11] Macrobius, *Somn. Scip.* II.x.6, quoted from Lovejoy and Boas 1965/1935: 381–2.
[12] Ovid, *Ars amatoria*, II.467–80, quoted from Lovejoy and Boas 1965/1935: 375.
[13] Pausanias 1797: 245, VIII.1.
[14] Varro, *De rustica*, II.1, 3ff, quoted from Lovejoy and Boas 1965/1935: 368.
[15] Empedocles, *Fragm.*, 130, quoted from Lovejoy and Boas 1965/1935: 32–3; Isaiah LXV; de Meun 1974/1270: 243; Ovid 1966: 44, 1.91–127; Virgil 1982: 6, 125–35.
[16] E.g. Aristotle, *Politica* I.1256b, 23–6, quoted from Lovejoy and Boas 1965/1935: 185.
[17] E.g. Pope 1993/1733–4: 109–10; Virey 1801, I: 100.   [18] Herder 1962/1784–91: 166.
[19] Porphyry, *De Abstinentia* IV.i.2, in Lovejoy and Boas 1965/1935: 94–6.
[20] Delamétherie 1802: 11.   [21] Pope 1993/1733–4: 109–10, *Epistle* III, vv. 161–8.

So we see that an old tradition of Western thought associates vegetarianism with the paradisal condition, while making hunting its opposite, linked with the subsequent state of imperfection, even at times responsible for that imperfection. The transition from peaceable vegetarianism to the meat diet of the murderous hunter is thus a part of the very popular class of myths relating to the 'original fall'. Later philosophical speculation has picked up the same sequence of events, while adding materialist significance. Naturalists like Delamétherie[22] or Virey[23] placed the first humans in 'a fair land' where gathering easily sufficed to satisfy all their needs; it was population growth that would force our ancestors later to supplement their diet with meat.

These notions foreshadow the view we find in our palaeoanthropological scenarios: the peaceable vegetarians are obliged, by an event that comes along to disturb the balance of their habitat, to hunt and kill. This conceptual infrastructure remains invariable, hypotheses competing to find naturalist explanations, illustrated by a few data chosen at random, that agree with the mythical theme of a transition from original vegetarianism to the cruel hunt. So new ecological data on the Plio-Pleistocene environment, cited today by scientific scenarios, merely provide some minor accessories to make the old mythical theme more credible.

Anthropologist Kim Hill[24] differs from other authors by attributing paradisal features to the hominids' new milieu: abundance of animal resources and absence of predators. In these conditions, the author asserts, hunting made it possible to maximise yields from efforts invested in provisioning, so that ecological change drove our ancestors, as unrepentant maximisers, to become hunters.

I have stated my reservations concerning that particular ecological view and the use of Optimal Foraging Theory by this author. I must now add that Hill's argument, with its 'new' image of the environment, is limited to reversing the chronological positions of 'mother nature' and 'stepmother nature', while maintaining the traditional sequences of the shift from vegetarianism to meat eating and from gathering to hunting. How changes in the way of life and of feeding are explained also remain the same: just as shortage of food in a hostile environment forced humans to become hunters, so abundance in a hospitable environment obliges them now to start living by hunting. So, whatever the environment, its impact on our ancestors is the same, and the logic of ecological determinism remains safe.

---

[22] Delamétherie 1802: 11.   [23] Virey, 1801, I: 100.   [24] Hill 1982.

FROM ECOLOGICAL CHANGE TO BIPEDALISM

No fewer than twenty-one scenarios in my sample consider bipedalism to be a distinctive characteristic of human species; the best illustration of its significance in scenarios of hominisation is that bipedal locomotion becomes sufficient in itself to explain the origin of eight other important 'human' characteristics.

Speculations about upright posture have a long history. When Plato spoke of the vertical posture of man, he said that the head, being the seat of the most noble of souls, has to be turned upwards as evidence that the human being is 'the heavenly plant', and as a sign of his 'affinity with heaven'.[25] This symbolic use of high and low, of vertical and horizontal positions, which serves to connote the distinction between humans and animals, occurs also in Xenophon,[26] Aristotle,[27] Pliny[28] and Vitruvius.[29] Ovid returns to it by developing its allegorical meaning: man was allowed to be upright and to turn his face up so that he might gaze at the sky.[30] Cicero declares that only man adopts the vertical posture, so that by contemplating the heavens he may come to know the gods.[31]

This tradition was perpetuated by Christian authors. Prudentius has God speak in these terms: 'I had created man perfect and I had commanded him to gaze on heavenly things, turned towards me in all his senses, to hold himself erect, to stand upright, to look upwards.'[32] For Gregory of Nyssa, the vertical attitude is the sign of the royal power of humans over all the other creatures, bent earthwards.[33] The same terms still appear at the beginning of the nineteenth century, although then they seem to be no more than vague metaphors, whose original significance has already been lost to an ornamental function; thus the naturalist J.-J. Virey is echoing the Ancients when he says that 'the human brow is raised heavenwards',[34] soon followed by Lamarck, for whom 'humans endeavoured to stand upright, moved by the need to dominate'.[35]

---

[25] Plato 1970: 90a.   [26] Xenophon 1872: I.IV.39.   [27] Aristotle 1968, I.15.
[28] Pliny the Elder 1947, XI.XCVIII.   [29] Vitruvius 1834, II.1.   [30] Ovid 1969, I.76–8.
[31] Cicero, *De rerum natura*, II.LVI.
[32] Prudentius 1948: II.259–65; see also Lactance 1987: 29–33, II.14–19.
[33] Gregory of Nyssa 1944: 106–7; this edition gives a bibliography of the same theme in other Fathers of the Church; Partides (1958) traces its presence in the Renaissance period.
[34] Virey 1801, I: 120.
[35] Lamarck 1820: 350; see also Virey 1827: 209; a detailed analysis of western conceptions concerning human bipedalism will be found in Stoczkowski 1995b.

Here again we are dealing with a system of terms arranged yet again in a series of binary opposites:

high/low
affinity with heaven/separation from heaven
knowledge of the gods/ignorance of the gods
domination/submission
humanity/animality
upright posture/bent posture

Bipedalism, associated with an upright posture, thus becomes a bearer of all the meanings on the left-hand side of these opposites and acquires its full sense as the antithesis of the contrasts on the right-hand side. 'Upright posture/bipedalism' will thus be a human characteristic symbolising union with the heavenly realm and abandonment of the animal condition. To illustrate how this symbolic system functions, remember the biblical story of King Nebuchadnezzar, related in the Book of Daniel (IV.30–3). The proud monarch, driven from men, dwelled a long time with the beasts of the field and ended up resembling them and taking on different animal traits, among them, as the text suggests and medieval iconography depicts,[36] the horizontal posture on all fours. But Nebuchadnezzar regained the human condition when he was able to stand upright again and lift up his eyes unto heaven.

It is in this symbolic sense that 'upright posture/bipedalism' creates humans, by turning them towards the heavens, whence they draw the strength necessary to rise above the animal state. That said, there is no reason to underestimate the criteria of upright posture and bipedalism, which indeed are fairly rare properties outside our biological family. This fact has not only been noted in the West: the ethnologist J.-P. Chaumeil reports that among the Amazonian Yagua, the criterion of 'verticality' of the species, expressed by the verb *uriane* (to 'get up', 'stand up', 'be standing on one's feet', as opposed to the 'crawling' position) is used to distinguish the higher from the lower animals and indicates their gradual climb towards humanity.[37] The fact remains that, while recognising the importance of this criterion, we should not forget its symbolic significance. In eighteenth-century Europe, this was simplified and reduced to two pairs of opposites: 'humanity/animality' and 'upright posture/bent

---

[36] See the illustrations in the tenth- and eleventh-century chronicles in Huband 1980: 8–9.
[37] Chaumeil 1989: 21.

posture'.[38] Thereafter, the role of 'upright posture/bipedalism' began to be perceived according to naturalist categories. Nevertheless, scholarly thought, following a symbolic tradition, continued to endow it with a strange 'creative' power: not only does upright posture distinguish humans from animals but it also produces humans out of animals, setting the hominisation process in motion almost single-handedly. Like Nebuchadnezzar, our ancestors only had to stand up on their feet to be transformed into human creatures.

We now know that bipedalism appeared very early (Kanapoi, $c.$ 4 million years ago; Laetoli, 3.5 million years ago), preceding a good many other 'human attributes', which may be an indication of the importance of its role in the hominisation process. But the way we see that role remains curiously faithful to the slant of the traditional imagery that still conditions the arguments of palaeoanthropologists.

Let us return to our main subject. An environment change would have been the principal reason for adopting an upright posture and bipedalism. Four scenarios[39] suggest a simple causal relationship that can be reduced to the following syllogism:

If at a certain period hominids started living in an open environment,

and if bipedal locomotion is linked with life in the open environment,

then the hominids adopted bipedal locomotion because they found themselves in an open environment.

The relationship between life in an open environment and bipedalism is explained by assuming that this kind of locomotion conferred great advantages in open country. Divergences between explanations go back to differing assumptions as to these advantages. Thus Kenneth Oakley[40] declared that upright posture made it easier to see above the tall grasses that covered the savannah. This hypothesis, which is plausible and corroborated by analogies with present-day primates who occasionally stand on their hind legs to look around, is none the less unverifiable (we should remember that the idea of a relation between upright posture and the

---

[38] E.g. Diderot 1754/1753: 66–7, XLVII; Ferguson 1767: 4–5; Herder 1962/1784–91: 104; Kant 1985/1786: 505; see also Stoczkowski 1995b: 26–9.
[39] Darwin 1871, I: 140–1; Oakley 1957: 207; 1968: 258; Niestourkh 1958: 233; Lumsden and Wilson 1983: 9–12.
[40] Oakley 1957: 207.

possibility of seeing a long way is already there in Xenophon and, in the eighteenth century, in Rousseau[41]).

Robert Ardrey assumes that bipedalism would have favoured survival in the savannah, where our ancestors would have been living with the constant menace of predators.[42]

Tanner and Zihlman's scenario[43] postulates that bipedalism was adopted by the first hominids because it was useful when carrying food back to group base sites concealed in safer clusters of trees, where the hominids took cover from predators. This hypothesis is plausible but would require empirical validation, which has not been attempted and seems difficult to imagine.

It is significant that all our authors try to explain the origin of bipedalism by looking for its 'usefulness', conceived in accordance with the traditional image they have of the natural environment, teeming with predators. Speculation about conceivable 'usefulness', when spared the imperative of validation, can evolve fairly freely and become a thought experiment, where more or less plausible conjectures rub shoulders at times with somewhat unexpected ideas. Thus R. W. Westcott believed that bipedalism was adopted because humankind's ancestor stood up on two feet so as to seem taller and so impress his adversaries.[44] According to A. Hardy, our ancestors, obliged to search for food and flee from predators, would have been led to live in the water somewhere along the coasts of Africa, where the upright posture would have proved useful in their new aquatic environment.[45] For W. Köhler, the first humans were living in a harsh climate, on ice-covered soil; they would have begun to stand upright so as to preserve their forepaws from the cold.[46] The boundary is easily crossed between these preposterous examples and the deliberately absurd explanation offered by David C. Batten in a text full of humour, daringly published in the *Journal of Anthropological Research*: our ancestors, living not in Africa but in Norway, would have been winter sports fanatics who became accustomed to the upright position to keep their balance on skis while freeing their hands to use the sticks. We have here even a test project: 'My research strategy has the elegance of simplicity. I and my team will simply position ourselves at the base of a glacier and wait for an australopithecine in knickers and goggles to melt out.'[47]

A joke out of place? At odds with the habitual seriousness of a scientific journal, Batten's article has the merit of showing how permeable is the

[41] Xenophon 1872, I.IV.39; Rousseau 1973/1755: 393. [42] Ardrey 1973/1961: 260.
[43] Tanner and Zihlman 1976: 597-9. [44] Wescott 1967. [45] Hardy 1960.
[46] Kohler 1959. [47] Batten 1986.

line between humorous fantasy and the gratuitous character of some scholarly hypotheses. The explanatory strategy is the same on both sides, since it is based on a quest for practical usefulness, more or less freely imagined, to explain the appearance of bipedalism. Obviously, this may be the right strategy. It is possible that a change of milieu was indeed at the origin of bipedalism, as suggested by chimpanzees in open country who resort more frequently to bipedal locomotion than those in a forest environment.[48] But how can we be sure, as long as scholarly explanations remain restricted to the same set of unverifiable conjectures?

FROM ECOLOGICAL CHANGE TO TOOLS

There has long been a fondness for representing primitive humans as hairy creatures, with an animal skin around their waists and a big, heavy club in their hands. Hairiness points to the still strong link with the animal world that our ancestors have only just left, while the tool in their hands and the furry 'loin cloth', modestly hiding their private parts, represent the first signs of the human condition. Tools have long been seen as one of the main attributes separating humanity from animality; countless myths tell of the origin of tools, whose appearance marks the transition from nature to culture. In the course of the eighteenth century, this theme would become one of the favourite topics of philosophical speculation, which would give it a naturalist dimension. But recent observations by primatologists undermine our habit of attributing the tool to humans and refusing it to animals. It turns out that chimpanzees and orang-utans not only use tools but actually make them.[49] What is more, the degree of complexity of these tools has moved certain anthropologists to compare them to the artefacts of some human groups.[50] When embarking on parallels of this type, the tendency to push them too far must, of course, be avoided and the disparities between the products of primates and those of the least advanced human groups remain beyond dispute;[51] but resemblances exist and they are indications that a rigid binary opposition can give only a perfunctory and imperfect picture of differences, which are none the less real.

[48] Robinson 1972: 258.
[49] Beck 1980; Boesch and Boesch 1983; Galdikas 1982; Goodall 1964; Jones and Sabater 1969; Jordan 1982; Kortlandt and Holzhaus 1987; Lethmate 1982; McGrew 1974; Nishida and Hiraiwa 1982; Struhsaker and Hunkeler 1971. It should be stressed that the use of tools by the apes has been known to naturalists since the 1830s and that in 1871 Darwin was able to cite several examples; Darwin 1871, I: 51–2.
[50] McGrew 1987.   [51] E.g. Wynn and McGrew 1989.

It is interesting to look closely at the types of tools ascribed to the first humans. The scenarios usually speak of natural, unshaped stones and all kinds of sticks:

Royer	stones/branches of trees
Darwin	stones/clubs
Coon	stones/sticks
Niestourkh	stones/branches
Washburn	stones/sticks
Ardrey	stones/bludgeons
Wolpoff	stones/sticks

The use of unshaped stones and of sticks would have marked the first stage in recourse to tools, even though it is only a matter of fortuitous tools, unprepared and eminently 'natural'. The term 'tools', moreover, is a rather poor one to describe them, since our scenarios make them more like weapons, conforming to the traditional view which sees defence and fighting as the first needs and occupations of our ancestors. And yet the example of the chimpanzees should inspire more peaceable conjectures: ancient tools may have served to crack nuts rather than heads.[52] It is only recently that less bloodthirsty hypotheses have been put forward, abandoning the patterns of conjectural anthropology to draw nearer to what is suggested by the tools of present-day non-human primates.[53]

But the fact that chimpanzees occasionally make use of stones and branches does not necessarily mean that these were the first tools of prehistoric hominids. There is not much likelihood that these hypotheses, based on analogies with present-day primates, will ever receive direct confirmation; it would need exceptional conditions (for example the transport of raw materials far from their naturally occurring deposits) for the prehistorian to be able to distinguish stones that have never found their way into the hands of hominids from those they might have occasionally used. Such discrimination is even less probable in the case of the occasional use of branches of trees, even supposing that some might be found one day on a hominid site.

Note too, that the idea of making stones the first human weapons does not come originally from the observation of primates. We find it in works of philosophers as early as the sixteenth century (Leroy, for example) up until the eighteenth century (for example Goguet and Voltaire),[54] who

---

[52] Boesch and Boesch 1984. [53] Chavaillon 1983.
[54] Leroy 1988/1575: 111; Goguet 1758, I: 74–5; Voltaire 1963/1756, I: 10.

borrow it from Lucretius.⁵⁵ Of particular interest is the history of the stick and the club. For a very long time, the club has faithfully accompanied early humans, and popular literature offers such lyrical descriptions of that union that I cannot resist the temptation to quote at least one of them:

The club had thus been his first companion. He loved it. It flattered him. He was proud of it.... At the moment of going into battle, he held it tight in his fist, as one holds the hand of a friend... after the battle, he caressed it just as the huntsman strokes his dog's back to show his appreciation; it was almost like thanks; the harder it had struck, the more esteem, attachment, trust and perhaps even gratitude he felt for it. He left it neither for food nor sleep; when it was not in his hand during a pause, it lay at his side, within reach; while he slept in the tree, he kept it on his chest.⁵⁶

To arm the hand of primitive man with a club seems perfectly natural to us, but we can find no trace of it in museum cases or in archaeological archives. The club is just not there. On the other hand, it has a very lively existence in the realm of the imaginary. Naturalists of the early nineteenth century,⁵⁷ as well as philosophers of the Enlightenment, frequently alluded to it.⁵⁸ But its birth certificate carries an earlier date, for the club or stick was already in the hands of the Wild Man – a character of medieval European folklore.⁵⁹ The historian Robert Bernheimer introduces us to this creature in the following terms:

It is a hairy man, curiously compounded of human and animal traits, without, however, sinking to the level of an ape. It exhibits upon his naked human anatomy a growth of fur, leaving bare only its face, feet and hands, at times its knees and elbows, or the breasts of the female of the species. Frequently the creature is shown wielding a heavy club or mace, or the trunk of a tree.⁶⁰

The Wild Man is encountered in French Arthurian romances and in the songs of the German minstrels, and later still, in Miguel de Cervantes or Edmund Spenser.⁶¹ But this character is not only found in books. During the famous *Bal des Ardents* in 1392 at the court of Charles VI, the banquet ended with the death of several lords, whose disguises of rough cloth covered with linen hairs caught fire; the unfortunate victims were wearing Wild Man masks and we can see them in an engraving of the period in costumes on which linen hairs imitated animal fur; great clubs

---

⁵⁵ Lucretius 1964: 85, v. 966–8.   ⁵⁶ Haraucourt 1986/1914: 116–17.
⁵⁷ E.g. Lacépède 1821: 376.
⁵⁸ E.g. Buffon 1825b/1778: 309; Burnet 1774–92, I: 399–400; Voltaire 1963/1756, I: 376.
⁵⁹ See the works devoted to him: Bernheimer 1970; Dudley and Novak 1972; Huband 1980.
⁶⁰ Bernheimer 1970: 1.   ⁶¹ Bibliography, see Bernheimer 1970: 2.

lie abandoned on the ground, gnarled tree trunks studded with sharp stones.[62] The masks of this tragic ball were probably modelled on those of popular carnival rites. At carnival time of year, and even recently, the spectacle of Wild Men dancing and carrying clubs could be witnessed in different regions of Europe.[63] The custom was particularly common in south Germany, and Goethe depicts it in Part II of *Faust*:

> The wild men of the woods they're named,
> And in the Harz are known and famed;
> In naked nature's ancient might
> They come, each one a giant wight,
> With fir-tree trunk in brawny hand,
> Around the loins a puffy band,
> The merest apron of leaf and bough.[64]

The popularity of this figure in folklore reached its peak in the fourteenth and fifteenth centuries, but some counterparts exist as far back as Greek mythology, where many creatures exhibit a mixture of human and animal traits, and carry clubs, sticks or tree trunks (Centaurs, Silenus); like our Wild Man or prehistoric man, they too use these weapons to fight off wild beasts.[65] Hercules, likewise, is constantly fighting wild animals, armed with a club, according to mythical narratives and to the iconography of all periods. Moreover in the eighteenth century he was called 'the lion tamer, because he makes all the wild animals disappear; because he forces them to yield possession of the Earth to him'.[66] A giant wielding a club exists in northern European folklore too, his great age being attested by the figure of the so-called Cerne Abbas Giant in Dorset (Great Britain) dating probably from the Roman or pre-Roman period.[67]

It is very likely that authors of Antiquity, when depicting early humans wielding clubs and sticks,[68] were inspired by the Wild Man figure borrowed from the imagery of popular culture. As far as Antiquity is concerned, we are reduced to conjecture, but with regard to the naturalist speculation of the eighteenth and nineteenth centuries, it is easy to find textual proofs of these borrowings. Thus, in Clémence Royer, 'primitive man is Hercules wielding his club, smooth, slender, and strong at the hilt, heavy, wider and knotty at the end'.[69] A similar association seems to make Voltaire believe that myths were a confused memory of the earliest times: 'Men could defend themselves against wild animals

---

[62] See, for example, Gaignebet and Lajoux 1985: 127.
[63] E.g. Bernheimer 1970: photo 3.
[64] Goethe, *Faust*, II. Act 1.3; trans. Bayard Taylor 1871.
[65] Bernheimer 1970: 94.
[66] Court de Gébelin 1773, I: 175.
[67] Willcox 1988.
[68] Lucretius 1964: 85, v. 966–8; Horace 1932: 99, I.iii.
[69] Royer 1870: 395.

only by hurling stones, or arming themselves with great branches of trees; and from that, perhaps, came the confused notion in Antiquity that the earliest heroes fought against lions and wild boars with clubs.'[70]

This was not the first time that the ancient folklore figure lent his attributes to our ancestors. When Charles V entered Bruges, masks of the Wild Man, representing the most ancient inhabitants of Flanders, were seen in the solemn procession.[71] In a pre-Shakespearian drama *Gorboduc*, the Wild Man is associated with the Ancient Britons, who peopled the island before the Anglo-Saxon invasion.[72]

In the era of great geographical discoveries, the Wild Man image began to be projected on to the primitive peoples of the Antipodes, who were thereafter given the name of savages, the very same name which had until then designated the imaginary Wild Man (in French *sauvage* or *salvage*; Middle English borrowed the word from Old French). So exotic *savages* emerge, also covered in hair, ceaselessly at war with wild beasts and using clubs.[73] These images fell on the fertile soil of ancient representations and were propagated with amazing success, despite the refutations of this 'common opinion', made from the middle of the sixteenth century on by certain travellers.[74] But the inertia of the imaginary is too great for proofs of its inadequacy to oust clichés very swiftly.

To ensure that exotic peoples conformed to the model of the Wild Man, they were endowed with animal characteristics; the reverse procedure served to project the same image on to orang-utans in the late seventeenth and eighteenth centuries,[75] the only difference being that this time it was not a human being cast in the role of an animal but an animal in that of a human.

Why did European imagination identify so completely our ancestors, aborigines and orang-utans with this strange figure from mythical iconography and carnival rites? As I have already noted, the Wild Man represents a mixture of human and animal traits. Although nearly human, the creature remains half beast, no longer wholly animal, but still lacking what is essentially human; the genuine 'missing link' in the natural order, which, as was said, *non facit saltum*. Le Brun wrote: 'all bodies are linked in the chain of Being; Nature everywhere is preceded and followed. In the constant order, her developing steps never conquer in leaps and bounds. Look at the Wild Man as a link in the existence of humans, diminishing the distance from them to the animals.'[76]

---

[70] Voltaire 1963/1756, I: 10; see also Burnet 1774–92, I: 399–400. [71] Bernheimer 1970: 120.
[72] Manly 1897: 215. [73] E.g. Hodgen 1964: 18–20. [74] Thevet 1982/1577–8: 58.
[75] Tinland 1968: 127. [76] Le Brun 1811/1760, II. 319–20.

In the eyes of the naturalists, the Wild Man, endowed with intermediary characteristics, became the ideal candidate to personify that 'missing link' in the economy of nature. Certain exotic peoples, orangutans, chimpanzees and – inevitably – humans of the earliest period were soon cast in the same role. Compared to the Wild Man, all these 'savage' figures, whether 'animalised' humans or 'humanised' animals, inherited his attributes, and, oddly enough, the club. In time, as journeys to the Antipodes became more frequent, and observation of 'primitive' peoples and primates allowed Europeans to build up a more relevant body of knowledge about these contemporary incarnations of the Wild Man, the vision of clubs, fights with wild beasts and 'bestial' properties suffered a process of erosion, as long as it was slow. On the other hand, in prehistoric archaeology, where verification of old beliefs is always more difficult, the Wild Man found his most secure refuge. His days are undoubtedly numbered, but the association of the hairy creature and the club still persists and will probably persist for as long as the conceptions of prehistorians and palaeoanthropologists rely less on empirical data than on that pernicious 'common opinion' which was already being denounced in the Renaissance.

The aim of this long digression was to show how the weapon of an imaginary figure could have found a place in the hominisation scenarios. Let us move on now to analyse the causal relation that associates the origin of tools with ecological change. We find this sequence in five scenarios, four of which offer arguments that can be reduced to the following two inferences:[77]

1. **If (a)** in their new milieu, hominids were threatened with attack from animals,
    and if (b) the hominids, lacking natural means of defence, were weaker than the animals,
    then (c) the hominids were physically too weak to survive in the new hostile environment.
2. **If(c)** *ibid.*,
    and if (d) tools can replace the somatic organs of defence,
    then (e) to survive in their new hostile milieu, the hominids were obliged to resort to the use of tools.

This argument calls on one of the most classic themes of naïve anthropology. Premise (*a*) brings the traditional image of a hostile nature into

---

[77] Ardrey 1973/1961: 252–71; Hockett and Ascher 1964: 140–1; Jolly, 1970: 21–2; Wolpoff 1974: 604–5; Tanner and Zihlman 1976: 599.

play with the attacks from 'wild animals'. Proposition (*b*) expresses the idea of human weakness, and those that follow *(c–d–e)* reconstitute the old conception of technique as a substitute for the teeth and claws that humans lack. This explanation is theoretically plausible and we cannot rule out the possibility that such was indeed the genesis of tools. But the essence of the problem stems from the fact that the hypothesis lacks empirical weight: it has never been confronted with palaeoanthropological or archaeological data and, indeed, it is difficult to imagine how it could be.

At the same time, it would be wrong to believe that the attachment to this explanation stems from the fact that it is the only one conceivable. Naïve anthropology claims that culture is born of practical necessities imposed by a hostile nature; but when these clichés are removed, they can easily be replaced by other conjectures, some of which may be inspired by observation of present-day primates. The research of M. A. Huffman,[78] who has described the use of stones in a group of macaques (*Macaca fuscata*), provides one of several examples: at the end of the year 1979, a macaque invented a game with stones, which consisted of picking up pebbles, piling them up, taking them in its hands and putting them down again on the ground, moving them from one place to another and finally rubbing or striking them against each other. Although these operations were linked to no practical needs, still less to any survival imperatives, the 'invention' was a great success. In 1984, five years after its first appearance, the game was being played by 49 per cent of the group, which then numbered 236 individuals. The author of these observations makes an interesting comment: once the game was over, the macaque abandoned the stones, but his interest revived as soon as he saw 'his' stones in the hands of another monkey. This behaviour is well known to all who have observed children playing (or who are able to observe the world of adults, while keeping slightly aloof): the most ordinary toy can become a desirable object for no other reason than that someone else possesses it, or is trying to appropriate it. It is worth emphasising the social nature of the stimulus that is capable of fostering behaviour of no direct link to the basic physiological needs. In primates, play constitutes an important, though often underestimated element in the use of tools.[79] More generally, laboratory research indicates that play has a considerable role in the life of social animals.[80] Such data as these allow us to imagine that the first tools might have appeared as the secondary outcome of

---

[78] Huffman 1984. [79] Menzel 1972. [80] Quoted from Bekoff 1972: 420.

a playful activity, and that they were propagated thanks to a system of social motivations, independently of any practical use. So the concept of 'useless tools' can be set against the idea of the pragmatic origin of tools. Of course, this is only a hypothesis and is itself unverifiable, but no more so than the one in our scenarios: from a methodological point of view, their value is equal, that is to say, very slight. And yet only one of the two is commonly accepted, and confidence is generally reserved for the one that is in perfect harmony with the notions of naïve anthropology.

The tradition that associates the origin of technique with human weakness and the constraints of survival is very ancient. We find its first trace in *Protagoras'* narrative of human creation:

> Once upon a time there were gods only, and no mortal creatures. But when the appointed time came that these also should be created, the gods fashioned them out of earth and fire and various mixtures of both elements in the interior of the earth; and when they were about to bring them into the light of day, they ordered Prometheus and Epimetheus to equip them and to distribute to them severally their proper qualities. Epimetheus said to Prometheus: 'Let me distribute and do you inspect.' This was agreed, and Epimetheus made the distribution. There were some to whom he gave strength without swiftness, while he equipped the weaker with swiftness; some he armed, others he left unarmed; and devised for the latter some other means of preservation. Upon those whom he clothed in diminutive bodies, he bestowed winged flight or subterranean habitations: those which he aggrandised with magnitude, he protected by their very size: and similarly with the rest of his distribution, always compensating. These devices he used as precautions that no race should be destroyed. And when he had provided against their destruction by one another, he contrived also a means of protecting them against the seasons of heaven; clothing them with close hair and thick skins sufficient to defend them against the winter cold, yet able to resist the summer heat, and serving also as a natural bed of their own when they wanted to rest; also he furnished them with hoofs and hair and hard callous skins under their feet... Thus did Epimetheus, who, not being very wise, forgot that he had distributed among the brute animals all the qualities which he had to give – and when he came to man, who was still unprovided, he was terribly perplexed. Now while he was in this perplexity, Prometheus came to inspect the distribution, and he found that the other animals were quite suitably furnished, but that man was naked and shoeless, and had neither bed nor arms of defence.[81]

Wishing to safeguard the existence of humanity, Prometheus stole from the gods not only fire but also a knowledge of the crafts by which the human race would be able to maintain life. The genesis of technique (*dêmitourgiké technê*) thus becomes a consequence of human weakness. As

---
[81] Plato, trans. Jowett 1871, I: 145–6.

I have already demonstrated, this theme is frequent in ancient, post-Platonic literature, and also in Christian thought. According to Gregory of Nyssa, 'a flaw in our nature is in fact an encouragement to dominate what is close to us'.[82] For man, weakness is a requirement to improve, without which he 'would be nothing but an unapproachable wild animal'; with no natural weapon, he finds himself forced to create tools, 'sturdier than defensive horns, sharper than the point of a tooth'.[83] By using tools, humans embarked on the path towards an improvement that would allow them to conquer and transform the world. Naïve anthropology wants everything that exists to be useful, so human weakness must be so too. Its significance takes on a finalist character, as in Origen, for whom man was created naked and indigent because his destiny was to conquer the world in a relentless struggle to which only his weakness could incite him.[84] The same idea lingers on in the nineteenth century in the anthropogenesis scenarios: 'Man is thus the child of his struggles, of his sufferings. All his greatness derives originally from an imperfection, his glory from his weakness, his felicity from his wretchedness, from his defeats at least as much as from his victories.'[85]

The weakness of human beings is no longer considered here to be a part of the divine plan, but its role in the genesis of culture remains the same. It is fascinating to note the extent to which the actual description of their weakness echoes that of Plato. The Russian palaeoanthropologist M. F. Niestourkh characterises it as follows: 'Our ancestors had no natural means of defence against attacks, neither sharp claws, nor large teeth, not horns, nor hooves, in other words, none of the specialised organs by means of which other mammals defend themselves against their enemies. Our ancestors could not even run very fast.'[86]

The thesis of the weakness of man is mobilised at different stages of their arguments by seven of the scenarios,[87] and three others adopt it implicitly.[88] Altogether, eleven scenarios deemed it essential to resort to this idea to account for the genesis of humankind and of culture. As for tools, human weakness is even considered to be a sufficient condition for their appearance, in conjunction with 'ecological change', and yet among animals there is no lack of creatures more 'disarmed' and more 'threatened', which nevertheless do not resort to clubs to defend themselves.

---

[82] Gregory of Nyssa 1944: 103.   [83] Ibid.: 103–4.   [84] Origen 1968, IV.76.
[85] Royer 1870: 169.   [86] Niestourkh 1958: 232, see also Ardrey 1973/1961: 252–3.
[87] Royer 1870: 152, 169, 392; Darwin 1871, I: 156–7; Oakley 1968: 258; Coon 1955/1954: 43–4; Niestourkh 1958: 232; Ardrey 1973/1961: 252–3; Wolpoff 1971: 605.
[88] Lamarck 1820: 151; Hockett and Ascher 1964: 141; Ruyle 1977: 144.

One of the five scenarios that envisage a causal relation between change of milieu and the appearance of tools offers a new explanation.[89] The first artefacts of our ancestors, it says, would not have been weapons, but a kind of baby sling, digging sticks and food containers, useful for gathering. It puts forward the *ad hoc* hypothesis of an incontrovertible need for such objects, and for good reason: it is directly connected to the premises of a feminist theory – which makes no secret of its ideological commitment – through a determination to 'prove' the primordial role of women in the hominisation process. Protection of children and gathering are attributed to females, and the authors of the scenario assert that it was these feminine occupations that inspired the invention of the first tools, which had become necessary in a new, more constraining environment in order to lighten the labour devolving on women.

This conception is as unverifiable as the classic hypotheses, but it is often considered to be 'new' and 'original'. Yet it hardly goes beyond the traditional pattern of naïve anthropology. In fact it is built on the basis of a transformation of the previous explanation, which associated the first tools with 'aggressive' and typically 'masculine' occupations, such as fighting and hunting; as a consequence of this, women became the passive object of cultural changes forged in the travails and fatigues that only men, 'the veritable creators of culture', were capable of facing. The feminist anthropologists invert this thesis: it is women who lay the foundations of culture, while the males wait passively in the wings until their more advanced lady friends design to 'hominise' them. In spite of this transposition, the mode of explanation remains classic: the women are deemed to start making tools under the pressure imposed, as usual, by a change of milieu. The metamorphosis of the canonical explanation is brought about by a new use of the traditional elements, subject to the minimal reworking essential to invert the respective roles and merits of the two sexes.

FROM BIPEDALISM TO FREE HANDS AND TO TOOLS

It is convenient to discuss these three elements together because in the scenarios they form a triad of almost inseparable characteristics that follow on from each other to form a pair of explanatory relations. I shall round off the presentation with a gloss on other consequences, apart from tools, ascribed to bipedal locomotion and free hands.

---

[89] Tanner and Zihlman 1976: 599.

The reasoning supporting these relations follows three stages, outlined below:

1. **If *(a)*** at some period, hominids adopted bipedal locomotion,
   and if *(b)* bipedalism frees the hands from the function of locomotion,
   then *(c)* following the adoption of bipedalism, the hands of the hominids were freed from their function of locomotion.[90]
2. **If *(c)*** ibid.,
   and if *(d)* the hands freed from the function of locomotion are available for other uses,
   then *(e)* as a consequence of the adoption of bipedalism, the hands of hominids have become available for other uses.[91]

The second inference is left tacit at times, as being self-evident, and the authors then move on directly to the following operation, which spells out the nature of the 'other uses' of free hands:

3. **If *(e)*** as above,
   and if *(f)* the uses of the hands freed from function of locomotion were:
   (i) making and using tools (nine scenarios),
   (ii) transporting tools (four scenarios),
   (iii) transporting food (four scenarios),
   (iv) gathering (one scenario),
   (v) hunting (one scenario),
   then *(g)* owing to the adoption of bipedal locomotion, hominids were enabled to practise one or other of the above activities (i–v).

No one will dispute that bipedalism does in fact free the upper limbs from the function of locomotion. The connection between human locomotion and free hands can be easily observed, and many authors mention it, from Antiquity on.[92] In the eighteenth century, this idea became a veritable commonplace,[93] and the naturalists of the early nineteenth century continued to use it frequently.[94] Just as ancient, but much

---

[90] Lamarck 1820: 151; Darwin 1871, I: 141; Engels 1971/1896: 58; Coon 1955/1954: 14–15; Niestourkh 1958: 233; Washburn 1960: 9; Leroi-Gourhan 1964: 108; Hockett and Ascher 1964: 140–1; Wolpoff 1971: 601–2; Ruyle 1977: 145; Tanner and Zihlman 1976: 600; Boriskovski 1979: 47–9; Lovejoy 1981: 345; Lumsden and Wilson 1983: 10.
[91] Darwin 1871, I: 141; Coon 1955/1954: 14–15; Lumdsen and Wilson 1983: 10.
[92] E.g. Xenophon 1872: 40, I.IV.39; Aristotle 1990: 134–5, 686a; Vitruvius 1834: 41, II.1; Gregory of Nyssa 1944: 103, 14d; 106, 144b.
[93] E.g. Herder 1962/1784–91: 104; Rousseau 1973/1755: 393.
[94] E.g. Bory de Saint-Vincent 1825: 393; Lacépède 1821: 350; Virey 1827: 12, 209; Lamarck 1820: 151.

more debatable, is the idea that the free hand is the exclusive prerogative of humans and the evidence of their superiority, setting them above the animal world.[95] In the hominisation scenarios in which the tool is held to 'create' man, the freeing of the hand that enables him to use tools[96] is considered to be the turning point in his genesis, the moment when, according to Haeckel, there opened up for him 'the career of unending progress he has been following ever since, moving ever further away from his animal ancestors'.[97] For the naturalists of the first half of the nineteenth century, the idea of the free hand was associated with the old opposition between the animal world and the human world: 'The upright position of the human body', wrote J.-J. Virey, 'which lifts our sight and our senses above the ground, which leaves our hands free, those marvellous instruments, makers of the other instruments, gives our brain an extraordinary preponderance over that of all other beings and makes man, in the words of Plato, a celestial plant.'[98]

Now, it had been known from the eighteenth century that neither bipedalism nor free hands are attributes reserved for human species alone, so they could not, consequently, provide an adequate explanation for the genesis of tools.[99] Moreover, even a limited bipedalism, mastered by some primate species, permits the use of tools.[100] The inadequacy of such an explanation becomes even clearer when we remember that hands can be freed not just by bipedalism but by sitting down; we should not forget that some 80 per cent of technical activities in so-called 'primitive' cultures are performed in a crouched or kneeling position.[101] So it would be just as conceivable that tools owed their origin not to bipedalism but to a seated position. On the other hand, if a free hand was a sufficient condition of the emergence of tools, one might ask why their use is so little developed among quadrumanous apes, for the seated position frees four hands in their case, which should doubly foster technical performances...[102]

These objections make no claim to show that the explanatory sequence 'bipedalism → free hand → tools' is wrong. It is more a case of underlining in the first place that this relation is not the only one possible (for example, an alternative version is conceivable ('seated position → free hand → tools'); in the second place, that its premises are inadequate.

---

[95] Aristotle 1990: 134, 686a–687a; Diodorus Siculus 1743: 16; Goguet 1758, I: 67; Kant 1985/1786: 191; Vitruvius 1834: 41, II.1.
[96] E.g. Cicero, *De natura deorum* LX.   [97] Haeckel 1868: 591.   [98] Virey 1827: 209.
[99] Lovejoy 1981: 343.   [100] Stoczkowski 1995b.   [101] Hewes 1961: 694.
[102] Cf. Richards 1986.

In search of causes 89

Indeed, since we know cases of bipedalism and free hands which do not imply the use of a tool, we could reinforce the left side of the explanatory sequence with supplementary conditions (for example, certain mental abilities), while reducing the role of the free hand and bipedalism to that of a circumstance favouring the use of tools.

The relation 'free hand → tools', which has been holding its own in the conceptions of anthropogenesis since Antiquity, has undergone a very characteristic transformation in recent scenarios. Palaeoanthropologists became aware that if bipedalism frees the hands from locomotion, the resulting consequences concern activities linked to locomotion more than to the use of tools in general. They immediately started to speculate about the benefits that free hands could have offered during locomotion: easier transport of tools, food or young, more efficient gathering or hunting, etc. The uses of the free hands are conceived in line with the idea the authors of the scenarios have of the activity that is crucial to hominisation. Formerly, when it was thought that the tool had created human species, a free hand was considered as the condition for tool use; nowadays, to the extent that an 'anthropogenic' function often comes down just to gathering,[103] or transporting food,[104] or even hunting,[105] the free hand becomes the condition for either gathering, transporting food or hunting. Thus bipedalism and free hands continue to hold the symbolic status of an essential condition for anthropogenesis that they already enjoyed in ancient conjectures.

FROM TOOLS TO BIPEDALISM

Nine of our scenarios assumed that bipedalism preceded the first tools and was their cause. Fewer of them reverse that relation, to assert that it was in fact the tools that had arrived before bipedalism and should therefore explain its genesis.[106] Does this new version get more support from the empirical data? Nothing is less certain, since the oldest indisputable trace of bipedalism, at Laetoli in Tanzania (about 3.5 million years ago) comes before the oldest known tools (sites at Omo Shungura and Hadar Kada Gona 2.3.4, in Ethiopia, dated respectively to 3 and 2.4 million years ago[107]). This objection could, however, be set aside if we accepted, according to the classic argument, that the first tools of flaked

[103] Tanner and Zihlman 1976.   [104] Isaac 1978a and 1978b.   [105] Lumsden and Wilson 1983.
[106] Engels 1971/1896: 57; Oakley 1968: 258; Washburn 1960: 9; Hockett and Ascher 1964: 140–1; Wolpoff 1971: 601–6; Ruyle 1977: 144–5.
[107] Chavaillon 1983; Harris 1986; Roche 1980.

stone had been preceded by others made of perishable materials,[108] so that bipedalism would have been favoured by the earlier use of artefacts whose traces have vanished for ever. But this solution implies that the first hypothesis (tools → bipedalism) must be based on the second (tools of perishable materials) – which is plausible and not disproved, since absence of proof is not proof of absence – but is incapable of validation since it cannot be proved wrong.

It is interesting to linger on the argument underlying the 'tools → bipedalism' relation. The primatologist Sherwood Washburn confined himself to stating in general terms that the tool favoured bipedal locomotion.[109] Other authors are more explicit and try to give an idea of the mechanism that might have been at work in this process. If the tool was at the origin of bipedalism, they say, it was because only that mode of locomotion could free the hands which were indispensable for using tools[110] or for carrying and using them while walking.[111]

The better to establish the sequence 'tools → bipedalism', two of the scenarios go further, accepting that bipedal locomotion is ineffective in itself and, as a consequence, its appearance must be linked to some other advantage, in this case the using of tools, which in turn is directly favoured by natural selection. However, the existence of bipedal animals proves that the tool is not necessary for preserving this type of locomotion through the process of natural selection. Furthermore, the theory of the general energy inefficiency of bipedalism seems fragile since certain experiments show that walking on two feet may be more energy-efficient than walking on four.[112]

So it is clear that the 'tools → bipedalism' relation is based on *ad hoc* arguments, of which some are incapable of validation and others have been disconfirmed, at least in a general form. This explanation is interesting because it has no antecedents in the speculation of naïve anthropology. Of course, it does not thereby acquire a special heuristic value, but it has the advantage of illustrating a mechanism underpinning the construction of new palaeoanthropological explanations. We observe

---

[108] Toth and Woods (1989) comment that our ancestors could equally well have made – besides tools of perishable materials like wood – retouched shell knives, shells being easily available along the lake shores where the sites of the earliest hominids are concentrated. Tools of that type are known in the Mesolithic and Neolithic (Vigie 1987). For the Plio-Pleistocene sites, this hypothesis cannot be verified at present: shells being fragile, it is impossible with current techniques to distinguish signs of retouching or wear from those due to fortuitous deterioration.
[109] Washburn 1960: 9.   [110] Ruyle 1977: 145.
[111] Oakley 1968: 258; Hockett and Ascher 1964: 140–1; Wolpoff 1971: 601.
[112] Rodman and McHenry 1980.

that the new sequence 'tools → need to have free hands → bipedalism' is just an inversion of the classic triad 'bipedalism → free hands → tools'.

So we see that a new hypothesis is formed by inverting a traditional scheme, and without enriching or completing it with new elements. The procedure is suggestive of the interplay of images in a kaleidoscope, the functioning of which has already served Claude Lévi-Strauss as a metaphor to describe one of the typical procedures of 'savage thought': by shaking the apparatus we can obtain a variety of configurations, the diversity of which, impressive in the first instance, is in fact the result of combinations of a few bits and pieces that are always the same.[113]

FROM THE USE OF TOOLS TO REDUCED CANINE TEETH

When we try to define human characteristics by contrasting them with those of apes, reduced canines stand out as an important specific feature. In fact, man is a primate with very reduced canine teeth. Since there used to be a tendency to compare humans with animals in general rather than with apes, reduced canines only appeared quite late in the list of human properties, in the nineteenth century.[114] Although Gregory of Nyssa,[115] in the fourth century, was already deploring the fact that the first humans did not have powerful teeth to defend themselves against animals, this was just a routine reference to Plato's dialogue *Protagoras*, in which lack of strong teeth constitutes one point in the vast inventory of human weakness. Reduced canine teeth acquired the status of a human attribute much later.

Charles Darwin was the first, as far as I have been able to ascertain, to associate reduction of canines in humans with the use of tools. So began the long history of an explanation that provides the curious and instructive example of an erroneous idea, the popularity of which was long resistant to counter-arguments, so that it is still perpetuated in certain hominisation scenarios. Its analysis provides an opportunity for a better understanding of the strength of the traditional imagery, which is capable of prolonging the existence of notions that hardly fit both factual and theoretical constraints.

---

[113] Lévi-Strauss 1962: 51.
[114] E.g. Lawrence 1849/1819: 124. We should, however, add that several naturalists since the seventeenth century have observed that apes are endowed with longer canine teeth than humans; nevertheless that observation has not led naturalists to make reduced canine teeth a distinctive character of human species; cf. for example, Perrault 1676: 121; Daubenton n.d.: 19.
[115] Gregory of Nyssa 1944: 104.

The relation 'tools → reduced canine teeth' appears in seven of our scenarios,[116] six of which offer the following argument:

1. **If (a)** at a certain time in hominisation, man's ancestor began to use tools,
   and if (b) from the very beginning, man's ancestor was endowed with large canine teeth and used them as a weapon in fighting,
   then (c) the first tools replaced their canine teeth in fighting.
2. **If (c)** ibid.,
   then (d) as a result of using the first tools, the canines of man's ancestor were reduced.

This last inference calls for comment: enigmatic in Carleton Coon's scenario, it becomes clearer in the other texts, thanks to complementary premises formulated as follows:

the disuse of parts [of the body] weakens them;[117]
an organ that the organism does not need becomes reduced;[118]
the take-over of the functions of canine teeth by tools favoured the reduction of the canine.[119]

We recognise here the classic principles of Lamarckism. In J.-B. Lamarck's *Philosophie zoologique* of 1809, they take the form of two 'laws', the content of which is worth remembering, for they contain ideas that play an important role in our scenarios:

First law: 'the more frequent and sustained use of any organ gradually strengthens that organ, develops it, makes it bigger and gives it a power proportional to the duration of that use; whereas lack of constant use of a given organ, weakens it imperceptibly, causes it to deteriorate, progressively diminishes its faculties and finally brings about its disappearance'.

Second law: 'everything nature has caused to be acquired or lost by an individual, through the influence... of the predominant use of a given organ, or by that of the constant disuse of such a part, nature preserves in new individuals through heredity'.[120]

In giving these principles the name of Lamarckism, I am respecting current usage, but it must be remembered that Lamarck was not their author and that his originality lay only in giving them a simple and explicit form and making systematic use of it. At the beginning of the nineteenth

---

[116] Darwin 1871, I: 144–5; Coon 1955/1954: 21; Washburn 1960: 9; Ardrey 1973/1961: 263–4; Ruyle 1977: 145; Hill 1982: 539–40.
[117] Darwin 1871, I: 144–5. [118] Ardrey 1973/1961: 263–4. [119] Ruyle 1977: 145.
[120] Lamarck 1809, II: 235.

century, these two 'laws' already belonged to a body of widely accepted ideas. Before being taken up by Lamarck, the principle of use and disuse appears, among others, in Virey, Delamétherie and Erasmus Darwin.[121] But in the eighteenth century there are already countless traces of it in the works of the naturalists or philosophers, and Diderot made himself a mouthpiece for the common opinion when he wrote that 'exercise strengthens all the members, just as lack of exercise obliterates them'.[122] Certain indications justify the idea that this popular conception took shape as a mistaken generalisation of observations concerning the phenomenon of so-called adaptability. This hypothesis is suggested not only by the passage from Diderot quoted above, but especially by the reflections of the naturalist Jean-Claude Delamétherie who, when seeking to justify the principle of use and disuse, offered this argumentation: 'A runner has very considerable strength in his legs; their muscles become larger and stronger. The same holds good for the arms of a blacksmith. A sailor has keen eyesight; a musician's ear is exceedingly sensitive; a gourmet has a very fine palate; the sense of smell of a perfumer is much keener.'[123]

The same reasoning would be taken up again later by Charles Darwin.[124] Thus the mechanism of adaptability, very real since that is what is responsible for the development of the impressive muscles of athletes, is credited with the ability to transform *all* organs *profoundly* and *permanently*. Centuries earlier, Plato introduced a similar idea in his metaphysical deliberations on souls, so formulating a sort of 'spiritual Lamarckism': 'one part [of the soul], if remaining inactive and ceasing from its natural motion, must necessarily become very weak, but that which is trained and exercised, very strong'.[125] Use strengthens, disuse weakens, and both are capable of transforming organs, even spiritual 'organs' – that is the common basis of the different manifestations of the same notion, as ancient as it is widespread.

Equally common was the conviction that acquired characteristics can be inherited (Lamarck's second law).[126] Its roots go back into Antiquity, witness the corpus of Hippocratic writings.[127] Aristotle took a particular

---

[121] Virey 1801, II: 164; Delamétherie 1800: liv; E. Darwin quoted from Szyfman 1982: 41.
[122] Diderot 1994/1778–80: 1279; see also Ferguson 1767: 5; Rousseau 1973/1755: 303–4; the American botanist Conway Zirkle (1946) drew up a long list of authors who touched on this idea in the eighteenth century.
[123] Delamétherie 1800: liv.   [124] Darwin 1871, I: 116–17.
[125] Plato, trans. Jowett 1871, III.89e: 777.
[126] Cabanis 1959/1802: 405–6; E. Darwin quoted from Szyfman 1982: 41; Delamétherie 1800: lvii; Diderot 1994/1778–80: 1312; Diderot 1994/1782: 636; de Maillet quoted from Gaudant and Gaudant 1971: 12; Rousseau 1973/1755: 304.
[127] *Des airs, des eaux et des lieux*, reproduced in Joly 1964: 83, see also Zirkle 1946.

interest in this subject: 'From deformed parents come deformed children, lame from lame and blind from blind, and, speaking generally, children often inherit anything that is peculiar in their parents and are born with similar marks, such as pimples or scars.'[128]

Aristotle was endeavouring, however, to distance himself from this notion, contrasting it with a few simple examples to the contrary. Moreover he was not the first or the last to notice them. And yet the popularity of the principle of the inheritance of acquired characteristics was hardly affected by them; it was not until Weismann's research in the 1880s[129] that a serious challenge was offered. The crucial experiments, in this particular case, took place in the 1950s, thanks to the development of molecular biology: they demonstrate that information acquired by proteins cannot be passed back to the nucleic acids and so be transmitted from one generation to another.[130] In spite of these decisive arguments, the Second Law has managed to maintain a certain credibility. The idea reappears in the doctrine of Lysenko who, it will be remembered, dominated Soviet biology between 1929 and 1964. Even in our own day, almost anywhere in the world, the public is happy to read articles that proclaim periodically in the popular press the inheritance of acquired characteristics 'scientifically demonstrated'. Popular culture is not alone in bearing witness to the life force of Lamarckism, and some of our scenarios carry its mark, as late as the 1970s.[131]

No one in anthropology today would dare to defend 'Lamarckism', at least not in the traditional form expressed in the two laws. Yet some students have attempted to safeguard the 'tools → reduced canine teeth' relation, by confining themselves to getting rid of its Lamarckian principles. The anthropologists C. L. Brace and M. F. A. Montagu have tried to replace the disuse principle by that of natural selection: the take-over of the warlike function of canines by the first tools would have rendered these teeth useless by freeing them from selective pressure which, until then, had fostered their great size. Consequently stochastic processes would have come into play and a directed accumulation of random mutations would have led to a reduction of the canine teeth.[132] This explanation is dubious, for a directed accumulation of random mutations is highly improbable without some favourable pressure of natural selection, and that is lacking in this argument. The flaw is so obvious that it is difficult to understand how it could have occurred. It should be noted that introducing positive selection would be tantamount to challenging

[128] Aristotle, trans. Ross 1910, VII. 6: 585b.   [129] Mayr 1989: 449.   [130] *Ibid.*: 511.
[131] E.g. Ruyle 1977.   [132] Brace and Montagu 1965: 227.

the decisive role of tools in favour of some other cause, unconnected with tools, that sets in motion a selection favouring a diminution of the teeth. So these authors would rather come into conflict with the principles of the theory of evolution than give up situating tools, as custom would have it, on the cause side. This attitude derives from a step typical of the process of tinkering with concepts; it consists in constructing new hypotheses from old elements, fitting them together despite their disparate nature and in spite of incompatibility with the assigned function.

The problems posed by recasting the old explanatory sequence are not restricted to a 'Lamarckism' that would have to be got rid of, and, incidentally, could not easily be replaced mechanically by a Darwinian formula. The traditional explanation was not only Lamarckian through and through but was linked to a simplistic view of nature, depicted as a bloodstained circus where all the creatures lead lives full of relentless struggle. In that setting, the great canine teeth could not fail to become a fearsome weapon in combat. Nevertheless, research on primates endowed with large canines shows that they rarely used these teeth in direct confrontations: although the canines constitute an important accessory in aggressive behaviour, they belong rather in the realm of a subtle combination of intimidatory ploys, threats and ritual acts. An analogy comes to mind, that of nuclear weapons, the significance of which lies less in use than in demonstration. Yet this simple dialectic escapes the naïve anthropologist who remains attached to the old image of our early ancestors engaged in ceaseless warfare and armed, in the absence of tools, with their teeth and nails. Were not Lucretius and, later, Leonardo da Vinci already saying that 'arms of old were hands, nails and teeth'?[133]

This tenacious view inevitably affected the first descriptions of exotic peoples whose existence was likened to that of 'ancient men'. Thus, Sir Francis Drake declared that the inhabitants of certain islands in the South Seas had only claws to defend themselves, while Le Mere asserted that the natives of New Guinea 'use their teeth as offensive weapons'.[134] So the traditional relation of 'tools → reduced canine teeth' brings the classic themes of conjectural anthropology into play, where the life of early humans is associated with struggle, and canines are seen simply as a weapon, just as the first tools were. On these premises, a type of hypothesis was constructed, of which Darwin introduced the scholarly version when trying to explain the reduction of canine teeth in humans. Before him, Leonardo da Vinci followed a partly analogous line of reasoning, this

[133] Lucretius, trans. Munro 1900, V: 147; Leonardo da Vinci 1942, II: 554.
[134] Quoted from J. Burnet 1774–92, I: 252, who considered the information to be credible.

time in connection with nails: 'the knife', he surmised, 'a forged weapon, deprives humans of the use of their nails, their natural weapon'.[135]

It would only need the addition of the disuse principle to obtain the complete model of the reasoning that would be adopted by eighteenth- and nineteenth-century naturalists. Starting from these assumptions, the hypotheses are directed towards the classic explanation: teeth and nails, rendered useless by artefacts, tend to reduce as a result of disuse.

It seems that the only way to get out of the straitjacket of this traditional opinion is to reject *en bloc* the whole sequence of 'tools → reduced canine teeth', which is based on a common-sense view that persists in attributing the same function to each of them. Alternative solutions have already been proposed and we can find some examples in our scenarios.[136] Certain authors mention selective pressure, which might have to do with a change of diet; indeed, teeth, even if they happen to be used as weapons on occasion, serve first and foremost for cutting and chewing food.[137]

Another plausible explanation refers to sexual selection. It is known that canine teeth are a manifestation of sexual dimorphism in primates, those of the males being bigger than those of the females. This phenomenon is often interpreted as an effect of sexual selection linked with the competitive behaviour to which males are prone.[138] The reduction of the canine teeth in hominids might thus be the result of a more moderate sexual selection than in apes. It is intriguing to note that Darwin came very close to this explanation. The greater part of *The Descent of Man* is devoted precisely to the different manifestations of sexual selection. When speaking of apes, Darwin stresses the absence of great canine teeth in females: for what reason, he asks, are they deprived of such a means of defence, if, indeed, the canines are used for defence?[139] And he concludes that their presence in males stems from sexual selection. Nevertheless, when Darwin ruminates on the reduction of the canine teeth in man's ancestors, the old clichés re-emerge under his pen: constant struggles, defence against enemies, fangs used as weapons, the first tools replacing them and the reduction of the useless organ as a result of disuse. It is amazing to see this great naturalist succumbing so easily to these commonplaces; proof that a critical mind and remarkable erudition are not always sufficient to triumph over the influence of traditional imagery.

[135] Leonardo da Vinci 1942, II: 453.
[136] Jolly 1970: 18; Tanner and Zihlman 1976: 605–6; Lovejoy 1981: 346.
[137] Cf. Jolly 1970: 18–22; see also Szalay 1975 and Leutenegger and Shell 1987: 356–7.
[138] E.g. Holloway 1967.   [139] Darwin 1871, II: 314.

FROM TOOLS TO LANGUAGE

The idea that the production and use of tools lie at the origin of language is found in four scenarios. André Leroi-Gourhan has proposed an interesting hypothesis, inspired by neurological data, on the link between cerebral zones governing technical behaviour and those controlling the faculty of language.[140] The linguist Charles F. Hockett and the anthropologist Robert Ascher, for their part, have pointed up the constraints of hunting which would have made the language of gestures impracticable and forced men to speak.[141]

The explanations proposed by Kenneth Oakley and Eugene R. Ruyle offer a broader justification for a causal relation between tools and language by assuming that the manufacture of tools requires a complex system of communication, a role filled of necessity by articulate language.[142] Oakley's scenario[143] specifies the nature of this connection:

1. **If (a)** at a certain period hominids started making tools,
   and if (b) the making of tools had to be learnt,
   then (c) with the appearance of tools, hominids began to transmit the knowledge essential to the making of tools.
2. **If (c)** *ibid.*,
   and if (d) learning to make tools demanded a system of communication (articulate language),
   then (e) making tools entailed, in hominids, the use of articulate language.

It is reasonable to accept that tool-making would go hand in hand with a learning process, but is it certain that, in order to obtain a stone flake or chopper, it was essential to talk about it? We do not at present know how complex a chain of operations has to be, if apprenticeship required more than simple visual demonstration.

Yet the conclusion of this argument (proposition *e*) could imply, in part, certain testable consequences, if it were possible to determine when the areas of the brain responsible for language appeared,[144] and to compare the chronology of their emergence with the evidence of the first use of tools (assuming the first stone artefacts were also the first tools).

It is striking that our scenarios attempt to explain the genesis of language solely by the need for it. They state that our ancestors began to

---

[140] Leroi-Gourhan 1964. [141] Hockett and Ascher 1964. [142] Ruyle 1977: 170.
[143] Oakley 1957: 208. [144] E.g. Tobias 1987; Vilensky, van Hoesen and Damasio 1982.

speak at the precise moment when vocal communication became necessary or simply useful: to explain procedures of tool-making, or in hunting, when hands are busy with weapons. Conditions sufficient for speech to appear are thus reduced to the pragmatic usefulness of language. Only Leroi-Gourhan[145] resisted this simplification; he was cautious enough to emphasise the role of the neurological basis of language, which could not have emerged from nothingness solely under the pressure of a need, had it not been preceded by the formation of different cortical structures essential to the use of words.[146]

Leroi-Gourhan's approach differs from that of the other scenarios, more eager to reduce the cause of emergent characteristics to a single factor. Generally, it is affirmed that the origin of language is due to tools, which made the use of words necessary, or at least very useful; if language did not exist before tools, it was because verbal communication had little point at that stage. Following this logic, as long as there were no tools, there was nothing worthy of being expressed and transmitted in speech. Language being the means of communication appropriate to cultural activities, we are back to the classic theory in which the tool is the first manifestation of culture. This notion has its place in the frame of naïve anthropology: the first humans had to devote all their time to satisfying a few elementary needs and they could only achieve that with tools, an essential condition for survival. So the first efforts of humans had to be directed to making tools, and it was only later that our ancestors would be able to take up other cultural activities, such as language communication or social life. According to this view, it is imperative that tools precede and explain language in one way or another, while the main premise leaves the field open to speculation as to the mechanisms of that causal relation (proximity of cerebral centres, usefulness for learning, etc.).

FROM LANGUAGE TO MENTAL FACULTIES

The idea that the use of speech led to the development of mental faculties in our ancestors rests on the conviction that language is necessary for exercising cognitive functions such as 'thought', 'memory' or 'foresight'.[147] This idea often passes wholly unchallenged: it seems obvious, remarks F. Lhermite, because 'language and thought are so intimately bound together in our mental activities that they may appear to be indissociable,

---

[145] Leroi-Gourhan 1964: 124–8.
[146] For other anatomical conditions, see Laitman 1986 and Duchin 1990.
[147] Lamarck 1820: 153; Boriskovski 1979: 166.

the more so as, if we work backwards, it is not possible to analyse our arguments, our sentiments, without resorting to language'.[148]

Yet this introspective evidence is fallacious. Many pieces of research, a portion of which was presented in the symposium eloquently entitled *Thought without Language*, show that complex cognitive processes can develop without speech.[149] Animals are capable of reasoning, of envisaging causal relations between phenomena and of acting accordingly.[150] But their cognitive capacities have limits. Experiments with chimpanzees learning a gesture language have proved particularly instructive: although they are able to assimilate and master a large vocabulary of several hundred words, chimpanzees lack the mental capacity necessary for combining words according to the rules of syntax that ensure the linear structure of the expression.[151] One can only conclude, without minimising the impact of language on thought, that the former does not constitute the source of all cognitive faculties but that it is rather a product of them.

The tendency to treat language as an indispensable condition for the development of mental faculties in our ancestors is, on the other hand, in perfect harmony with one of the profound convictions of naïve anthropology. Back in the eighteenth century, it was often thought that reason cannot exist without language and that only speech can lead to the combination of 'ideas', and make 'reasoning' possible.[152] To prove that thought cannot exist without language, descriptions of 'wild children' were then invoked, like the 'bear-man' of Lithuania, who 'so long as he was deprived of the use of words and speech ... displayed no operation of the understanding and showed no sign of reason'.[153] 'Without language', wrote Herder, 'all the operations of our mind ... would never have taken place, the elaborate structure of our brain would have remained idle, the whole purpose of our Being unaccomplished, as the instances of men who have fallen among beasts sufficiently prove.' *Homo sapiens* must first be *homo loquens*, for 'language is the mark of our reason, by which alone it acquires and propagates forms'.[154]

A portion of modern scenarios of hominisation shares this opinion, and the justifications that accompany it have their place in the line of

[148] Lhermite 1982: 15.
[149] Weiskrantz 1988, cf. in particular Premack 1988, likewise Premack 1985.
[150] Dunbar 1989, see also Griffin 1983; Walker 1984.
[151] Gardner and Gardner 1969; Premack 1976.
[152] Herder 1962/1784–91: 151; cf. also Rousseau 1973/1755: 315; Turgot 1973/1750: 48.
[153] Wolf, *Psychologia rationalis*, 1734; quoted from Tinland 1968: 197.
[154] Herder 1784–91, trans. Churchill 1800: 233–4, see also Lacépède 1821: 375.

speculative tradition where common sense and naïve introspection reign supreme.

FROM CULTURAL BEHAVIOUR TO INCREASED BRAIN SIZE

It is convenient to discuss these kinds of causal relations together, since our scenarios attribute the development of brain size in our ancestors to different items of cultural behaviour, considered separately or together, such as tools, language, hunting or cooperation. The underlying reasoning is the following:

If hominids began to practise activities x, y, etc.,

and if activities x, y, etc. imply (cause, necessitate, entail, etc.) an increase in the brain volume,

then as a result of activities x, y, etc., the brain volume in hominids increased.

Divergences of opinion are restricted to the nature of the activities involved:

Scenario	x	y
Engels	tools	language
Oakley	tools	cooperation
Washburn	tools	language
Hockett and Ascher	tools	language
Laughlin	tools	–
Hill	tools	hunting

All the versions accept that cultural activities preceded expansion of the brain; this idea is formulated most succinctly by Sherwood Washburn, who writes that 'the reason that the human brain makes the human way of life possible is that it is the result of that way of life'.[155]

The development of the brain becomes necessary, according to our scenarios, when culture already exists. One might wonder why a large brain, which was not necessary for culture to appear, suddenly becomes indispensable when culture has taken shape. If culture emerges without this vast brain, why could it not have continued to exist without it?

The authors left implicit the mechanism that might have governed this process. A comment by Darwin ('the continued use of language will

[155] Washburn, 1960: 13.

have reacted on the brain, and produced an inherited effect'[156]) suggests that we may have 'Lamarckian' reasoning here: culture (tools, language, cooperation, hunting, etc.) involves a more intense use of the brain, the continual exercise strengthens it and makes it grow; these effects, according to Lamarck's second law, are hereditary; therefore 'culture' implies a large brain. Darwin appealed to premises such as these when he was trying to understand the difference between the brain volume in domestic and wild rabbits: 'I have shown that the brains of domestic rabbits are considerably reduced in bulk in comparison with those of the wild rabbit or hare; and this may be attributed to their having been closely confined during many generations, so that they have exerted but little their intellect, senses and voluntary movements.'[157] According to this type of reasoning, culture would be the main factor requiring the use of the brain, previously immersed – as naïve anthropology imagines – in a numbing dullness: without culture, the cerebral organ would have been little used and this disuse made its development impossible.

While 'Lamarckism' has foundered in disgrace, the 'culture → large brain' relation has survived its disappearance. We find it again in Washburn's scenario, supported this time by a Darwinian argument: the author assumes that the handling of tools, the use of speech and other human activities are subject to control by specialised areas of the brain whose development may have been fostered by the existence of culture. Lacking the competence to assess the plausibility of this explanation, I will confine myself to reminding readers that the author himself declares this to be unverifiable.[158] But the example deserves attention, for it raises another interesting question: how is it that a 'Lamarckian' formula can be so easily replaced by a Darwinian one? The reason may be that the traditional explanations lend themselves easily to Darwinian reformulations, without the classic 'causal' sequences being in any way challenged.

FROM THE USE OF TOOLS TO FREE AND SKILFUL HANDS

This relation furnishes another example of the move from 'Lamarckian' arguments to 'Darwinian' explanation. The first is clearly revealed in the reasoning of Engels:[159]

---

[156] Darwin 1871, II: 390.   [157] *Ibid.*, I: 146.   [158] Washburn 1960: 13.
[159] Engels 1971/1896: 57–8.

1. **If (a)** hands play an increasing role in labour (identified as the use of tools),
    and if (b) development of the activity of an organ strengthens and perfects it,
    then (c) the hands of human ancestors were strengthened and perfected following the use of tools,
2. **If (c)** *ibid.*,
    and if (d) the acquired characteristics are hereditary,
    then (e) strong and perfected hands became a lasting characteristic of the human species.

Engels' text was the principal reference of the Soviet prehistorian P. I. Boriskovski[160] who, by the way, proclaims his Marxist orientation explicitly, and on several occasions. In 1979, he returns to the 'tools → free and skilful hands' relation as part of the 'Marxist' heritage, without, however, explaining the mechanism by which the hand develops; we can only suspect that his conception remains as Lamarckian as that of Engels: the tool that replaces the canine teeth, and so causes their reduction from lack of use, accentuates, in parallel, the use of the hand, which develops as a result.

Yet Darwinian rhetoric too can provide a justification for this causal relation: the anthropologist Kim Hill assumes that using tools favoured changes in the morphology of the hand.[161] The argument is fairly vague: although the author seems to invoke natural selection, no precise mechanism is envisaged. The substitution of 'Darwinian' for 'Lamarckian' explanations is an interesting problem, to which I shall return later when the different categories of palaeoanthropological explanations will be compared. I shall merely observe here that both variants of the argument take for granted that the hand was less used before the appearance of tools (a paradisal state in which hands do not get blistered?) and that its intensive use is connected only with tools, the sole and unique pretext for manual manipulations. This crucial role, arbitrarily vested in the tool, is a recurrent idea in naïve anthropology, which sees the tool as the first and main attribute of man's cultural condition.

FROM MENTAL FACULTIES TO A LARGE BRAIN

Some scenarios attribute encephalisation in *Homo* to the use of tools and language; for others, the enlargement of the brain has rather to

---

[160] Boriskovski 1979: 47.   [161] Hill 1982: 540.

In search of causes 103

be explained by the development of our ancestors' mental faculties. This reasoning is indeed curious: the large brain, the organ of thought, would have appeared when human cognitive capacities already existed. Darwin[162] made explicit 'Lamarckian' principles underlying this unexpected process, and R. Ardrey later affirmed it still more explicitly, saying that our ancestors developed their brain by thinking.[163] In other words, the increased cognitive faculties would have intensified brain use, as a result of which the cerebral organ would have increased in size, like the biceps of an athlete. So 'mental faculties' would have acted on the brain in the same way as the principle of use, just as tools and language did in the explanations we have already analysed.

This notion provides a singular view of human history, divided into a thought-less prehuman period, in which the brain was used little or even not at all, and a thought-full human period, where the brain is used daily. For Ardrey, these two periods coincide with the demarcation line separating the period of paradisal inertia from the subsequent times of struggle for existence, in the course of which human beings were forced to emerge from 'numbing dullness'.[164]

A similar notion can also be found in the works of Conjectural History, which set primordial man in a paradisal environment 'where he wandered at will in the peace and freedom of vast solitudes',[165] his brain unused since no ingenuity was required to satisfy the basic needs.[166] The cataclysm that opened the period of struggle against hostile nature and imposed the necessity of social life made the use of brain essential: 'The great preponderance of the cerebral organ', imagines Virey, '... increased still more with its continual use in the social state.'[167] 'The intellectual faculties of social man', added Delamétherie, 'take up considerable energy, because the thinking organ is perfecting itself by all the exercise it is given.'[168]

These arguments, based on the Lamarckian principle of use, are wonderfully well adapted for the scheme of transition from mother nature to stepmother nature. Thought becomes a logical consequence of the end of the paradisal condition. Furthermore, since thought here comes before the large brain, and the social state comes before thought, the latter has the modest role of an epiphenomenon in the hominisation process.

---

[162] Darwin 1871, I: 145.
[163] Ardrey 1961: 316–17; in the 1973 reissue, these passages have been omitted. [164] *Ibid.*
[165] Virey 1801, I: 95.
[166] E.g. Boulanger 1766, II: 388; Ferguson 1767: 46; Kant 1985/1786: 508; Virey 1801: 95–7.
[167] Virey 1801, I: 180. [168] Delamétherie 1800: lxii.

'Mental faculties' are thus confined in explanations to the effects side, as if they could clarify exclusively the genesis of a few human characteristics and were of no significance for the origin of others.

FROM MENTAL FACULTIES TO PERFECTIBILITY

According to six of the scenarios, 'perfectibility' constitutes a distinctive feature of humanity.[169] In the eighteenth century, it was widely believed that perfectibility had to be considered as a peculiarity of man, and was deemed as important as language itself.[170] In the prolific debate on the soul of animals, that had been going on since the seventeenth century, there were some attempts to extend that faculty to the animal world, but Buffon acted as a mouthpiece for the dominant opinion when he asserted that 'animals invent nothing and perfect nothing' (this idea was also expressed by the very influential Bossuet[171]). There was general agreement to associate perfectibility with the faculty for transforming and 'improving' culture (tools, society, laws, language, etc.). This restricted perfectibility to our species, since all these cultural attributes were held to be non-existent, or at least rudimentary in animals.

Three of our scenarios declare that the origin of human perfectibility stems from 'mental faculties' which, as they developed, would have led our ancestors to perfect their 'labour' and 'language',[172] to improve hunting tactics,[173] to invent and manufacture tools.[174]

Similar views were already appearing in Lucretius, for whom the development of culture was due to 'intellectual experiments'.[175] In the eighteenth century, Rousseau was not alone in thinking that 'the clearer the mind became, the more industry improved'.[176] The discoveries and technical innovations of the Enlightenment were sufficiently numerous to suggest the idea of a causal link between intellectual effort and the progress of civilisation, until it became commonplace.

It must be acknowledged that this relationship, transposed into prehistory, provides perfectly plausible explanations for cultural change.

---

[169] Engels 1971/1896; Coon 1955/1954; Washburn 1960; Ardrey 1973/1961; Hockett and Ascher 1964; Laughlin 1968.
[170] E.g. Herder quoted from Tinland 1968: 200–11; Kant 1985/1786: 511; Burnet 1774–92, I: 147–9; Condorcet 1971/1793: 77; Goguet 1758, I: 79; Holbach 1822/1773: 273; Rousseau 1973/1755: 314; Virey 1801, I: 90; Voltaire, quoted from Duchet 1971: 285.
[171] Buffon 1954/1749: 359; Bossuet 1722: 344. The opposite opinion can be found, for example, in Le Roy 1994/1768a: 129; and in Smellie 1790, I: 437–40.
[172] Engels 1971/1896: 62.   [173] Ardrey 1973/1961: 269.   [174] Hockett and Ascher 1964: 143.
[175] Lucretius 1964: 102, V. 1448–57.   [176] Rousseau 1973/1755: 350.

The problems that arise here are quite different. In the first place, our scenarios set out the relation between mental faculties and cultural improvements in an exceedingly vague way, which is difficult to test: nothing is said about the nature of these 'mental faculties' or the precise nature of 'improvements'. Second, any attempt to define the notion of improvement would bring us back to the old sterile and tedious debates about progress. If we accept the current meaning of the word, it is difficult to avoid tautology because dictionaries define perfectibility as 'the character of what is perfectible' (*Petit Robert*); at the same time, we will have to admit that perfectibility is not exclusively human property, associated with cognitive faculties that permit a teleological anticipation, since 'improvement', as everyday language understands it, may also be the outcome of the process of selection, operating through interactions between living beings and their milieux.

An explanation that places 'mental faculties' on the side of the causes provides an opportunity to reflect on the role of cognition in the anthropogenesis scenarios. Our authors introduce 'mental faculties' into hominisation at a point where the process is far advanced: our ancestors are not only walking upright with free hands, they are also making tools, hunting in groups, living in society and using language. Indeed, recent palaeoanthropological data confirm that important anatomical transformations, such as bipedalism and its morphological consequences, preceded brain growth; so the development of certain 'mental faculties' would have come later and could not explain earlier phenomena. Consequently, it is no longer possible to defend theories that seek, for example, to make the origin of bipedalism a result of 'mental faculties'.[177] However, it is intriguing to observe that cognition also plays almost no part in explanations of cultural phenomena. Thought would have had no part in the genesis of culture and served only to 'perfect' it. This is a strange, yet common view, with numerous paleoanthropologists considering any contrary notion as a fantasy based on prejudices peculiar, they say, to intellectuals with an irritating tendency to overestimate the significance of thought.[178]

Yet if we cling to cultural evolution, there is no alternative but to recognise that both these views, one that overvalues the impact of mental faculties in this process and one that underestimates it *a priori*, have very few arguments in their favour. Just one important difference separates them: the first option – let's call it 'idealist' for want of a better word – barely disguises a philosophical inspiration that sees the human mind as

---

[177] See their summary in Bowler 1986: 156–67. [178] Ruyle 1977: 136.

the only driving force in our history; the 'naturalist' view, on the other hand, claims to be free of such assumptions and therefore superior, and at the same time the only legitimate option, because it is so self-evident that it claims to have no need of verification. Yet the 'self-evidence' is dubious and it seems necessary to examine what underlies it.

The life of our ancestors was 'just a frantic search for food', states C. Coon, and they 'spent most of the day' at it.[179] According to P. I. Boriskovski, at the starting point of hominisation, 'the level of development of the forces of production was so low that it hardly outstripped the problems of the search for food',[180] so that men's thinking was of necessity reduced to issues directly concerned with their basic needs. Ardrey believed that, for our ancestors, thought could not flourish until their 'daily life was freed from the eternal munching'.[181] So the opinion that the difficulties of primitive existence were so great that they left neither time nor energy for exercising mental faculties is widely shared (as if the constant quest for food could not equally well be an occasion for exercising the mind).

We have already noted the presence of this idea in schoolbooks. Now we must add that it also figures among the well-known themes of *histoire raisonnée*. Condorcet wrote: 'There is a feeling that the uncertainty and difficulty of providing for subsistence, the necessary alternatives of extreme fatigue and absolute rest, never left room for a state of leisure in which man can indulge in thought and enrich his understanding with new combinations of ideas.'[182]

So too for Voltaire, we had first to wait for culture to improve our ancestors' lives 'before anyone was to be found who had leisure enough for meditation'.[183]

According to J. Millar, even 'savages' who already possess the rudiments of culture, but are still reduced to hunting, gathering and fishing in order to live, will never be able to indulge in reflection because they are obliged to devote all their energies to satisfying basic needs.[184] In the same period, Burnet[185] and Boulanger[186] were describing primitive life as an unthinking state, and, a few decades later, J.-J. Virey was adding that human minds, emerging unsullied from nature, 'were dead, or rather sleeping in lifeless indifference... Sleeping, eating and reproducing – such was their entire existence.' We had to wait until people had learnt

---

[179] Coon 1955/1954: 11.   [180] Boriskovski 1979: 213.   [181] Ardrey 1973/1961: 317.
[182] Condorcet 1971/1793: 78.   [183] Voltaire 1963/1756, I: 12.
[184] Millar 1979/1771: 183; likewise in Home (1744: 88): 'No time nor zeal for studying conventions'; see also Goguet 1758, I: 179; Lamarck 1986/1802: 88.
[185] Burnet 1774–92, I: 159.   [186] Boulanger 1766, II: 388.

to free themselves from the basic necessities in order to see 'the human heart filled with artificial needs, the tireless instigators of all efforts to perfect our species'.[187]

It is clear from this that the traditional, broadly accepted image of the precarious existence of the first humans fits in well with the conviction that the role of mental faculties must have been negligible in the earliest stages of anthropogenesis. I merely note the compatibility of these two views without claiming that one is derived from the other. Indeed, the significance of 'thought' in the genesis of culture is also underestimated by authors who reject the view of a hard life and place the first humans in the bosom of bountiful nature. This was already the case in the period when Rousseau was writing that 'everything seems to distance savage people from the temptation and the means to cease to be so... Their imagination conjures up nothing, their heart asks for nothing. Their modest needs are so easily to hand and they are so far from the knowledge necessary to make them desire to acquire more, that they can have neither foresight nor curiosity.'[188]

So, whatever view is taken of primitive nature, naïve anthropology finds sufficient reasons to ascribe thoughtlessness to the first humans. If nature is hostile, it leaves no energy for exercising the intellect; if it is paradisal, it provides no stimulus for reflection. It goes without saying, therefore, that our ancestors did not think. The way in which their environment is represented merely provides a framework for *ad hoc* arguments that will justify this main thesis one way or another – a thesis that clings to the image of primitive bestiality, depicted in conformity with the principle of contrast: since the existence of modern humanity is dominated by thought, thought must be absent from the life of primordial humanity. This absence is an attribute of its animal condition, as is hairiness or nudity. Consequently, the evolution of 'mental faculties' is often envisaged as a process leading from nothing to everything, or – as E. Haeckel put it – from '*homo stupidus* to *homo sapiens*'.[189]

FROM HUNTING TO COOPERATION

It has long been maintained that the emergence of cooperation was an important landmark in the transition from the animal state of nature to the social stage of culture. Some of the scenarios make the first forms of cooperation a direct consequence of hunting. The general argument is

---

[187] Virey 1801, I: 117; see also Le Roy 1994/1786b: 150. [188] Rousseau 1973/1755: 316.
[189] Haeckel 1898: 43.

that cooperation would be indispensable to hunting.[190] Only one of our authors[191] develops this idea more fully, as follows:

1. **If (a)** at a certain period hominids began hunting,
   and if (b) hunting activities cause exposure to great risks,
   then (c) the first hunters were exposed to great risks.
2. **If (c)** ibid.,
   and if (d) the cooperation of several individuals reduces risks when hunting,
   then (e) cooperation appeared as a consequence of the first hunting activities, in order to reduce risk.

This explanation may be plausible but it is not the only one conceivable; moreover, it gives rise to several objections. First, cooperation is also seen in animals, and although it sometimes coincides with hunting,[192] it cannot be restricted to that type of activity alone, while forgetting other occupations for which it is useful or necessary. Second, both primatology and ethnology provide descriptions of hunting methods that do not expose the hunter to the slightest risk. Thirdly, no palaeoanthropological data can confirm or disprove this hypothesis. That being so, on what do our authors base their affirmation that all hunts are dangerous, that they require cooperation and that this was the origin of the earliest forms of cooperation?

To answer these questions we have to bear in mind the meanings with which the notion of hunting is charged in our scenarios. We should recall that conjectural anthropology was very attached to the image of continual warfare between primitive men and animals, which would have compelled our naturally weak ancestors to join forces to confront the menace of the beasts.[193] Traces of this view are also apparent in our palaeoanthropological scenarios and three of them express it explicitly, positing that the earliest humans had been obliged to cooperate to defend themselves against wild animals. In underlying arguments it is easy to find the classic notion of human weakness and incessant attacks

---

[190] Jolly 1970: 22; Ruyle 1977: 144; Boriskovski 1979: 49.
[191] Hockett and Ascher 1964: 142.   [192] E.g. Teleki 1973; Strum 1981.
[193] To cite a few more examples in support: 'being often attacked by fierce beasts, they felt the need for mutual aid' (Diodorus Siculus 1737: 18); 'did they not very swiftly seek to band together, firstly for defence in numbers and then for a concerted effort to make themselves a dwelling and weapons' (Buffon 1825a/1764: 308–9); 'so they had to unite to overcome powerful animals so as to escape from them and feed on them' (Virey 1801, I: 113). An analysis of the context from which this idea emerged in ancient Greek tradition will be found in Schnapp 1997: 18–23. That society is a consequence of the mutual aid individuals can give each other is a common idea in the eighteenth century; cf. for example Le Roy 1994/1764: 96.

by 'fierce beasts'.[194] The parallel between the relation 'struggle against fierce beasts → cooperation' and the sequence 'hunting → cooperation' is obvious. The similarity can be explained by the juxtaposition of the notion of hunting and that of struggle against animals. Philosophical conjectures provide abundant historical testimony to this kind of assimilation. So, for A.-Y. Goguet, 'most peoples of Antiquity considered that hunting was the occupation of the primordial men. They took to it as much from the need for subsistence as from the necessity of defending their lives against attacks by wild animals.'[195] This opinion finds an echo in J.-J. Virey: 'so they had to unite to overcome powerful animals so as to escape from them and feed on them.'[196] This explanation, traces of which can still be found in a recent text,[197] leads to attributes traditionally associated with a struggle against 'fierce beasts' being projected on to hunting activities. Thus, in the imagery of naïve anthropology, primitive hunting became synonymous with a dangerous confrontation with savage monsters in which the solitary hunter constantly defied death. And hunting took on not only the attributes of a 'bloody struggle', but also its function, that of the chief cause of cooperation. This transformation offers us yet another example of the conceptual change in which a new arrangement of old elements preserves the trace of former meanings.

FROM COOPERATION TO SOCIAL LIFE

Herbert Spencer stated that 'society exists only when to juxtaposition is added cooperation'.[198] This opinion was widespread in Conjectural History, for which social life is simply a function of cooperation; according to this, the beginnings of society would mix with the emergence of cooperation, which had been reduced, as we have seen, to subsistence activities.

The same idea turns up again in three of our scenarios,[199] and not a single one of the twenty-four casts doubt on it. Yet even leaving aside the meagreness of the verifiable implications offered by such a hypothesis, its bias seems striking. Social life is reduced to a purely utilitarian and economic function, from which a whole universe of arbitrary conventions, rivalries and conflicts is quite simply missing. Society becomes a rational

---

[194] Royer 1870: 152, 166, 392; Niestourkh 1958: 232–3; Boriskovski 1979: 160.
[195] Goguet 1758, I: 79–80.   [196] Virey 1801, I: 113; see also Buffon 1825b /1778: 310.
[197] Hockett and Ascher 1964: 141–2.   [198] Quoted from Durkheim 1973/1895: 21.
[199] Hockett and Ascher 1964: 140–2; Tanner and Zihlman 1976: 605; Zihlman 1978: 15; Boriskovski 1979: 49.

creation of individuals and would have been formed for the same reasons as those that caused cooperation: to make it possible for individuals to survive in their struggle against hostile nature. This narrow view can hardly account for the social life of modern hunter-gatherers or even of chimpanzees. On the other hand, it fits perfectly into common-sense imagery.

The above constitutes a typical example of the attitude that depicts evolution as transition from nothing to everything. Since society is the fruit of necessary cooperation, it is believed that this necessity did not exist previously, and that man's ancestors led individual, presocial lives. It is easy to recognise the ancient view of a period of paradisal abundance, when 'each one went his own way in search of fruit and herbs',[200] all then being capable of obtaining food without the help of others. Lucretius and Diodorus Siculus[201] were already painting a similar picture of the primordial existence, and in the eighteenth century the idea of the solitary life of the earliest humans became more firmly embedded in popular imagery.[202] In the twentieth century, colourful speculations concerning that grave event, the first encounter between two humans, still persist. Here is how E. Haraucourt imagined it in a 'prehistoric novel' which portrays the first *tête-à-tête* between a male and a female:

> A punch on the forehead stunned but did not defeat her and she returned to attack. She buried her teeth in the shoulder of the male who had grabbed her round the waist; it was his turn to scream; picking up a stone, he dealt her such a vicious blow on the top of her head that she collapsed: circles of light were whirling in front of her and she was vaguely aware of a violent mass hurling its weight on her back... When she reopened her eyes, the conqueror was still clasping her but was not devouring her.[203]

This is a good illustration of the firm belief that existence was originally solitary and that the first meeting was not without some difficulties. This view conforms very well to the old habit of defining the original state as a mirror-image of ourselves; because civilised man is a *zôon politicon*, the lives led by prehuman creatures must necessarily be presocial and individual.

FROM SOCIAL LIFE TO LANGUAGE

The reasoning underlying this relation can be reduced in the three scenarios[204] to the following inference:

---

[200] Goguet 1758, I: 71–2.   [201] Lucretius 1964: 85, v. 958–61; Diodorus Siculus 1737: 18.
[202] E.g. Boulanger 1766, II: 388; Burnet 1774–92, I: 257; Delamétherie 1802: 11; Home 1774: 62; Locke 1947/1690: 17; Rousseau 1973/1755: 340.
[203] Haraucourt 1988/1914: 43.
[204] Coon 1955/1954: 18; Washburn 1960: 13; Boriskovski 1979: 50.

If (a) at a certain period our ancestors started living in society,
and if (b) life in society required the use of 'language',
then (c) 'human language' appeared as a consequence of life in society.

In the second premise (proposition *b*) the term 'language' has been placed in inverted commas because our authors give it a meaning that varies from one scenario to another. Thus they speak of the language that corresponds to the needs of the group,[205] of the development of language,[206] of a flexible means of communication,[207] of a system of symbolic communication[208] or simply of a means of communication.[209] These terms are as varied as they are vague and it is impossible to evaluate the main assumption of this reasoning ('life in society requires the use of language') without specifying what is understood by 'society' and by the 'language' deemed indissociable from it. If it is a question of articulate language, the generalisation is faulty, since such language does not exist in animal societies; if it is a question of a system of communication in general, the proposition is inadequate to explain the origin of articulate speech.

C. F. Hockett and R. Ascher present a more elaborate piece of reasoning. They declare that the need for a flexible means of communication (language) appeared with a 'complex social organisation'. Recourse to communication by means of gesture language was impossible, these authors argue, because, during the hunt, the hands of the earliest men were holding weapons and their eyes were constantly watching the movements of their prey. Furthermore, since bipedal creatures had free hands, they were no longer obliged to transport food by holding it in their teeth; the mouth had thus been freed for speech, which thenceforward became established as the most effective means of communication.[210] This reasoning rests on several perfectly unfalsifiable premises and illustrates a mode of conjecturing that is typical of most of our authors, for whom language, like many other human characteristics, would result solely from economic constraints, in this case the necessity of the hunt.

In all these arguments, the origin of language is explained by the need to communicate, which is supposed to emerge as soon as our ancestors engaged in social relations. That being so, the previous absence of language would merely be due to the absence of social life; and here we are back again with the vision of that presocial state, so dear to naïve

---

[205] Coon 1955/1954: 18.   [206] Washburn 1960: 13.   [207] Hockett and Ascher 1964: 141–2.
[208] Jolly 1970: 22.   [209] Boriskovski 1979: 50.   [210] Hockett and Ascher 1964.

anthropology. According to an ancient idea, the earliest humans did not speak because, living alone, they had no need of speech.[211] This notion becomes a recurrent theme in speculations on the origins of language that flourished during the Enlightenment. Rousseau asserted that 'not interacting with each other, and with no need to do so, humans do not conceive of any necessity for such an invention [language], nor any possibility of it, unless it were indispensable'.[212] For J. Burnet, 'although a solitary savage might in process of time acquire the habit of forming ideas, it is impossible to suppose that he would invent a method of communicating them, for which he has no occasion'.[213]

The 'utilitarian' premises of that notion found particularly clear expression in J.-J. Virey: 'Without the ties of immediate usefulness to unite them [humans], it would be neither possible nor useful to create a language.'[214] Thus society makes its appearance for a utilitarian reason, as does language, necessary for social intercourse. Society made language possible because it made it useful; and if language did not exist in the 'presocial period', it is because humans had no need of it.

It is interesting to observe that our scenarios pay little heed to the biological conditions indispensable for an articulate language (larynx, cerebral centres, oral cavity of a particular shape).[215] Of course, social life may favour vocal communication, one means of which is language, but we should not on that account neglect anatomy and neurology. This disparaging attitude had some justification in the eighteenth century, when the first dissections of primates provided the authority: naturalists frequently referred to the work of Edward Tyson, who concluded, after examining the remains of a young chimpanzee, that its tongue, larynx and brain were identical to those of humans.[216] By pointing to decisive factors outside biology, this mistaken conclusion subsequently determined the way in which the origin of language was envisaged for more than a century. So it was asserted that apes, who some authors stated to be ignorant of life in society, are deprived of speech because they have no need to communicate; later it was deduced that 'language' is a result of that need, which appeared with social life. Certain palaeoanthropologists still argue on those lines, although they know that the brain of humans, just like the larynx or the oral cavity, is different from that of apes.[217] In spite of that, our authors restrict the conditions for the

---

[211] E.g. Lucretius 1964: 88, v. 1029; Diodorus Siculus 1737: 18.
[212] Rousseau 1973/1755: 320.   [213] Burnet, 1774–92, I: 215.   [214] Virey 1801, I: 107.
[215] Cf. Laitman 1986; Varney and Varney 1980; Duchin 1990.
[216] Buffon 1825g /1766: 110; Dunbar 1774: 62; Tyson 1699: 51–7.
[217] One of the first to stress that the anatomical differences in the larynx prevent the apes from articulating sounds was Georges Cuvier in 1798 (Cuvier 1798: 96).

emergence of language to social factors alone, which means that they continue to favour explanations that fit, not today's empirical data, but those of two centuries ago.

FROM HUNTING TO SEXUAL DIVISION OF LABOUR AND FOOD-SHARING

Nine of our scenarios assume that sexual division of labour and food-sharing appeared in the wake of the development of hunting.[218] Five of them, taking this explanation further, suggest that hunting had first imposed a sexual distribution of subsistence tasks and that later this would have led to food-sharing. As most of the authors associate the division of labour with the sharing of its products, I shall examine jointly these two supposed consequences of hunting.

On this subject, the scenarios offer two distinct arguments. The first appears in one text only, that of Carleton Coon.[219] The author considers that man's ancestors began hunting small game as soon as they left their tree shelter to live on the ground. Then, with time, as their skills progressed, they attacked big herbivores as well, such as antelopes. Added to this hypothesis is the conviction that the males would have been the first to indulge in the new hunt for big game. This leads to the following generalisation: 'in every shift of occupation of which we know throughout history, women have taken over the jobs formerly held by men as the men have moved on to something new and more specialised'.[220] Aside from the naïve reference to a 'law' claiming to be based on one of the invariants of History, but stemming in reality from a fiction of misogynist 'common sense', no supplementary argument is adduced to prop up this apparently universal rule, which is also found, although more rarely, in other works of American anthropology of this period.[221] Coon claims that hunting big game became a masculine task, while women continued to catch small, slow animals: thus the first division of labour was born. This reasoning implies a singular view of both sexes: the male, enterprising and endowed with an inventive spirit, the creator of progress, is contrasted with a passive female, obliged to await the fruits of masculine ingenuity. The misogynist character of this conception, added to the complete impossibility of confirming or disconfirming it with archaeological data, exempts me from further comment on its epistemological

---

[218] Ardrey 1973/1961: 269; Leroi-Gourhan 1964: 215; Laughlin 1968: 318; Jolly 1970: 21–2; Isaac 1978a: 100; Hill 1982: 533; Lumsden and Wilson 1983: 11; Kelso and Quiatt 1985: 209; Coon's scenario (1955/1954: 47–8) restricts the consequences of hunting to food-sharing only.
[219] Coon 1955/1954: 47–8.   [220] *Ibid.*: 45.   [221] E.g. Murdock and Prevost 1973: 212.

relevance. However, we shall see later that such arguments, quite apart from the sexism for which they are commonly criticised today, convey a whole body of traditional beliefs of naïve anthropology.

Meanwhile, we shall analyse the second type of argument, which is shared by more of the scenarios. Its core can be set out as follows:

If *(a)* at a certain period, our ancestors began to practise hunting,

and if *(b)* hunting necessitates a sexual division of labour and food-sharing,

then *(c)* when they started hunting, our ancestors were obliged to inaugurate sexual division of labour and practise food-sharing.

Only one scenario stops short at such a summary argument, in which nothing is said about the reasons why hunting should always impose division of labour and food-sharing. In other texts, the data base proves richer and allows the analysis to probe more deeply. First of all, we shall note the general character of the tasks that devolve to both sexes:

Scenario	*Men*	*Women*
Coon	hunting large animals	hunting small game
Ardrey	?	?
Leroi-Gourhan	hunting	gathering
Laughlin	?	?
Jolly	hunting	gathering
Isaac	hunting	gathering
Hill	hunting	gathering
Lumsden and Wilson	hunting	gathering
Kelso and Quiatt	hunting	gathering

With the exception of Coon's scenario and two other texts that do not specify the nature of masculine and feminine occupations, while asserting they were distinct, the five authors agree in assigning hunting to men and gathering to women.

Gathering would be the most ancient means of subsistence and the introduction of hunting, added to gathering, would lead inevitably to a division of labour. Leroi-Gourhan summed up the usual explanation of this phenomenon by a very clear formula: 'The very slow growth of children rendered women naturally less mobile; given the double character of Palaeolithic subsistence, based on hunting and gathering, the primitive group had no other organic solution than that of men hunting and women gathering.'[222]

[222] Leroi-Gourhan 1964: 215.

The sexual division of labour among hunter-gatherers would thus have been linked, on one hand, to the weight of the reproductive functions with which women are burdened, and on the other, to the greater difficulty of hunting compared to gathering. Let us look first at our authors' views of the biological differences between women and men:

Scenarios	**Men**	**Women**
Jolly	predisposed to hunting activities	–
Isaac	–	hampered by children, less mobile
Hill	–	less fitted for hunting, maternal duties
Lumsden and Wilson	–	reduced mobility because of child care
Kelso and Quiatt	–	procreative function, protection of children, predisposition to gathering

Thus natural frailty, frequent pregnancies and above all the care lavished on children would render women incapable of facing the difficulties of the hunt. These assertions quite clearly imply a particular view of hunting, seen as the pursuit of animals, demanding 'virile strength' and 'mobility'. If we accept these assumptions, we are led to believe that any human group living from hunting and gathering is obliged to share out these tasks between the two sexes. It is 'the only organic solution', declares Leroi-Gourhan. The sexual division of labour would have been subject to biological determinism that would make it a purely natural phenomenon. The scenarios grant it the status of a general law, asserting that masculine hunting and feminine gathering are the rule not only among recent hunter-gatherers but also among chimpanzees and baboons. This rule, raised to the status of a law of nature, valid at all times and in all places, could thereafter be projected into the prehistoric past of our species and form a solid deductive basis for bold reconstructions.

However, this status of a 'universal law' must be challenged. In the first place, women are not always barred from hunting. The example of the Agta of the Philippines is well known: Agta women hunt big game and are even reputed to be good archers.[223] Women hunters were also known

---

[223] Estioko-Griffin and Griffin 1981.

among the Northern Ojibwa,[224] the Melscalero Apache, the Eastern Cree,[225] the Copper Eskimo[226] and the Tiwi of Australia.[227] So it would be difficult to maintain that women are by nature incapable of hunting.

One could object that this criticism is irrelevant. Apart from the Agta, women go hunting only rarely, sometimes only in the case of the sickness or death of their husbands;[228] so the fact that women hunt in exceptional circumstances does not disconfirm the principle of a habitual division of labour between the sexes. It might be said to be more judicious and more efficient that women, hampered by pregnancies and childcare, should leave hunting to men. The division of subsistence tasks, therefore, would be the result not of absolute and inevitable necessity, but of a concern for efficiency (this version is found in the authors who assume that food was abundant in the first hominids' environment).

This kind of argument rests on certain assumptions, the weaknesses of which were clearly perceived by Alain Testart:[229]

Premise 1 Hunting demands great mobility
Hunting techniques exist that do not require great mobility,[230] whereas gathering may sometimes involve covering long distances. As an example, Testart recalls that a !Kung woman, frequently carrying a young child, covers an average of 2400 km a year.[231]

Premise 2 Women are immobilised by their maternal duties
The care lavished on children may indeed reduce women's mobility, but it does not follow that they are thereby excluded from hunting. Among the Agta, mothers undoubtedly hunt less than girls or old women, but it is not unusual for them to go hunting, leaving their children in the care of grandparents, older brothers and sisters or husbands.[232] Since the authors of our scenarios have no hesitation in corroborating their 'laws' with zoological observations, we in turn remind them that in the case of African wild dogs who go hunting, juveniles are always left at their base site under the protection of an adult guard, who is often not the mother, nor even a female.[233]

Premise 3 By reserving the heavy hunting tasks for men, hunter-gatherers are aiming at economic efficiency
If it is not unusual for women to take part in hunting and be burdened with the same tasks as men, they are often barred, on the other

---

[224] Landes 1938: 153.   [225] Flannery 1935: 83.   [226] Jennes 1922: 88.   [227] Goodale 1971: 154–6.
[228] E.g. among the Ojibwa and the Cree, Flannery 1935: 83; Landes 1938: 163.
[229] Testart 1986.   [230] Examples in Testart 1986: 12–14.   [231] Lee 1979: 314.
[232] Estioko-Griffin 1981: 131.   [233] Kuhne 1965.

hand – notes Alain Testart – from using the same tools.[234] For example, the Northern Ojibwa men fish using lances and nets while the women may only use nets.[235] Among the Central Eskimo, the men hunt seals with harpoons, whereas the women hunt only with bludgeons, less efficient tools, the use of which makes long-distance hunting impossible, so reducing the chances of success.[236] When the Copper Eskimo fish for salmon, the harpoon is reserved for men, while the women are allowed to catch fish only with their bare hands.[237] When beaters are being employed, women often make up the group of beaters, whose work is the hardest and demands the greatest mobility.[238]

In the face of these observations it is difficult to maintain that the sexual division of labour is *always* 'natural' or 'organic' in character. Although there were groups of hunter-gatherers living in environments which made this kind of division of labour efficient, there were numerous societies in which, far from freeing the women from drudgery, this custom makes their duties still heavier.

What is more, the highly prized view of the 'natural' solution is not the only conceivable one. It is equally possible to seek the reasons for the sharing out of tasks by sex in the realm of beliefs rather than of biology and practical imperatives. Robert Lowie observed that the sexual division of labour seems to a large extent to be a matter of convention. That is to say, it has nothing to do with the physiological characteristics of the two sexes; this can be proved by comparing the different rules in force, sometimes in neighbouring tribes.[239] Taking a large number of examples, Alain Testart has observed that many taboos exist among these peoples, barring women from contact with hunting weapons such as spears, javelins, harpoons, bows and arrows, etc.[240] So it may be that we were wrong to speak of a *division* of labour, in so far as cross-cultural data demonstrate[241] that men can and sometimes do perform all kinds of womanly tasks, while women find themselves excluded from certain occupations strictly reserved for men. It would seem to be more a matter of *prohibition* than of division. Thus, still according to Alain Testart, it is not so much hunting that is forbidden to women as the use of certain weapons without which hunting may be impracticable. So what is conventionally called 'division of labour' among hunter-gatherers would be the result of a taboo, which leads, perhaps indirectly, to the exclusion of women from certain types of hunting.

[234] Testart 1986: 11–18.   [235] Landes 1938: 132.   [236] Boas 1888: 484.   [237] Jennes 1922: 88.
[238] E.g. Tiwi, Goodale 1971: 169; Copper Eskimo, Jennes 1922: 88; see also Testart 1986: 13.
[239] Lowie 1969/1920: 78.   [240] Testart 1986: 31.   [241] Murdock and Prevost 1973: 207.

But why do the beliefs of so many peoples impose this separation between women and certain hunting weapons? Testart notes that the arms in question are the ones that penetrate the animal's flesh and cause blood to flow, or else come into direct contact with the blood of the prey.[242] Moreover, the ban is particularly strict for women during their periods. There are very widespread beliefs that their contact with the tools of hunting could have particularly harmful consequences: 'Any hunting tools that she touches or steps over will become unusable', say the Siberian hunters, 'the gun won't fire, fish will flee the nets and fur animals the traps'.[243]

The Kwakiutl believed that if menstrual blood contaminated their hunting tools, game would no longer allow itself to be caught.[244] According to the Bella Coola, who lived by fishing, menstrual blood possesses a very malignant power: 'At certain periods, women do not have the right to bathe for fear that a drop of blood might blind the fish and prevent them finding their way.'[245] On the other hand, for hunting practices that do not shed blood, as Lévi-Strauss has already noted, women may exert a beneficial influence during their periods.[246] So the essential point of these practices would be to separate animal blood from menstrual blood, by virtue of a theory that Testart considers to be universal among hunter-gatherers.[247]

I am mentioning Testart's hypothesis here not because I am convinced by his argument, but because it offers us an alternative to the traditional explanations, which, from this very fact, can no longer be held to be the only conceivable ones. Furthermore, this theory accounts for the ethnological data much better than explanations in which the division of labour by hunter-gatherers is presented as a purely 'natural' or 'pragmatic' phenomenon. But we must stress that the hypothesis of the universality of 'blood ideology' has not been tested and does not accord with some of the available information, for example concerning hunting Agta women. Alain Testart is right when he states that the sexual division of labour is more easily and effectively explained by the *doxa* than by the *praxis*, but it remains to be verified whether 'blood ideology' always underlies this phenomenon and whether it is really universal.

Setting aside these objections, we stick to the conclusion, however imprecise it may be, that women are in fact often excluded from some

---

[242] Testart 1986: 31. [243] Lot-Falk 1953, quoted from Testart 1986: 32–3.
[244] Ford 1941, quoted from Testart 1986: 32.
[245] McIlwraith 1948, quoted from Testart 1986: 81–2. [246] Lévi-Strauss 1952: 68–9.
[247] Testart 1986: 79.

In search of causes 119

cynegetic activities because of a belief in the malign and dangerous potential of menstrual blood.

There is no need, moreover, to go looking for other examples of such ideas among non-Western cultures, or solely in connection with hunting: they have existed and still do exist in our own Western culture. The historian J. Delumeau notes that, in the Middle Ages, many theologians, referring explicitly to Pliny's *Natural history*, asserted that menstrual blood contains an evil force that prevents plants germinating, kills vegetation, rusts iron and sends dogs mad. 'Penitentials forbid women to take communion during menstruation, or even to enter a church. Hence, more generally, the ban on women celebrating mass, touching sacred vessels, having access to ritual functions.'[248]

This type of taboo, whose roots in the Bible (Leviticus)[249] and in Antiquity (Pliny)[250] are well known, has persisted in our culture down to the nineteenth century, as Victor Hugo's observation bears witness:

A part of the catacombs in Paris is devoted to growing button mushrooms. No woman is allowed to enter it. It is claimed that the mere presence of a woman at a certain time of the month is enough to make a whole planting of mushrooms fail and rot. This periodic indisposition has strange and mysterious effects. It is certain for instance that it makes powder and rouge fall off the cheeks of actresses.[251]

The mechanism responsible for women being excluded from hunting among certain so-called primitive peoples is very reminiscent of the one that, in our culture, has led to their exclusion from ritual functions and from cultivating mushrooms. It is intriguing to observe that anthropologists, themselves raised in a cultural tradition that eliminates women from certain tasks for purely symbolic reasons, continue to treat a similar exclusion among others as a simple effect of biologico-economic factors. This attitude stems from another tradition, a materialist one this time, still firmly anchored in the common sense of today.

'Man is more courageous, pugnacious and energetic than woman and has a more inventive genius', wrote Darwin.[252] It is a long time since the conviction appeared whereby the social status of women is simply the consequence of their physical frailty (for example in Buffon[253]) and of the 'deficiency' of their mind which 'is not capable – according to Delamétherie – of great schemes or profound conceptual combinations'.[254] 'Due to her weakness', wrote Cabanis, 'woman ... has

---

[248] Delumeau 1978: 313.   [249] Leviticus XV. 19–24.   [250] Pliny the Elder 1977: 61.
[251] Hugo 1972/1887: 441; see also Verdier 1979.   [252] Darwin 1871, II: 316.
[253] Buffon 1984/1749: 98.   [254] Delamétherie 1802: 464.

had to stay inside the house or hut. Particular indispositions and child care have kept her, or constantly returned her, there... Unable to bear the fatigues, face the hazards, withstand the tumultuous impact of great assemblies of men, she has left to them those heavy tasks, those dangers they had chosen for preference.'[255] Rousseau likewise attributed to purely natural reasons the fact that 'women became more sedentary, grew accustomed to looking after the hut and the children, while the men went in search of their common subsistence'.[256]

In eighteenth-century historical conjectures, hunting was already associated with hardships and fatigue which only men were capable of facing, while gathering, considered easy work, was assigned to women.[257] This vision of the hunt, moreover, came to be loaded with all the negative connotations linked to subsistence appropriate to humans banished from paradise. Gathering, on the other hand, a feature of life in the Garden of Eden or in the Golden Age when vegetarian humans were still living in harmony with animals, conveys all the symbolic charge of a paradisal occupation, hence it is light and easy.[258] This view is combined with the old theory of 'the imbecility of the female nature', the written history of which can be traced back to Plato.[259] Such a superposition of ideas leads to the belief that at the time when humans were obliged to kill to survive, the sexual division of labour must have been the only possible solution. Condorcet concluded that 'the frailty of women excluded them from hunting'.[260] That is why hunting became the man's duty while 'paradisal' gathering was assigned to 'frail' woman.

Here we have an eloquent example of the way naïve anthropology lays the foundations of its inferences, resting them on 'general laws' which are deemed to sanction the validity of deductive reasoning. The ideas of the 'hardships of hunting', of the 'frailty of women' and of the 'organic necessity' of the sexual division of labour among hunter-gatherers provide typical illustrations of this type of 'law'.

Let us return to hominisation scenarios. I have no intention, as a result of what has just been said, of bringing all the differences between the sexes down to a social convention. Males do not give birth to children nor do they breast feed them, and it was the same 3 million years ago. Neither do I want to deny that a genuine distribution of tasks can exist without a 'blood ideology', indeed, without any ideology at all. Even among

---

[255] Cabanis 1959/1802: 292, see also Lacépède 1821: 355.
[256] Rousseau 1973/1755: 351; see also Home 1774: 172.
[257] E.g. Burnet 1774–92, I: 445, 452–3.   [258] Ibid.   [259] Delumeau 1978: 327.
[260] Condorcet 1971/1793: 89.

primates we often observe differences in subsistence activities of males and females, as in chimpanzees, where females spend more time gathering insects, whereas the males hunt more.[261] But it is none the less true that the woman's place in human or prehuman society is not 'naturally' in the hut, and that if women do not hunt it is not because they are incapable of it. Hypotheses concerning the origin of the division of labour should not be constructed on the basis of the conviction that there is only one 'organic solution', imposed by the biological differences between the sexes.

This has interesting consequences for the way we envisage hominisation. If the division of subsistence tasks derived from the eternal nature of both sexes, we should be entitled to propose convincing conjectures about the division of labour among the hominids of a few million years ago, the male still being male and the female female. But what if 'femininity' and 'masculinity' are not determined by biology alone, but are decreed, in part at least, by social conventions? These conventions being diverse and often arbitrary, what can we say about the ones that prevailed in the distant past, almost the only traces of which are stone tools and fossil bones? To accept the theory that gender and its social role arise in part from arbitrary cultural notions deprives the traditional 'organic solution' hypothesis of its deductive justification, which had served for centuries as the foundation of the 'naturalist' hypothesis of the origin of the sexual division of labour.

FROM FOOD-SHARING TO SOCIAL LIFE

Food-sharing is often considered to be the essential reason for the emergence of human social bonds in the first hominids.[262] Yet the notion of 'human social bonds' remains obscure; only their comments on the connection between those bonds and exchange or reciprocity can throw light on the properties our scenarios bestow on the social life of primitive humanity. Palaeoanthropologists quite rightly insist on the fact that complex systems of reciprocity govern a very considerable part of social phenomena in the cultures described by ethnography. More suspect is their attempt at the same time to reduce society solely to the constraints of food exchange. Yet, even among animals – primates,[263] dogs or bats[264] –

---

[261] Galdikas and Teleki 1981.
[262] Coon 1955/1954: 66; Hockett and Ascher 1964: 140–1; Isaac 1978a: 106; Lumsden and Wilson 1983: 11–13; Kurland and Beckerman 1985: 73, 86.
[263] E.g. Gilk 1978; Lefebure 1982; McGrew 1975; Teleki 1975; de Waal 1989.
[264] Kühme 1965; Wilkinson 1990.

food-sharing does not explain their whole social life; moreover, it does not involve such complex phenomena of reciprocity as among humans.

It is interesting to note how insistently some of our scenarios tend to reduce the first human society to an epiphenomenon of nutrition, with food exchange and mutual relations presented as its direct consequences. The testimony of ethnographic data proclaims unanimously that the contrary is just as conceivable: food-sharing may be not the cause but the effect of social bonds that determine more or less arbitrarily the duties of reciprocity. Of course, when the hypothesis based on this last possibility is applied to prehistory, it is hardly open to verification, but the opposite conjecture, that our scenarios accept so readily, is no more testable.

It is significant that of the two hypotheses, both equally weak in methodological terms, it is again the hypothesis in closest agreement with the traditional view that is favoured: the hypothesis whereby society is a product of economic constraints defined by the basic needs of the individual; the hypothesis whereby social life emerged from cooperation between hunters joining forces to overcome powerful animals and to confront 'ferocious beasts'.

FROM HUNTING TO THE USE OF TOOLS

The last relation of those which appear at least three times in our scenarios associates the origin of tools with hunting activities.[265] The reasoning is as follows:

If *(a)* at a certain period, our ancestors started hunting,

and if *(b)* hunting requires the use of tools,

then *(c)* the use of tools appeared as a consequence of the first hunting activities.

This formula may be completed with propositions indicating the different reasons why tools would have been indispensable to the first hunters. The primatologist Clifford Jolly and the prehistorian Glynn L. Isaac insisted on the necessity of dismembering animal carcasses, while the anthropologist Eugene E. Ruyle assumed that hunting was impracticable without tools. The authors thus follow the typical strategy of classic explanations: to clarify the origin of a human characteristic (*tools*), a condition is posited and assimilated to the 'cause' (*hunting*); subsequently,

---

[265] Laughlin 1968: 318; Jolly 1970: 22; Ruyle 1977: 144; Isaac 1978a: 100.

a practical usefulness is sought (what could *tools* have been used for?) which might justify the necessity for the emergence of the characteristic whose origin they are trying to explain. Thus, causal hypotheses evolve in the fixed framework of a determinism that reduces history to a chain of inevitable events.

THE RULES OF CONJECTURE

I have dealt with enough examples now – too many, perhaps, for the reader's taste – to allow me to refrain from scrutinising the other explanatory relations in our scenarios: they would simply be a pretext for renewed excursions into the realm of naïve anthropology. So I shall summarise the provisional conclusions that can be drawn from the preceding comments.

First of all, the previous analyses suggest that the credibility enjoyed by the twenty-one causal explanations that occur most frequently in our hominisation scenarios has more to do with their conformity to premises of common-sense anthropology than with their conformity to empirical data or to the absence of alternative conceptions. To illustrate the historical persistence of the 'successful' explanations widely accepted in modern palaeoanthropology, I have drawn up a table that brings together the first mentions in western literature of the 'relations' underlying these etiological structures. A mere glance reveals that, of these twenty-one most widespread causal explanations, fourteen are based on 'relations' postulated before 1800 (eight even date from Antiquity), four were proposed in the second half of the nineteenth century, and we are indebted to contemporary anthropologists for only three (Table 5). As to the list of the thirty-seven 'human characteristics' at stake in the construction of the hominisation scenarios, no fewer than twenty-two are already attested to in the literature of classical Antiquity, while seven appear in works published in the eighteenth and mid-nineteenth centuries; only seven originate in works of twentieth-century science (Table 6).[266]

[266] It should be remembered that, in this list, we are dealing with features considered to be either distinctive of humans in general compared with animals, or else distinctive of the early humans compared with their direct ancestors. I have excluded the concept of 'culture' from this list; it is mentioned in one scenario but the significance proved too variable over the centuries for historical comparisons to be possible. As to the other positions on this list, it is undeniable that contemporary scientists do not define 'tools', 'bipedalism' or 'sociability' in the same way as the ancient authors or the philosophers of the Enlightenment. Table 6 is just an *aide mémoire* intended to illustrate succinctly the debt still owed by modern palaeoanthropology to earlier philosophical speculation; it should in no way be seen as a 'proof' that concepts are historically immobile.

Table 5. *First mentions of the 'causal' relations most frequent in our sample of the scenarios of hominisation (the first figure [Q] indicates the number of scenarios in which these relations appear)*

Q	Relation	Date	Author	Reference
11	Bipedalism → free hand	Fourth century BC	Aristotle	*Partibus animalium*, 687a
9	Free hand → tools	Fourth century BC	Aristotle	*Partibus animalium*, 687a
9	Environmental change → hunting	First century BC	Virgil	*Georgica* 1.121–46
8	Environmental change → bipedalism	1871	Darwin	Darwin 1871, I: 140–1
7	Tools → reduced canines	1871	Darwin	Darwin 1871, I: 144–5
7	Hunting → sexual division of labour	1774	Burnet	Burnet 1774–92, I: 445–53
6	Tools → voluminous brain	1896	Engels	Engels 1971/1896: 62
6	Tools → bipedalism	1968	Oakley	Oakley 1968: 258
5	Food-sharing → social life	1954	Coon	Coon 1955/1954: 66
5	Language → mental faculties	1784–91	Herder	*Ideen zur philosophie...*, viertes Buch, s. 136
5	Environmental change → tools	First century BC	Virgil	*Georgica* 1.139–45
5	Hunting → tools	First century BC	Virgil	*Georgica* 1.139–45
5	Social life → language	First century BC	Diodorus Siculus	*Bibliotheca historica* 1.8
4	Tools → free hand	1870	Royer	Royer 1870: 154
4	Sexual division of labour → food-sharing	1755	Rousseau	Rousseau 1973/1755: 351
4	Hunting → cooperation	1774	Home	Home 1774: 62
4	Tools → language	1957	Oakley	Oakley 1957: 208
4	Mental faculties → voluminous brain	1801	Virey	Virey 1801, I: 180
3	Hunting → food-sharing	1755	Rousseau	Rousseau 1973/1755: 351
3	Cooperation → social life	First century BC	Lucretius	*De rerum natura*, v. 958–61
3	Mental faculties → perfectibility	First century BC	Lucretius	*De rerum natura*, v. 1448–57

Table 6. *The first mentions in European literature of distinctive characteristics either of humans in general, or of primitive humanity in particular*

Characteristics	Date	Author	Reference
Tools	Fourth century BC	Aristotle	*Partibus animalium*, 687a
Bipedalism	Fourth century BC	Aristotle	*Partibus animalium*, 688a
Free hands	Fifth century BC	Anaxagoras	Quoted in Aristotle, *Partibus animalium*, 687a
Language	Fifth/Fourth century BC	Xenophon	*Memorabilia* I.IV.39
Social life	Fifth/Fourth century BC	Plato	*Protagoras*, 322b
Voluminous brain	Fourth century BC	Aristotle	*Partibus animalium*, 653a
Superior mental faculties	Fifth century BC	Anaxagoras	Quoted in Aristotle, *Partibus animalium*, 687a
Reduced canine teeth	1849	Lawrence	Lawrence 1849: 24
Cooperation	Fifth/Fourth century BC	Plato	*Protagoras*, 322b
Sexual division of labour	1755	Rousseau	Rousseau 1973/1755: 351
Food-sharing	1755	Rousseau	Rousseau 1973/1755: 351
Hunting	Fifth century BC	Sophocles	*Antigone*, vv. 342–6
Perfectibility	Fifth/Fourth century BC	Xenophon	*Memorabilia* I.IV.39
Family organisation	First century BC	Lucretius	*De rerum natura* V. 1011–12
Reproductive success	First century BC/First century AD	Ovid	*Metamorphoses* 1.60–91
Prolonged childhood	Sixth century BC	Anaximander	Quoted in Pseudo-Plutarch, *Stromates*, 2
Absence of oestrus	Fourth century BC	Aristotle	*Historia animalium*, v. 8
Carnivorous diet	Third/Fourth century AD	'Common opinion'	According to Porphyry, *De abstinentia* 1.13

Table 6. (*cont.*)

Characteristics	Date	Author	Reference
Large cranium	1801	Virey	Virey 1801, I: 180
Sociability	First century BC	Lucretius	*De rerum natura*, V. 1015–27
Cranium and jawbones modified	Fourth century AD	Gregory of Nyssa	*De hominis opificio*, 148d
Sexual dimorphism	1871	Darwin	Darwin 1871, II: 316
Scavenging	1953	Bartholomew and Birdsell	Bartholomew and Birdsell 1953
Omnivorous diet	1801	Virey	Virey 1801, I: 243
Protection of elders	First century BC	Lucretius	*De rerum natura*, V. 1024
Menopause	1982	Hill	Hill 1982: 359
Reduced incisors	1960	Washburn	Washburn 1960: 9
Strong incisors	1982	Hill	Hill 1982: 539
Large molars	1982	Hill	Hill 1982: 539
Reduction of the sexual dimorphism	1976	Tanner and Zihlman	Tanner and Zihlman 1976: 606
Burial of the dead	First century AD	Pliny the Elder	*Historia naturalis* VII.5
Religion	Fifth/Fourth century BC	Plato	*Menexenus*, 237d
Magic	Second/Third century AD	Origen	*Contra Celsum* IV.86
Longevity	1982	Hill	Hill 1982: 539
Fire	Fifth/Fourth century BC	Plato	*Protagoras*, 321d
Moral sense	1773	Helvétius	Helvétius 1773, section V, chap. III
Labour	1746	Pluche	Pluche 1746, V: 129

It is worth noting that, among the recurrent 'causal explanations', those that have been proposed more recently do not seem particularly revolutionary with regard to common-sense anthropology. In the nineteenth century, only one relation – the one put forward by Darwin (environmental change → bipedalism) was a true innovation, in so far as it was based on the new concept of natural selection. The other two (tools → reduced canine teeth; tools → large brain) rest on Lamarckian premises which themselves are derived from a set of ideas dating back to Antiquity. For the twentieth century, only the relation linking the emergence of language to the use of tools[267] is a genuinely new one, although it is based on the traditional conviction whereby the tool was the first manifestation of culture. In the end, the remaining innovations are combinatory rearrangements of conventional ideas:
(a) 'tools → bipedalism'[268] is only an inversion of the relation 'bipedalism → tools';
(b) 'food-sharing → social life' is a transformation of the classic sequence '[collective] hunting → social life', where the food-sharing, a logical consequence of collective hunting, left tacit in the arguments of naïve anthropology, is made explicit so as to become an intermediary element between 'hunting' and 'social life'.

It is obvious, therefore, that the core of the knowledge employed in hominisation scenarios is based on a relatively inert structure that prolongs the tradition of conjectural anthropology and has not been remodelled, in its broad outlines, either under the influence of new palaeontological and archaeological discoveries or as a consequence of the theoretical developments in biology.

This observation is confirmed when the arguments underlying the relations are analysed. Their content reveals a whole stock of ideas stemming from ancient common-sense imagery. We are struck first by the powerful influence still exerted by the idea of transition from a prehuman, paradisal state to the toiling human existence of the subsequent period. The impact of this conception is particularly plain to see in the way ecological changes are viewed, but it has left much more important traces in our scenarios. This conjectural scheme provides the authors with a whole spectrum of attributes of the prehuman and early human periods, which can be reduced to a system of binary oppositions:

[267] Oakley 1957: 208.   [268] Oakley 1968: 258.

Prehuman period	**Early human period**
hospitable nature	hostile nature
mild climate	harsh climate
abundance of food	shortage of food
absence of predators	threat from predators
natural gentleness	cruelty
vegetarian diet	carnivore diet
leisure	toil
individual life	social life

In scholarly anthropology as in its conjectural antecedents, this scheme loses the symbolic meaning it used to have in the myths and becomes a basis for purely naturalist inferences, for example:

If 'vegetarian diet', *then* 'gathering'
If ' carnivore diet', *then* 'hunting'
If 'leisure', *then* 'brain (or hands) disused'
If 'toil', *then* 'frequent use of brain (or hands)'
If 'individual life', *then* 'language useless and so absent'
If 'social life', *then* 'language necessary and so present'

Thus the body of traditional oppositions is expanded by a series of inferences, so as to include new pairs of contrasts, such as:

gathering/hunting,
disuse of brain/frequent use of brain,
absence of language/language, etc.

This primitive scheme can be further enriched along other lines than those of naturalist inference. As the very earliest 'paradisal' period is often identified with an animal state, another system of opposites is grafted on to the antinomy of the periods, this time contrasting bestiality and humanity, so that 'bestial' attributes are added to the left-hand column of the original scheme and 'human' properties complete the right-hand column. From that moment, the prehuman condition of the paradisal period is found to be associated with a bent posture, non-bipedal locomotion, absence of tools, and the non-existence of characteristics such as social life, family organisation, cooperation, food-sharing, sexual division of labour, etc., so many opposites to the properties assigned to the following, early human period, whose features are found in the right-hand column of the scheme. Their use in the explanatory arguments follows immediately. For example, absence of cooperation, which stands on the left-hand side next to gathering is straight away 'explained' by means of an *ad hoc* argument that establishes a 'necessary' link between the two characteristics ('gathering does not require cooperation'), and the same procedure is followed with cooperation, which abuts hunting on the right-hand side of the relation and so is thereby 'explained' ('hunting requires cooperation'). So the juxtaposition of the attributes in the two opposite columns gives rise to a set of mutual explanations, sustained by makeshift arguments whose chief virtue is their plausibility in the eyes of common sense.

A third way of using and transforming the primitive scheme remains: by inversion. The 'paradisal' attributes can be moved to the right-hand side of the binary structure (period B), while the negative properties take their place on the left-hand side (period A). This type of permutation does not change the explanatory procedure itself: for example, the attributes of a 'mother nature' can replace those of a 'stepmother nature' without modifying the part played by ecological change, which continues to 'explain', in a determinist manner, the origin of hunting, of tools, of bipedalism, etc.

The system of opposites can also suffer amputation of one of its two poles: the result is a static image of a single period, endowed with one type of characteristics, either positive or negative.

Thus the tradition of naïve anthropology offers us a set of ideas, the content of which may be developed or transformed by operations that prolong the broad lines of the primitive scheme, still capable of nurturing quite an abundance of anthropological speculation.

In addition to this well-structured matrix, the authors of our texts turn other common-sense topics to good account. The examples are legion: the projection onto primitive humans of the attributes of the Wild Man, a folklore figure; the anthropogenic role of bipedalism with all the symbolic connotations that philosophical and theological traditions assign to upright posture; a still lively Lamarckian principle, always about to resurface in the arguments that claim to be in harmony with the most up-to-date evolutionary theory; the idea of the natural 'frailty' of women, linked with the ancient symbolic system of a weak, soft womanhood contrasted with a hard, strong manhood well adapted to hunting; the references to proverbs ('necessity is the mother of invention'), or to illusions of introspection ('thought is impossible without language').

More generally – and this will be the first of our conclusions – the differences between the vernacular or philosophical opinions about anthropogenesis and scientific explanations of hominisation, these latter supposedly founded on newly acquired palaeontological and archaeological data, are amazingly slight. Each of them is constructed out of the same conceptual matrix.

This phenomenon might be explained by a kind of selection of ideas taking place in the field of palaeoanthropology. On the one hand, we have noticed many times in the course of these analyses that the sum total of the hypotheses put forward by scientific experts is far from covering the whole extent of the conceptual possibilities. On the other hand, although anthropological speculation very often hovers, empirically speaking, in the undecidable, we can observe a consequent selection of ideas, the criterion of which is now clearly apparent: the palaeoanthropological literature is more willing to retain explanations which, without being flagrantly at odds with empirical data, correspond to schemes of naïve anthropology, either by perpetuating its patterns textually or by subjecting them to a few simple permutations. This procedure allows for the establishment of a certain consensus, the stability of which, for all its relative nature, can only reassuringly lead to the belief that the conjectural method, despite its fragility, ultimately produces some intersubjective results, easily accepted by the majority of the scientific community.

I have attempted to show that this consensus, far from proving the strength of the method, rather tends to reflect the weakness of our imagination, still remaining under the sway of common sense. The consequence is that the diversity of the hypotheses proposed continues to be limited – a state of affairs which helps us to avoid the risk of an unsavoury hubbub where anything may be said because, in the realm of the undecidable, nothing is prohibited. Naïve anthropology is thus the compass that allows us to navigate with confidence on the ocean of the conceivable, while kindly leaving us the illusion of steering the right course.

From this angle, conjectural anthropology, clinging to common-sense wisdoms, also seems to be a trap. In studying it, I have in mind not so much the history of ideas, rather their possible future: being more aware of the trap, we might be able to avoid it. And the pitfall here is in fact twofold. Naïve anthropology, by conditioning our imagination, not only leads us to sift the hypotheses following a criterion that is not cognitively efficient (by their conformity to the old conjectural schemes and not by their empirical or theoretical relevance); it is also responsible for reducing the variability of those hypotheses, and since scientific knowledge develops by competition between rival ideas, excessive standardisation of our conjectures jeopardises the progress of knowledge. For these two reasons, it seems to me important to be awake to the limits imposed by the conceptual schemes of naïve anthropology on our attempts to imagine the process of hominisation.

CHAPTER 4

Evolutionary mechanisms: the constraints of nature or of imagination?

The general is honoured because it reveals the cause.
Aristotle, *Posterior analytics* 88a 5

COMMON SENSE AND EVOLUTION

A study of the components and 'causal' relations that form the structural framework of our scenarios gives only a fragmented image of the way they are constructed, since each of the explanatory sequences also presupposes a mechanism for evolutionary change. In this regard, the explanations can be divided into three groups:

1. 'Traditional' explanations, which appeal neither to the mechanisms of Darwinian evolution nor to 'Lamarckian' principles.
2. 'Lamarckian' explanations, which refer, explicitly or not, to the principle of use and disuse, as well as to the inheritance of acquired characteristics.
3. 'Darwinian' explanations, in which I have included those that allude to the mechanisms of natural and sexual selection, or, more generally, those that have recourse to Darwinian terminology (for example, the terms of fitness, preadaptation, etc.), indeed even to a terminology commonly considered as such (for example the notion of adaptation). A separate group in this category consists of explanations that refer to the mechanism of 'correlated variation' or 'correlation of growth'.[1]

The logicist reconstruction to which all the hominisation scenarios have been subjected enables us to distinguish a total of 216 explanatory sequences, each expressed by one or more inferential operations. Since the authors under consideration (leaving Lamarck aside, of course)

[1] Cf. Darwin 1871, I: 130–1.

proclaim their attachment to the Darwinian or neo-Darwinian theory of evolution, it is surprising to find that almost 74 per cent of the causal sequences make no reference to Darwinian mechanisms. These appear in only 20.4 per cent of cases, so they play a very modest role in our scenarios, barely three times greater than Lamarckian principles, which are called on in 6 per cent of the causal sequences (Table 7).

Because almost half the scenarios construct their explanations of anthropogenesis without recourse to Darwinism, I suppose that the arguments of these texts would not have suffered overmuch if the theory of evolution had not existed. If Darwinism is commonly accepted, why do our texts make such limited use of it? Is it because their authors are under the illusion that they are using Darwinism? Or it is rather because they do not need it? And if they do not feel the need for it, is it because Darwinism brings very little that is new to the ancient explanatory framework? But, in that case, is it really Darwinism, rather than one of its naïve applications, that our authors may have found credible and relevant? In order to answer these questions, it is necessary to examine more closely the nature of the 'traditional' and 'Darwinian' explanations so as to throw more light on the differences separating them, and especially to delimit the points they have in common, which reveal the limitations to which both the 'ancient' and 'modern' explanatory patterns are subject.

'TRADITIONAL' EXPLANATIONS

The form of the 'traditional' explanations is very stereotyped and can be reduced to two versions, one simple, the other more complex. The simple version is of the type: *If (x), then (y)*, where x designates either a characteristic of the environment or a 'human' characteristic (rarely a group of characteristics) which are accorded the status of cause, while y denotes a 'human' characteristic (rarely a group of characteristics) deemed to be the effect of the above: for example, *if* 'hunting' (x), *then* 'cooperation' (y).

The complex version includes a complementary proposition in the aforesaid formula, indicating the nature of the relation between the left-hand side (x) and the right-hand side (y): *If (x), and if $[(x) \rightarrow (y)]$, then (y)*, where (x) and (y) have the same values as above, while $(x) \rightarrow (y)$ signifies that a characteristic (x) commands (leads to, is linked to, necessitates, contributes to, stimulates, liberates, allows, makes possible, etc.) another

Table 7. *Explanatory sequences extracted from our sample of hominisation scenarios and classified according to the mechanism of evolutionary change they presuppose. The Roman numerals refer to the numbering of the texts in Table 2; the Arabic numerals indicate the number of occurrences (detailed analysis in Stoczkowski 1991).*

Scenarios / Mechanisms	I	II	III	IV	V	VI	VII	VIII	IX	X	XI	XII	XIII	XIV	XV	XVI	XVII	XVIII	XIX	XX	XXI	XXII	XXIII	XXIV	Total	%
'Traditional' mechanisms	5	5	5	11	12	6	6	8	6	2	16	8	7	3	12	5	5	11	4	7	10	1	1	3	159	73.6
'Lamarckian' mechanisms	–	–	3	2	1	–	–	3	2	–	–	–	–	1	1	–	–	–	–	–	–	–	–	–	13	6.0
'Darwinian' mechanisms	–	–	5	–	–	2	–	4	–	5	–	–	4	–	1	5	2	1	3	8	–	1	3	–	44	20.4
TOTAL	5	5	13	13	13	8	6	15	8	7	16	8	11	4	14	10	7	12	7	15	10	2	4	3	216	100

characteristic (y). For example:

> **If** 'hunting' (x).
> **and if** 'hunting' requires 'cooperation' ($x \rightarrow y$)
> **then** 'cooperation' (y).

So the 'traditional' explanations rest on statements that postulate a relation between the characteristics, in which the connection between the left-hand side (cause) and the right-hand side (effect) is sometimes made explicit, sometimes not (a distinction corresponding to that made by Greek rhetoric between *syllogismós* and *epicheírema*).

As we have already observed, this arrangement of characteristics in causal sequences is subject to certain rules and limitations which reflect a particular view of humankind and of culture. The broad lines of this conception can be defined by four axioms that I have called *environmental determinism*, *materialism*, *utilitarianism* and *individualism* (see chapter 1).

Environmental determinism

Most of the palaeoanthropological scenarios explain the beginning of hominisation, in its biological and cultural aspects, by the impact of the environment. The influence of the milieu would thus play a key role in triggering the process, the whole of which would be merely the chain of logical consequences of that first impetus.

There is no reason to cast doubt on the importance of the environment in the mechanisms of evolution. As to hominisation, the role played by the environment is plausible because the climatic changes of the Plio-Pleistocene are coeval with important evolutionary changes, not just in the hominid family but also for a large part of the flora and fauna of East Africa.[2] None the less, this correlation does not prejudge the nature of the mechanism at work, which might be associated either with new selective pressures, with a reproductive isolation resulting from environmental factors, with both causes working in tandem, or, on another level, with a climatic influence on foetal development.[3] Furthermore, even if the environment played a decisive part, it would be rushing things to seek to explain hominisation by limiting the spectrum of the hypotheses to external factors, without also taking the structural constraints of the organisms into account.

---

[2] See, for example, the collected texts in Coppens 1985.
[3] This last hypothesis, cf. Vrba, Denton and Prentice 1989.

The precise character of the influence which the environment has been able to exercise on hominisation cannot therefore be taken for granted. Despite this, our scenarios, which often cast ecological change as a catastrophic event, seem inclined to depict the action of the milieu in terms of the most perfunctory formula: ecological constraints would have traced the straight and narrow path of necessity for the hominids, a single track along which alone the evolutionary process could proceed. So our ancestors would have been faced with a simple choice: to perish or to 'hominise' ('the refusal of some unidentified species to become extinct made possible... the human condition', says Robert Ardrey[4]). The adoption of such a perspective inevitably affects the explanations put forward: 'when we ask why this change', one of our scenarios asserts, 'we must remember that our ancestors of the time were not striving to become human. They were doing what all animals do: trying to stay alive. Thus, in searching for causes of the change, we must look to conditions pertaining at the time.'[5]

So, to quote a few examples, a meat diet and hunting are perceived as the only chance of survival in a new environment where vegetarian food is sorely lacking; bipedalism is the only form of locomotion conducive to rapid flight and staying alive in an open milieu; tools and cooperation become indispensable, either for defence against more powerful animals or for obtaining the necessary food, etc.

Explaining evolutionary transformation would therefore amount to showing how, in given conditions, the change allowed escape from death and the realisation of what is held to be the supreme imperative of the animate world: 'to stay alive'. This watchword, raised to the status of a law, makes nature the arena of the strictest determinism, in which just one road is open, outside which there is no salvation.

Biologists today reject this oversimplistic view. Of course the survival imperative influences living organisms, but it is far from accounting entirely for their transformations. From the point of view of the problems of survival, 'it is difficult', wrote François Jacob, 'to see any necessity in the fact that trees bear fruit. Or that animals age. Or in sexuality. Why should it take two to make a third?'[6] The demands of the same environment can be met by very different anatomical constructions and behavioural responses;[7] in other words, external constraints are insufficient to explain the options that were in fact chosen in the process of evolution.

[4] Ardrey 1973/1961: 246.   [5] Hockett and Ascher 1964: 136.   [6] Jacob 1981: 18.
[7] Devilliers and Chaline 1989: 70.

If the axiom of environmental determinism does not meet the complexity of evolution, it nevertheless reflects very clearly the simplicity of the common-sense representations. I have already shown in a number of examples that pre-empirical speculation envisaged anthropogenesis as a process subject to a strict inevitability. Holbach became the spokesman for this opinion when he declared: 'Everything should have convinced man that, at every moment of his existence, he is a passive tool in the hands of necessity . . . So it is nature, ever active, that marks each of the points along the line that man must follow.'[8]

From their inception, anthropological conjectures have been accompanied by the avatars of ecological determinism.[9] It is striking to observe the lasting success still enjoyed today by theories explaining the diversity of cultures and the important moments in human history by the influence of the natural environment. Their popularity, the faith and trust vested in them, are no smaller in numerous scholarly works than in popular literature; might this once again be the consequence of the weight of the traditional imagery, in which the speculation of Hippocratic theory flourished for so long?[10] This ancient doctrine proposed a symbolic structure, in which, on the four physical qualities, arranged in two pairs of opposites (cold/hot, dry/moist), a whole system of associations is juxtaposed, including four elements (fire, air, earth, water), four physiological humours (yellow bile, blood, black bile, phlegm) and four temperaments (choleric, brave, melancholic, phlegmatic). Through the medium of climate, food and drink, primitive elements were deemed to influence the humours, which governed temperaments, and these subsequently determined both the anatomy and the mentality of human beings, their customs and social organisation. Thus the climate, and the food that depends on it, acquired the extraordinary and limitless capacity to shape humankind.[11] And since anatomy, like culture, would be determined by the natural environment, all their transformations would have to be explained by ecological changes.

This line of thought, fostered by the writings of Hippocrates, Aristotle and Galen, has long been a strand in western culture. An upsurge in its popularity marked the Renaissance period;[12] it reached a high point in the eighteenth century and lasted on into the first half of the

---

[8] Holbach 1821/1770: 90.   [9] Greenwood 1984.
[10] E.g. choice of texts from the Hippocratic corpus, Joly 1964.
[11] Myers 1908: 162–4; see also Greenwood 1984.   [12] E.g. Bodin 1951/1572.

Evolutionary mechanisms 137

nineteenth.[13] This system of symbolic associations, based originally on identifying the human microcosm with the elements and the qualities of the macrocosm, was swiftly 'naturalised'. Many authors saw in it a way of explaining rationally the differences, both anatomical and cultural, between human beings. The general conclusion was always the same: 'Three causes, therefore', wrote Buffon, 'must be admitted, as concurring in the production of those varieties which we have remarked among the different nations of this earth: 1. The influence of the climate; 2. Food, which has a great dependence on climate, and 3. Manners, on which climate has, perhaps, a still greater influence.'[14] So climate would be the first and principal cause of differentiation of humans and cultures, because it is on climate that the other two causes, food and custom, depend. Buffon adds: if 'the Samoiedes, the Zemblians, the Borandians, the Laplanders, the Greenlanders and the savages to the north of the Esquimaux... resemble one another in figure, in stature, in colour, in manners and even in singularity of customs',[15] it is precisely because they all live in the same climatic zone and consume identical food. Not even the most trivial details of culture escape the impact of a determinism so rigorous that it extends to generating identical 'singularity of customs'. The connection between these speculations and the symbolic system of Hippocratic anthropology is obvious: at least until halfway through the nineteenth century, references to humours and elements can be found in debates on the connections between climate/food and temperament/anatomy/culture.[16]

The success still enjoyed by similar arguments in our own day testifies to how deeply this theory has infiltrated the universe of common sense. In the nineteenth and twentieth centuries they are found in the popular literature of countless *Universal geographies*, which offer colourful descriptions of nations and ethnic groups whose characters are said to have been determined with great precision by local climates.[17] A veritable arsenal of fanciful images and racist or xenophobic clichés finds a 'rational' and 'scientific' justification there, reducing the differences between people to differences in climates and geographical situations. This view is still firmly anchored in our contemporary culture, where it is conveyed by products of everyday consumption. Analysis of Gérard de Villiers' *SAS*

---

[13] E.g. Bory de Saint-Vincent 1825, VIII: 278–339; Buffon 1831/1749; Cabanis 1959/1802: 316–512; Ferguson 1767: 165–85; Helvétius 1988/1758; Herder 1962/1784–91, Books VI–VII; Montesquieu 1979/1748, I, Books XIV–XVIII; Virey 1801, II; 1827: 179–207.
[14] Buffon, trans. W. Smellie, 1771: 132.   [15] *Ibid.*: 63.   [16] E.g. Virey 1841.
[17] E.g. Granger 1922.

adventure stories, for example, reveals a perfectly coherent view of correlations between climates and the temperaments and cultures particular to this or that region of the world.[18] Thus the temperate climate is associated with discipline, reserve, a peaceful character, a taste for cleanliness, honesty, whereas the tropical climate is deemed to generate spontaneity, lack of discipline, exuberance, qualities that go hand in hand with cruelty, dishonesty and corruption. Gérard de Villiers' hero journeys through just such a world, and the mythical anthropology that peers out from the peregrinations depicted in the previous century by Jules Verne was practically the same.[19] Besides, how many of us still believe Nordic people to be reserved or phlegmatic, and are astonished to find no joviality in a Southerner?

The theory of climatic determinism is thus embedded in an ancient tradition that still seems to condition judgements based on common sense: since we are convinced that humans are entirely determined by the environment, we believe that anatomical and cultural transformations are due to its changes.

Materialism

Just as the principle of *ecological determinism* tends to oversimplify the mechanisms of nature, so that of *materialism* oversimplifies the mechanism of culture. The anthropology built on these premises makes material constraints the only authoritative explanation of cultural phenomena; even when cognition and social conventions are clearly in evidence, they are thought to be a mere reflection of the material reality, as in the classic formula of Marx and Engels, according to which 'thought and the intellectual commerce of men appear as the direct emanation of their material behaviour'.[20] Thought and the arbitrary conventions it generates have no place among the causes of cultural phenomena, and consequently become a factor of no importance in the genesis of culture. Some such principle seems to govern the 'traditional' explanations in the hominisation scenarios. Tools, language, cooperation, social life, sexual division of labour, food-sharing appear only under the impact of material circumstances, which would have entirely determined the life of our ancestors.

This view of the origins of culture is not unconnected with a popular theory of 'human' nature, clearly expressed by the primatologist

---

[18] Stomma 1986. [19] *Ibid.* [20] Marx and Engels 1968/1846: 50.

Adrienne Zihlman in an address to an annual meeting of the American Association of Anthropologists, in which she summed up discussions on the origin of mankind in this sentence: 'As with most things in life, the debate centers on two themes: food and sex; or to give it a proper academic tone: diet and reproduction.'[21]

Whether the tone is academic or not, the idea remains the same and this quote sums it up very well: the human being is first and foremost hunger and the sexual instinct. These are the stimuli that would order its behaviour in the 'state of nature' and they are still the prime movers of civilisation.

It would be extremely difficult to defend this view on the grounds of ethnological research, where contemporary humans are studied across a multitude of cultures. There we discover humans bogged down everywhere in systems of arbitrary conventions imposed on them by society, often running counter to the logic of material constraints. What is more, the human being thinks, so he creates representations of the world that are far from being only a reflection, whether simplified or distorted, of the material universe. Of course, cognition feeds on certain elements of the physical world, but it also has the faculty to generate entities whose existence, although restricted to the realm of imagination, can in turn affect human beings in all the spheres of their lives with as much force as stimuli from the material world. As our scenarios often refer to the cultures of hunter-gatherers, it is worth remembering the important function of dreams and their interpretations, both influenced by local beliefs, in the lives of these peoples.[22] Another eloquent example of the role of cognition and social constraints in culture is provided by the phenomenon of the sexual division of labour, reduced by naïve anthropology to biological necessity alone. It is fascinating to observe how vain are the efforts of ethnologists who try to convince their audience that the relation between humans and external reality is mediated by conceptual schemes, that the subjective does not follow from the objective, that cognitive constraints are sometimes as important as material circumstances.[23]

There will be objections that this line of argument is concerned only with contemporary or relatively recent cultures, accessible to direct observation or to historical enquiry. What happens when we turn to look at our remote ancestors? In fact, our knowledge of the cognitive capacities

---

[21] Zihlman 1987: 11.   [22] E.g. Rogers 1962: D32, D5; Martin 1978: 74; Tanner 1979: 108–10.
[23] Cf. for example Lévi-Strauss 1962 or Sahlins 1976.

of the first hominids is virtually non-existent, so it is difficult to prejudge their mental faculties and their aptitude for creating the arbitrary social conventions that might have played a part in the genesis of certain cultural phenomena. This ignorance, of course, leaves us free to imagine our ancestors' existence as reduced to 'sex' and 'food', but it does not follow that this is the only possible view. There is no obligation to accept *a priori* a reduction of primitive man to *homo stupidus* obsessed with the incessant quest for food and females; some kind of cultural logic is equally conceivable as a necessary element in the explanation of certain stages of anthropogenesis. Most of our scenarios pass over this eventuality in silence, as if it were indisputable that the explanations not only can but also must restrict themselves to materialist premises.

Yet the history of anthropology provides examples of studies that have adopted the opposite point of view, in which thought is considered as the prime mover of hominisation.[24] In 1828, K. E. von Baer maintained that upright posture is the consequence of the development of brain and intelligence. In 1895, a similar hypothesis was put forward by L. F. Ward. W. J. Sollas asserted in 1909 that an intelligent ape with a large brain had chosen the human way of life because he had realised its advantages. In the same spirit, G. E. Smith declared in 1912 that hominisation had started with the development of the brain and the intelligence, and that upright stance and language were merely secondary effects; if the transition from the forest to an open milieu seemed to be the key moment for this process, the only reason for it, according to Smith, was that our ancestors, having become intelligent, understood the superiority of life in the new milieu.

Clearly, this type of reasoning can easily be transformed into an all-purpose explanation that will lend itself to every situation. Humans 'understood' or 'decided' – just one act of the intellect and the will provides all the explanations you want, as easy to make up as they are difficult to refute. The 'materialist' school of anthropology, aware of these weaknesses, rejected this procedure. The materialist search for causes was intended to supply the alternative solution, as Engels emphasised when he wrote that 'it is to the mind, to the development and activity of the brain that all the credit for the swift development of society must be attributed; men grew accustomed to explaining their activity by their thinking rather than by their needs . . . the result of this was that, with time, the idealist world-view emerged, which, particularly since the decline

[24] Cf. Bowler 1986: 161–73.

Evolutionary mechanisms 141

of Antiquity, has dominated people's minds. This kind of view still prevails, so that even materialist scholars of the Darwinian school could not always get a clear idea of the origin of man.'[25]

Yet Engels was wrong when he claimed the materialist approach as a nineteenth-century innovation; anthropological speculation had been using it constantly since Antiquity. The 'materialist' and the 'idealist' explanatory formulae alike belong to the *longue durée* structures of western thought: although contradictory, the two remain paradoxically linked, heirs to the same anthropological view, which we might call the conception of 'stratified man'.

In both cases the human being is conceived as a creature with strata, consisting principally of two layers. One is natural, physical, biological, animal, material, instinctive and predictable. The other is cultural, suprabiological, human, moral and cognitive, therefore arbitrary and unpredictable. The demarcation line separating them is presented as clear and easily discernible. The layers are superimposed in such a way that one forms a plinth, while the other is the pinnacle. Consequently, all that remains is to decide which of these strata is fundamental: either thought–culture has pride of place and decides about materiality–nature or the reverse. This is the essence of the old anthropological debate between 'idealism' and 'materialism'.

It is the materialist option rooted in the old naturalist tradition that dominates in our palaeoanthropological scenarios. Anthropological conjectures of the eighteenth and early nineteenth centuries again and again alluded to the 'stratified man', in which the natural layer appeared as the base for the cultural layer. 'We are born, so to speak, apes, it is education that makes us men', wrote J.-J. Virey.[26] In Diderot, this ontogenetic summary was echoed in a historical development: 'There existed a natural man: into that man an artificial man was introduced.'[27] Still according to Diderot, the ancient fundamental layer lies buried in civilised man, but it can get the upper hand again in difficult circumstances which 'return man to his early simplicity, reducing him to the constraints of the most elementary needs'.[28] So, faced with the menace and hardships of the struggle for existence, humankind regresses to its animal dimension; and no one should be surprised, since the strata are distinct and the base level can exist in isolation from its pinnacle. There is thus no doubt, Conjectural History asserted, that in earliest times, everyone was entirely engaged in the 'vital struggle' (the term

[25] Engels 1971/1896: 67.   [26] Virey 1827: 23.   [27] Diderot 1972/1830: 183.   [28] *Ibid.*

used by the Enlightenment when speaking of what was later called the 'struggle for survival') and human nature, subject to primary needs, was limited to its fundamental layer. Philosophers of every age delight in discovering this popular wisdom, according to which, in the beginning, mankind was reduced to digestion and sex. So Engels, in his funeral eulogy for Karl Marx, paid tribute to his master and friend, saying that 'just as Charles Darwin discovered the law of the development of the organic world, so Marx discovered this simple fact, shrouded until then by ideological biases, that human beings must first eat, drink and find shelter before they can indulge in politics, science, art, religion, etc.'[29] Two hundred years earlier, Giambattista Vico had made a similar 'discovery': 'humans are first of all in search of what is necessary for life; after that they seek useful things, the comforts of life, then they yearn for pleasure.'[30]

The idea that leisure and release from material preoccupations are necessary before humans can rise to activities going beyond their elementary needs had already been widely accepted since Antiquity.[31] It would be just as easy to amass references in support of the opposite conception, equally ancient and widespread, that gives priority in humans and in culture to the 'moral' and 'cognitive' layer alone.

Consequently, what must be borne in mind is the favour enjoyed among philosophers and scholars alike by the view of man as 'stratified' and capable of being 'dismantled', in either of these versions. The basic scheme is in perfect harmony with the traditional anthropological thesis. In Christian theology, in gnostic and cabbalistic speculations, as in other esoteric currents, the human being is made up of two parts, different in nature, either of which may achieve mastery of him: soul and body, New Man and Old Man, *pneuma* and *anti-mimon pneuma*, the holy soul (*nischmata*) and the bestial soul (*néphesch haîa*), etc. The words of Faust spring to mind, when he cries out in tragic desolation:

> Two souls, alas! reside within my breast,
> And each withdraws from, and repels, its brother.[32]

The idea of this duality in humans still persists in our contemporary culture, where it takes the most varied forms. Not only does a good deal of literature tell us of the eternal struggle being fought out deep within us between the Beast and the Angel, but certain scientists declare from time to time that they have just discovered an ancient, forgotten residue

---

[29] Engels 1949: 155. [30] Vico 1953/1744: 83, paragraph L.XVI. [31] Lloyd 1974: 149–50.
[32] *Faust I*, trans. Bayard Taylor, 1871: 54, cf. Goethe.

in human beings, knowledge of which will allow a better understanding of our true nature (for example the revelations by Desmond Morris of the ape concealed in man; similar conceptions are legion).

The theory of the 'stratified man' is heavy with consequences for the explanations of anthropogenesis, since it authorises the breaking down of the human being into layers or levels for which independent modes of functioning are envisaged. It is then deemed necessary to reduce humankind to characteristics derived from just one of those levels and to explain anthropological phenomena in terms of the monovalent logic peculiar to such a level, that is, either by purely cognitive operations or, as in our palaeoanthropological scenarios, by material constraints alone.

Utilitarianism

To explain the origin of new characteristics in terms of the principle of utilitarianism means showing in what way an innovation was useful. In our scenarios, such a procedure implies a particular view of usefulness, adapted to the image we have made of our ancestors' life. As most of the authors lean to the belief that primitive existence consisted chiefly of a struggle for survival, they attribute a usefulness for safeguarding life to the first human characteristics to emerge at the beginning of hominisation. If hunting appears, it is because it alone allowed enough food to be found in the savannah; social life was vital in order to face up to the mortal danger from predators; tools were essential for defence, etc. Thus, in the beginning, usefulness would derive from absolute necessity. Then, with time, these first 'human' characteristics bring about the need for other innovations: language is essential for transmitting technical skills; cooperation is necessary when hunting, which in turn implies the usefulness of a sexual division of labour, which then makes food-sharing necessary.

A notion of usefulness reduced in this way to the elementary necessities is typical of 'traditional' explanations, and fits in well with their determinist principles. So it is rare for usefulness to be invoked in connection with a mere benefit, possible but not essential (for example the merit of bipedalism to facilitate observation in the savannah; the advantage of tools for swifter butchering of carcasses).

In line with the principle of 'materialism', any usefulness of a cultural type, decreed by social convention, is ruled out of these explanations. Cultural logic affects neither family life, social organisation, exchange, hunting techniques nor the choice of food. If this cultural usefulness is absent from the hominisation scenarios, it is certainly not by virtue of information provided by ethnology about the cultures it has access to; everything seems to indicate that it is more a question of respecting materialist axioms and the image they impose of what early man's existence was like.

However, the essential problem faced by the palaeoanthropologists is not only how to recognise clearly the exact nature of the usefulness that can be referred to in the explanations; it is chiefly a matter of deciding whether invoking usefulness is sufficient, or even necessary, to explain the origin of things. Emile Durkheim was already recommending extreme prudence in this respect and his remarks have lost none of their topicality:

Making plain the usefulness of a fact is not the same as explaining how it arose or how it is what it is. For the uses to which it can be put imply specific properties that characterise it but do not create it. Our need for things cannot make them be this or that and, consequently, it is not need that can draw them out of nothingness and confer being on them.[33]

Yet explanation by usefulness, or better still by necessity, remains a popular and *a priori* credible procedure. 'The old maxim "necessity is the mother of invention" is quite applicable to both the human and the later Neolithic revolutions', a commentator on Hockett and Ascher's paper confidently declares, so giving an accurate picture of the explanatory principle put forward in their text.[34] 'Need is the father of the arts', wrote J.-J. Virey[35] a century and a half earlier, in order to lay the foundation of his own 'prehistoric' speculations. Marx and Engels made the same rule the basis of their understanding of history, stating that 'any revolution and the results that are its outcome were determined by the conditions of existence of the individuals, by needs'.[36]

Explanation of genesis by needs was a commonplace already in the seventeenth and eighteenth centuries. Hobbes spoke then of 'need, the mother of all inventions', and Goguet echoed him later calling need 'the master and tutor of men'.[37] Diodorus Siculus, in the first pages of his *Universal History*, was already using those words ('need has been the master of men'[38]), and the same idea was put to the task by the Fathers of the Church: 'God', wrote Origen, 'wishing human intelligence to be

---

[33] Durkheim 1973/1895: 90.   [34] Livingstone 1964: 150.   [35] Virey 1801, I: 116.
[36] Marx and Engels 1968/1846: 415.   [37] Hobbes 1996/1651: 21, Ch. IV.2.
[38] Diodorus Siculus 1743: 16; see also Lucretius 1964: 88, v. 1029.

exercised in every connection, that it might not remain idle and ignorant of the arts, created man destitute: so his very need would constrain him to invent arts, some in order to feed himself, others for protection.'[39] The folklore of different European countries preserves this idea in proverbs ('necessity is the mother of invention'; 'le besoin fait tout faire', etc.), and we shall not try to discover, in this particular case, whether it was fathered by philosophy or by ordinary thought. Let us rather reflect that the same theme is still widespread in scholarly anthropology as well: elementary needs are assigned such a large part in culture that they are believed to be sufficient to elucidate its genesis.[40]

Explanation by usefulness is itself very useful, since it enables us to explain practically everything. It is easy to attribute some kind of function to everything that exists, especially to past phenomena, of which traces are fragmentary and knowledge is uncertain. The writings of ethnologists show that this formula is applied just as commonly in the interpretation of contemporary cultures, even though the data available on the subject are richer and should impose stronger empirical constraints.[41]

When we accept the theory that everything that exists is useful and that, if something exists, it is because it is useful, the task of etiological explanation becomes child's play: if we want to understand a characteristic, a phenomenon, an event, we need only give it a function. We are reminded of Metternich: 'I wonder', he is supposed to have said on learning that the Tsar of Russia was dead, 'what can have been his motive?'

---

[39] Origen 1968, II: 375, IV.76.

[40] *Histoire raisonnée*, for its part, assimilated the notion of necessity to that of needs, which were contrasted with desires. In earliest times, the needs of man would have been limited to the simple necessities of biological existence and it was only later, with the development of culture, that the list of elementary needs would have been enriched with superfluous desires whose powerful presence henceforth had an influence on the vicissitudes of human history (for example Burnet 1774–92: 19; Delaméthrie 1802: liv; Lacépède 1821: 380; Virey 1801, II: 227).

[41] The discussions on the social organisation of hunter-gatherers in particular are a good illustration of the mechanism of explanation by usefulness. Take, for example, the debate on the rules for postmarital residence. The traditional explication (e.g. Service 1962: 67) holds that all hunting peoples are patrilocal, since, by allowing the solidarity between men of the same group to be preserved, that system is useful for hunting activities, the sharing of meat and war. Yet it turns out that some groups of hunter-gatherers, quite a lot in fact, especially among the Northern Athabascans (Canada) are matrilineal. Why? The explanation of this phenomenon, the opposite of the previous one, also appeals to usefulness. R. J. Perry (1989: 47) proposes the following argument: since men spend their time hunting in small bands, the base camp, inhabited chiefly by women, becomes the main setting for social life. So it is important that friendship and harmony reign there. The rule of matrilocality, then, was established so as to regroup women of the same origin together. With that kind of reasoning, it is easy to 'explain' any cultural phenomenon and, by the same token, its opposite, because the usefulness of either can be imagined in a flash.

Individualism

'The proper study of mankind is man': this famous line by Alexander Pope, quoted at the head of a work by Cabanis,[42] could also be the motto for the 'traditional' explanations. Because if the origin of the characteristics of human beings can be explained by their needs, these are no more than individual. 'Culture grows out of the activity and needs of individuals', we read in a hominisation scenario.[43] The dialectic of conflict between individual needs and those of the social group is missing from this type of explanatory reasoning. Society, our authors maintain, is formed to satisfy the needs of the individual; so how could it not be subject to the latter's demands? Emile Durkheim gave a penetrating analysis of the close link that exists between the principles of utilitarianism and of individualism:

> Indeed, if society is just a system of means instituted by humans in order to achieve certain ends, those ends cannot but be individual; for, before society, only individuals could exist. So it is from the individual that emanate the needs which have determined the formation of societies, and if it is from him that everything comes, it is through him that everything necessarily must be explained.[44]

Now, according to Auguste Comte whose ideas are the target of Durkheim's criticism, 'social facts would derive so immediately from human nature that, during the earliest phases of history, they could be deduced directly from it, without any recourse to observation'.[45]

The 'traditional' explanations used in almost three quarters of our causal sequences show a strong resemblance to those of naïve anthropology. The principles of *environmental determinism, materialism, utilitarianism* and *individualism* establish apparently solid bases for deductive reasoning. Their strict application reduces mankind and culture to what is thought to be a 'natural' dimension, in which the causes of the phenomena studied could be inferred directly from the 'laws of nature'. This was already the classic method of Conjectural History, which endeavoured to remove the social and the arbitrary so as to make 'naturalist deduction' possible. Thus the aim was to satisfy the crucial condition for telling history backwards, of which Kant spoke in these terms:

> But if we were to start reconstructing history entirely on conjectures, we would be doing little more, it seems to me, than sketching out a novel. Moreover, such

---

[42] Pope 1993/1733–4: *Epistle* II, vv. 1–2; Cabanis 1959/1802. [43] Ruyle 1977: 149.
[44] Durkheim 1973/1895: 98. [45] Quoted from Durkheim 1973/1895: 98.

a work would not even merit the name of Conjectural History, but at the very most that of pure fantastic fiction. Nevertheless, what we should not dare to do for the course of the history of human actions, we may well attempt to establish through conjecture for the first beginnings of that history, in so far as there are the works of nature then at stake.[46]

So the danger of ending up with fiction has not passed unnoticed, and the chief justification claimed by deductive conjectures consisted in bringing the vision of humankind down to a natural and individual level, held to be predictable. The four principles I have just reviewed are the axioms of this view; their usefulness is consequently beyond question in any attempt at deductive reconstruction of prehistory.

It is tempting to explain the origin of these principles precisely by their usefulness in conjectural reconstructions, but then we would just be following the explanatory procedure adopted by our scenarios themselves. To avoid that trap and point up the weakness of such an approach, I have highlighted the fact that these four principles are part of a common-sense knowledge, deeply embedded in popular imagery, which took shape independently of speculations about the origins of humankind. Anthropology, both scholarly and naïve, when it tries to explain anthropogenesis, draws on the same set of ideas, while retaining only those that are 'useful', but which had been in existence long before, and their genesis has nothing to do with their 'usefulness' for speculation on the origin of man and of culture.

I began this chapter by indicating that 'traditional' explanations establish relationships between 'human' and 'ecological' characteristics and give them a causal status. For the present, having analysed the rules governing these relationships, I can pinpoint the standard procedure of the palaeoanthropological scenarios: to explain the origin of a new human characteristic y by the previous existence of characteristic x (the sequence $x \rightarrow y$) is to state that, in the presence of x, y becomes necessary or useful for the survival and subsistence of the individual, whose elementary needs are determined by the constraints of the natural environment.

'LAMARCKIAN' EXPLANATIONS

The arguments based on 'Lamarckian' premises persisted in anthropology into the second half of the 1970s, surrounded, paradoxically, by the

[46] Kant 1985/1786: 503.

aura of a classic Darwinian theme, Darwin's 'Lamarckian' hypothesis concerning canine teeth reduction having become particularly popular. Furthermore, on these same bases, certain scenarios try to explain incisor reduction, increased brain size, the perfecting of manual skill, cranial modifications and jaw reduction.

According to Lamarck's original formulation, evolutionary change unfolds as follows: circumstances modify needs, which modify the uses of organs, and the used organs grow stronger and bigger, while the disused organs become weaker and smaller. The useful and used organs develop, and degeneration affects only those conformations that remain disused and therefore useless. Use flows from usefulness, and usefulness depends on need; thus Lamarck concluded: 'needs alone will have done everything'.[47]

Reference to these principles makes it easier to understand the claim, current in our scenarios, that the organ no longer needed by the organism is reduced,[48] or again that 'need creates its organ'.[49] This last proposition can be employed to support a line of reasoning in which the need for language explains the origin of the human larynx and the anatomy of the oral cavity essential for speech. According to Lamarck's first law, need is able to bring about more frequent use of those parts and so transform them. Diderot was already alluding to a similar mechanism in *Le rêve de d'Alembert*, imagining that 'needs produce organs'.[50]

The popularity of this thesis in the eighteenth century is easier to understand when we turn to the assumptions shared by the naturalists of the period. According to the maxims that then summarised the general view of nature, it 'abhors a vacuum', 'does nothing in vain', 'does nothing superfluous'. It goes without saying that in such a world, usefulness is the first *raison d'être*, while lack of usefulness becomes a death sentence. Kant wrote:

> An organ that does not have to be used, a conformation that does not fulfil its objective is a contradiction in the teleological doctrine of nature. Indeed if we depart from this principle, we are no longer dealing with a nature that obeys laws but with a nature that operates with no purpose, and a distressing indeterminism takes the place of the vital lead of reason.[51]

The principle of use and disuse meets perfectly the demands of the 'natural order' established by the Architect of the Universe in accordance

---

[47] Lamarck 1809, I: 357.   [48] Ardrey 1973/1961: 263.   [49] Engels 1971/1896: 60.
[50] Diderot 1994/1782: 635.   [51] Kant 1985/1786: 189.

with the immutable logic of universal laws. Atheists were in agreement with theologians on this point: whatever the forces hiding behind her wisdom, nature 'does not play aimlessly'.

It is fascinating to see the extent to which the 'Lamarckian' view of usefulness agrees with the 'traditional' explanations of common-sense anthropology, which for centuries has been making usefulness the very principle of its explanatory reasonings. In both cases, external circumstances determine needs, needs decide on the nature of the usefulness, and everything that comes into being finds its explanation in usefulness. The theory common to both naïve anthropology and 'Lamarckism' is that the genesis of things is the genesis of their usefulness.

'DARWINIAN' EXPLANATIONS

I have agreed to designate as 'Darwinian' any explanation showing some rhetoric or lexical sign of a possible connection with the theory of evolution, whether Darwinian or synthetic. So I shall attach this label to explanations that allude to notions such as natural selection, selective advantage, fitness, reproductive success, adaptation (the explanatory sequences that call on the principle of correlation of growth form a separate group, which will be discussed later). The terminology provides a criterion general enough to flag up the arguments that do indeed rest on the Darwinian or neo-Darwinian principles, and also those in which the use of these theories might be only apparent.

Although this definition is very wide, the number of 'Darwinian' types of explanation in our corpus does not exceed 20 per cent, and half the scenarios offer no trace of it at all (Table 7). Yet all our authors – with the exception, of course, of Lamarck – accepted the Darwinian theory (*sensu lato*) unreservedly, declaring more than once that its principles must lie at the base of evolutionary explanations. If they state their attachment to Darwinism in this way, and subsequently make only modest use of it, it is perhaps because their vision of Darwinism is very specific and deviates from the definition I have chosen. However, the methodological statements in our scenarios refer to absolutely classic Darwinian notions, which should be easily identifiable with the aid of my terminological criterion.

In short, the question remains: what does the Darwinism in the palaeoanthropological scenarios really amount to and why is its role so restricted? In order to attempt an answer, let us examine the concrete uses made of Darwinian concepts.

Natural selection

Natural selection is the paramount notion of 'Darwinian' explanations in our scenarios. To explain the origin of an organ, of a function, of a type of behaviour or of an artefact is to indicate the selective pressure responsible for propagating it.

The general pattern of the causal chains is as follows: when certain characteristics or states appear (x), they imply the action of natural selection which begins to favour other properties (y). For example, it is assumed that the emergence of sexual division of labour and food-sharing (x) in turn activates natural selection which favours the emergence of family organisation (y).[52] In certain cases, this kind of succinct explanation is expanded by a proposition establishing a functional relation between x and y. Kim Hill's scenario offers a typical example: the hominids, the author imagines, started eating meat, but their digestive system was not producing the enzymes that usually aid the assimilation of flesh in other carnivores. Consequently, long and tedious mastication was required, which was decidedly difficult. Strong incisors and large molars then became useful to facilitate mastication; so natural selection favoured the development of just such dentition.[53] What is it that is being favoured here? Something that is useful. The functional relation between x and y comes down to the usefulness of y in relation to x. By extension of this argument, it is accepted that if selection favours a, and if b is useful for a, selection must favour b equally. For example, when natural selection promotes reciprocal aid between brothers and sisters, and if the learning of mutual aid from the mother helps to reinforce this mutual assistance, then natural selection also favours the development of that learning.[54] So selection is a direct support of what is useful and an indirect support of what is useful to what is useful.

What is the nature of this usefulness? Notably useful is anything that:

(a) ensures better access to food;[55]
(b) allows food to be obtained at the maximal possible rate;[56]
(c) allows maximisation of the yield (in calories/hour) from the effort invested in foraging.[57]

[52] Isaac 1978a: 106. [53] Hill 1982: 538–9. [54] Tanner and Zihlman 1976: 605.
[55] Hill 1982: 537. [56] Kurland and Beckerman 1985: 74. [57] Hill 1982: 532.

Evolutionary mechanisms 151

So, the notion of usefulness comes down to efficiency in the quest for food. This finding is revealing. Since our authors accept, in accordance with the rules of Darwinian theory, that natural selection gives advantage to characteristics favourable to reproductive success, they go on to reason as if ability to reproduce were limited only by alimentary problems. And we are back again to the traditional view of nature, in which lack of food is the only worry for all creatures, and the course of evolution is governed by the struggle for food. This view alone could justify assimilating the action of selection solely to the problems of obtaining food.

Fitness

The same principle seems to govern the use of the term fitness. Consider, for example, the explanation proposed by Kim Hill's scenario. Male-hunter hominids were able to obtain food more efficiently than the female-gatherers, and so they had some free time; they devoted this leisure – supposedly unknown until then – to increase their fitness: taking advantage of their free time, they hunted more and so obtained a surplus of meat, which they then exchanged for additional copulations with females.[58]

Leaving aside this singular and unverifiable idea of primeval prostitution, it seems surprising that fitness should be determined exclusively by the amount of time free from subsistence activities, which would have been lacking before the emergence of hunting. Here again appears the old idea of the 'frantic search for food', supposed to dominate the original human existence.

Adaptation

According to our scenarios, if a characteristic displays adaptation in relation to another characteristic, that simply means that the first presents a certain usefulness in relation to the second. Bipedalism is an adaptation to open country, adopted because this locomotion was useful for getting about in that environment.[59] Reduction in anterior tooth size is an adaptation to chewing vegetable food, because the anterior teeth, when reduced, are useful for that task.[60] A large oral cavity is an adaptation to the prolonged chewing of plant food because it is useful for it,[61] etc.

[58] *Ibid.*: 533. [59] Oakley 1968: 258; Washburn 1960: 9. [60] Jolly 1970: 18. [61] *Ibid.*

Since the publication of G. C. Williams' *Adaptation and natural selection*,[62] which has become a classic, we are aware of the ambivalence of the term 'adaptation' and the tautological traps to which casual users of it may be exposed. By assimilating adaptation to usefulness, and usefulness to natural selection, the hominisation scenarios provide a good illustration of this. The basic reasoning is as follows: since natural selection favours only adaptive characteristics and since natural selection is the only force responsible for the proliferation of new characteristics, everything that is propagated in nature is adaptive: 'all existing features of animals are adaptive. If they were not adaptive, then they would be eliminated by selection and would disappear.'[63]

If everything is adaptive, it follows that everything is useful, because only useful features – according to our scenarios – are adaptive. The teleological doctrine seems to govern everything in this particular version of 'Darwinism', exactly like in 'traditional' and 'Lamarckian' explanations.

Sociobiology and optimisation models

It is worth emphasising the role played in 'Darwinian' explanations by the formulae that appeal to the principles of sociobiology and to optimisation models (for example Optimal Foraging Theory). Sociobiological theory and optimisation models are not inseparable but they are often applied jointly, combining their main concepts: that of inclusive fitness and of optimisation (or maximisation). Both concepts relate to natural selection. According to sociobiology, selection favours inclusive fitness, that is the properties of the organism that are useful not only for increasing its own chances of survival and reproduction, but also for ensuring that parents carrying similar genetic information have the same opportunities.[64] According to the premises of Optimal Foraging Theory, natural selection should favour anything that allows maximisation or optimisation of yield from the effort invested in obtaining food. The principles of the two theories can operate separately, with the concept of natural selection as their common base; they can also be combined, the inclusive fitness of sociobiology becoming the objective of optimisation. However the concept of fitness is defined (individual or collective), natural selection can sometimes be considered as a process aimed at optimising or maximising fitness.[65]

[62] Williams 1966; see also Gould and Lewontin 1979.
[63] W. Bock 'The Use of Adaptative Characters in Avian Classification' (1967), quoted from Gould and Vrba 1982: 6.
[64] E.g. Tanner and Zihlman 1976: 588–9. [65] Pyke *et al.* 1977.

The conviction that natural selection tends towards optimisation has often been criticised,[66] even by sociobiologists.[67] Despite that, the fashion for optimisation models has had considerable success in anthropology, especially in the United States, where – as Arthur S. Keene, a representative of that trend, was well aware – it soon took the form of a belief in an omnipresent and omnipotent optimisation: 'Optimal behaviour is adaptive behaviour; all creatures optimise, and it is our task to figure out what they are optimising. Archaeologists working with these methods have tended to find optimisation lurking behind every artefact.'[68]

A similar orientation is displayed in some of our scenarios as well. The authors who invoke optimisation seem convinced that early hominids were tending to go that way, and they consider this premise to be the solid foundation of deductive inferences, regardless of the fact that the optimisation models are only applicable in particular conditions.[69]

A. S. Keene was justifiably amazed at the success achieved by his colleagues and himself in trying to demonstrate that prehistoric hunter-gatherers optimised the use of resources.[70] Their success is less surprising when we take into account the convergence between some of the assumptions of these models and the schemes of naïve anthropology. A single example will suffice: the use of optimisation models implies acceptance of the postulate of the scarcity of resources, the latter often reduced to scarcity of food.[71] To assume that the process of optimisation was at work in hominisation is to suppose that food shortage was constant among prehistoric hominids, and this links up with an idea easily accepted by naïve anthropology.

In spite of the terminological and theoretical innovations peculiar to this type of explanation, the mechanism envisaged remains very similar to that underlying other 'Darwinian' formulae: fierce competition rules the search for food which is always too scarce, and omnipresent selection favours anything that is useful in that struggle. The chief modification concerns a widening of the field of usefulness: what was difficult to understand with reference to individual usefulness alone (for example altruism or reciprocal aid) becomes now explained through usefulness to the group.

This rapid review enables us to note that, in the hominisation scenarios, the concepts stemming from the theory of evolution – selection, fitness,

[66] E.g. Gould and Lewontin 1979.   [67] Lumsden and Gushurst 1985: 15.
[68] Keene 1983: 155–6.   [69] Definition of these conditions in Pianka and MacArthur 1966.
[70] Keene 1983: 146.   [71] Pianka and MacArthur 1966; Smith 1983: 625.

adaptation, optimisation – are reduced to the principle of usefulness. The Darwinian explanation of hominisation would therefore consist in claiming the usefulness of new human attributes. The nature of that usefulness corresponds to the image we have of our ancestors' life: as the struggle for survival and the frantic search for food are deemed to be their major occupations, efficiency in acquiring food becomes the chief criterion of usefulness. Just as, in naïve anthropology, the origin of things is explained by their usefulness for survival and for satisfying elementary needs, so, in this naïve version of Darwinism, everything is explained by natural selection, which favours usefulness for survival and for satisfying elementary needs.

THE ARCHITECTURE OF PALAEOANTHROPOLOGICAL EXPLANATIONS

'Traditional' and 'Lamarckian' explanations are constructed on a pattern that can be reduced to the following formula:

If (x),
and if (y) is useful for (x),
then (x) is the cause of (y).

The majority of the typical 'Darwinian' explanations (I shall discuss the exceptions later) introduce a simple rhetorical change:

If (x),
and if (y) is useful for (x),
then (x) makes natural selection favour (y).

That is just another way of saying that '(x) causes (y)', since natural selection is held responsible for every widespread form or function. The explanation by natural selection (adaptation, advantage for fitness) is modelled on the traditional explanation by usefulness. So, in order to be 'Darwinian', it is enough to reuse the explanatory pattern of naïve anthropology, taking care to replace the vague notion of 'cause' by that of natural selection, both of them associated with the notion of usefulness.

Let there be no misunderstanding: none of this means that I consider Darwinian theory to be a rhetorical device based on a simple modification of vocabulary. First, 'Darwinian' reasonings in our scenarios, in most cases, represent only a very simplified use of the theory of evolution. Second, explanation by usefulness, or by selection favouring useful features, notably for acquiring food, remains *a priori* plausible. Third, even these simplistic arguments can occasionally provide perfectly acceptable hypotheses, particularly when these have verifiable implications.

My conclusion is, in fact, limited to showing that the explanatory formulae keep returning, throughout the two hundred years or so covered by our scenarios, to the same premises, the very ones that naïve anthropology has been using for two millennia. Although these assumptions may occasionally lead to reasonable hypotheses, they have the drawback of always generating the same explanations of evolutionary change and of ignoring several other equally plausible ones. I am not claiming, therefore, to put my finger on explanations that are necessarily 'wrong', although there may be errors, but rather to highlight a conditioning that limits the variability of hypotheses and reduces them to a simple pattern, the main features of which I have tried to define.

So the 'convincing' explanation proposed in all our scenarios amounts to envisaging the entity subject to evolutionary change as an assemblage of separate characteristics, and tying the origin of new characteristics to their usefulness. This notion of usefulness has the same classic content virtually everywhere. In the 'traditional' version it is linked with satisfying the elementary needs of the individual determined by the constraints of the environment. In the 'Darwinian' version, that aspect remains dominant, even if a new kind of usefulness is invoked, for reproduction, which naïve anthropology neglects. The biggest innovation is apparent in the works that appeal to sociobiology, where the field of usefulness is extended from the individual to the group.

It is surprising to note the extreme simplification to which the theory of evolution has been subjected in many of these supposedly 'Darwinian' explanations. The impression given is that our authors have carried out a genuine selection – hardly natural in this case – so as to retain only those elements of Darwinism already present in the assumptions of naïve anthropology. Thus, 'Darwinian' explanations move closer to 'traditional' explanations and these in turn seem like twin sisters of the former. If Darwinism can be reduced in this way to naïve anthropology, every naïve explanation appears to be Darwinian. This, no doubt, is the reason why references to Darwinian theory so often accompany explanatory inferences that in fact manage very well without the theory of evolution.

If we held to this view of Darwinism, even Prince Metternich in our anecdote would be Darwinian. Doctor Pangloss – aptly chosen by S. J. Gould and R. Lewontin[72] as the personification of naïve Darwinism – would be Darwinian too: was not the chief motto of his *metaphysico-theologo-cosmolo-nigological* doctrine that 'everything is made for a purpose'?[73]

Voltaire intended Pangloss' speculations to be a satire on the kinds of explanation that abounded in the scholarly works of the period (see C. Thacker's critical edition of *Candide*[74]). For example, according to Boyle, if cats have pupils with a vertical slit, it is because they feed mainly on rats and mice which 'are animals that normally move up and down walls and other steep places, and the most convenient situation for the pupils [of cats], so as to detect those objects swiftly and follow them, is to be vertical'.[75] The Abbé Pluche tried to elucidate the phenomenon of tides from the fact that they are useful to ships, which, thanks to them, can enter port more easily. Fénelon explained the degree of fluidity of water by its usefulness for supporting vessels without impeding their progress, and went into raptures about the fact that cattle and sheep are always more numerous than bears and wolves: 'Is it not wonderful that the most useful animals should also be the most prolific?'[76] The Panglossian *metaphysico-theologo-cosmolo-nigological* doctrine may indeed seem laughable but its continuing popularity is less so. Even Voltaire – author of *Candide* – was unable to free himself from the hold of that explanatory procedure he had been so prone to criticise, as can be seen in his essays on *histoire raisonnée* that I have already mentioned.

In that, Voltaire, as much as the seventeenth- and eighteenth-century naturalists and philosophers, was merely carrying on an old tradition of Western thought. Was not Origen already saying that 'everything was created for its use'?[77] It is strange that this idea should remain so persistent, not only in the palaeoanthropological scenarios analysed here, but more generally across the human sciences. The conviction that everything can be explained by its usefulness for some purpose seems to be a characteristic feature of our intellectual tradition: from the Old Testament Job who pondered on the function of his sufferings, seeking to understand the reason for them, right across theological and naturalist doctrines to modern folklore conceptions, such as the conspiracy theories that are so often used nowadays to explain historical events by their usefulness to some Machiavellian plan.[78]

The simplicity of the explanation by usefulness is very attractive, and its vacuity is rarely perceived clearly. Darwin himself, very well aware of

[72] Gould and Lewontin 1979.   [73] Voltaire 1968/1759: 102.   [74] *Ibid.*: 267–9.
[75] Quoted from Roger 1971: 227.   [76] Quoted from Ehrard 1970: 54.
[77] Origen 1968, II. 377.   [78] Cf. Cubitt 1989.

some of the traps into which his explanatory procedure could lead, gave the instructive example of one possible defective argument: the sutures in the cranium of young mammals are admirable 'adaptations' facilitating parturition; their advantage in that regard is beyond doubt. But can that usefulness explain the genesis of the sutures? Darwin answers no, for the same sutures exist in the cranium of young birds and young reptiles that need only emerge from a broken egg.[79]

This example shows that too mechanical a transition from usefulness to the 'cause' can easily lead to important errors. Important, but none the less 'convincing', which means that explanation by usefulness can retain its status as an *a priori* credible formula, so much so that our palaeoanthropological scenarios even make it the cornerstone of their arguments. With or without Darwinian rhetoric, everything can be explained along that track. This power should be worrying, but it is rather the opposite that occurs and many researchers treat that feat as a quality. In this regard, we cannot but be struck by Nobel prize-winner Peter Medawar's slip of the pen when he sought to defend the theory of evolution in these words: 'It is too difficult to imagine or envisage an evolutionary episode which could not be explained by the formula of Neo-Darwinism.'[80] Indeed, explanations in line with a certain Darwinian scheme are a magic key that opens every door; and since it would be impossible – in Medawar's words – to imagine a lock that the key would not fit, it could be inferred that the 'utilitarian' formula is virtually tautological.

One way of justifying the traditional procedure might be that the explanations by usefulness must necessarily be the rule, simply because they are the only ones conceivable. Everything that exists would be, one way or another, useful for something, on pain of slipping back into nothingness; so any etiological explanation must imply some usefulness, and the only problem is to determine the nature of that usefulness correctly.

Are we obliged to bow the knee to this assumption? Does it match the mechanisms of evolution, or those that rule our thought, impeded by an imperfect view of nature?

ANOTHER VIEW OF EVOLUTION

From the outset, Darwinism was perceived as a theory that made usefulness an adequate explanation of all the conformations observed in

[79] Darwin 1859: 197.   [80] Quoted from Ruse 1982: 294.

living species. Darwin was already trying to correct this mistaken view,[81] but it slipped quickly into common use, where it was made into either an unjust objection to the theory of evolution, or, more often, the guiding principle for hypotheses that, rightly or wrongly, claimed to be Darwinian. The theory of evolution itself progressed along more and more sophisticated lines, always finding some alternative to explanations by usefulness, without, quite obviously, denying it some role in its view of nature. We shall now examine some of these complementary options, as they are presented in recent literature, including, in some cases, our palaeoanthropological scenarios.

The stratigraphy of functions

A first alternative, proposed by Stephen J. Gould and Elisabeth Vrba,[82] attempts to build a bridge between conventional explanation and versions that might remedy some of its deficiencies. The authors acknowledge the plausibility of explanations by usefulness: it is obvious that the process of natural selection fashions certain features in accordance with their usefulness at the time. Thus, with the example of bipedalism, it is possible that our ancestors became bipeds because natural selection favoured that type of locomotion, for the same advantages – such as the ability to carry objects in the hands – that we still enjoy today. But it is equally legitimate to think, as do Gould and Vrba, that a characteristic's present function has nothing whatever to do with its genesis, which may have been linked to another function, now vanished.

This version is still not very far removed from the classic positions. The only difference consists in making a clear distinction between a former usefulness, responsible for the genesis (adaptation), and a current usefulness (exaptation). Darwin was aware of this possible 'stratigraphy' of functions, but he only evoked it to reply to critics who stressed the existence of characteristics apparently devoid of 'usefulness'.[83] The biological literature of our own day often deals with a similar phenomenon under the term 'preadaptation', and one of our scenarios does indeed bring this concept into play. It presents the reduction of anterior tooth size as an adaptation (original usefulness) to the mastication of grass seeds or annual herbs, and the freeing of the hands as an adaptation to gathering; these two features are deemed to become later, in the course

[81] Darwin 1859: 199–202. [82] Gould and Vrba 1982. [83] Darwin 1859: 195–6.

of hominisation, a preadaptation (secondary usefulness) to the use of tools.[84] In the same way, a large oral cavity and a muscular and mobile tongue would, in the first place, have been an adaptation to the prolonged chewing of food and would subsequently have assumed the character of an exaptation to the use of articulate speech[85] (these features had been 'preadaptive' to...).

The concept of exaptation, used in this sense, corresponds therefore to that of preadaptation. Yet a new term was essential – Gould and Vrba argue[86] – in order to take a second type of exaptation into account, one that dissociates genesis from usefulness. In the process of evolution, the reason why a feature is propagated may be independent, not only of secondary usefulness, observed at present, but also of any former function. It is possible that certain conformations proliferate totally unconnected with usefulness ('nonaptive' features in the authors' terminology). This eventuality requires us to envisage entities subject to evolution as if they were systems composed of 'communicating parts'.

Communicating parts

There are two explanatory formulas that allow genesis and function to be separated either partially or completely. They both rely on notions that I shall call, for the convenience of this brief account, the conception of 'communicating characteristics' and the conception of 'communicating levels'.

Our scenarios define human beings, the end result of hominisation, by a list of very distinct characteristics. A particular usefulness is subsequently attributed to each of them in order to explain their origin. And yet these conformations can also be envisaged in the form of 'communicating vessels', in which the change undergone in one part brings about transformations in some of the others. The idea is hardly new. Darwin mentions it under the name of 'correlation of growth', which for him becomes one of the three main sources of change, alongside natural selection and the principle of use and disuse[87] (nowadays terms are pleiotropic mechanisms or allometric phenomenon[88]). Thereafter, if certain parts are correlated (the mechanism involved is another problem), natural selection, acting on one of them because of its usefulness, may change others whether useful or not.

[84] Jolly 1970: 18–22.   [85] *Ibid.*   [86] Gould and Vrba 1982: 12.   [87] Darwin 1859: 143, 466.
[88] E.g. Gould and Lewontin 1979: 591.

This type of explanation is very rare in our scenarios. We find it in Sherwood Washburn's text;[89] he associates reduction in the ridges of bone over the eyes and a decrease in the shelf of bone in the neck area with the suppression of aggressive behaviour in our ancestors. Natural selection is thought to have underpinned endocrinological changes which contributed to restricting aggressiveness within the earliest human groups; certain 'non-utilitarian' transformations in the morphology of the cranium would have resulted as a secondary effect. Likewise, the reduction in the bony birth canal, a secondary result of bipedal locomotion and upright posture, would have had no usefulness in itself.[90]

A. Leroi-Gourhan's scenario provides another example of a similar explanatory formula. Upright posture, a first cause – it appears, incidentally, like a *deus ex machina* – is thought to set in motion a whole chain of morphological transformations in human ancestors. Their skeleton is thought of as a structure in dynamic equilibrium, in which change in one part must lead to modification in others linked to it, and subject to the same system of mechanical constraints. Leaving aside the initial stimulus and its function, the explanation of the other changes, that follow almost automatically, does without any references in Leroi-Gourhan to natural selection and usefulness, even though it is true that any new characteristic may acquire a practical significance with time.[91]

This type of explanation is curiously rare in our scenarios, despite the fact that the 'communicating parts' concept has led to some verifiable hypotheses. For example, S. J. Gould and D. Pilbeam obtained positive results by applying the data test to the hypothesis which linked the differentiation of cranial capacity in the Australopithecines to differences in the size of the body.[92] Positive results are also mentioned in connection with the hypothesis relating to the cause of the reduction in canine dimorphism and canine size in *Australopithecus afarensis*; these are attributed to selection favouring the growth of the occlusal surface of the premolars, to the detriment of the space available for the development of late erupting canine teeth.[93]

Another way of avoiding explanation by usefulness is to resort to the conception of 'communicating levels'. Traditional Darwinism made the

---

[89] Washburn 1960: 9–11.   [90] *Ibid.*: 14.   [91] Leroi-Gourhan 1964: 87–8.
[92] Gould and Pilbeam 1974.
[93] Jungers 1978; Leonard and Hegmon 1987; certain allometric hypotheses have nevertheless been invalidated (e.g. Wood and Stack 1980) so this key does not open all doors.

individual the main entity subject to natural selection.[94] This principle is being increasingly contested. Sociobiology speaks of selection at group level but it can also be thought of at the level of the genome, the population or the species.[95] In order for natural selection to come into play, it is enough for the following factors to come together:

1. Variation: different entities in a population have different characteristics (morphological, physiological, behavioural, etc.).
2. Reproduction: different characteristics have different rates of reproduction and survival.
3. Heredity: the characteristics are transmitted from one generation to the next.[96]

These three conditions are fulfilled at each level of organisation of living matter, the respective stages of which fit together to form a hierarchical system. Thus the domain of natural selection can be widened to open the way to broader views of the possible connections between usefulness and the genesis of new characteristics.

The hierarchical conception avoids, in particular, arbitrary assimilation of the selective value of a characteristic, expressed by the reproduction and survival rates, to its usefulness for the individual situated in a given milieu. If it is assumed that the hierarchical levels are interconnected, selection that favours a certain characteristic on one level because of its usefulness, may at the same time, on other levels, give rise to a non-utilitarian sorting of other characteristics. It is logical, for example, that the selection responsible for eliminating certain organisms should proceed at the same time to a sorting of genomes, but it is equally possible that the selection favourable to certain characteristics of the genome may give rise to a sorting of organisms. And it may also happen that what is useful for the genome is not useful for its bearer. For example, the sperm of the house mouse contains a total 85 per cent of t-allele, although at the level of the organism that is disadvantageous, since male homozygotes bearing two t-alleles are sterile. The strong t-allele content in the sperm would be explained by the support this allele receives through the selection present at the level of the genome.[97]

---

[94] E.g. Darwin 1859: 459, but see also p. 76, where Darwin speaks of the struggle for survival between species.
[95] E.g. Arnold and Fistrup 1982; Doolittle and Sapienza 1983; Gould 1982; Hull 1980; Lewontin 1970; Vrba 1980, 1983; Vrba and Gould 1986; also the controversial works of Wynne-Edwards 1962 and Dawkins 1976.
[96] From Lewontin 1970: 1. [97] Lewontin 1970: 14.

In order to distinguish these different manifestations of selection arising from various 'causes', Elisabeth Vrba and Stephen J. Gould proposed replacing the general notion of selection by the following two terms:

1. Sorting, that is the differential birth and death among varying entities (without prejudging its 'cause');
2. Selection, that is a particular kind of sorting that appears in the interaction with the environment and which always remains linked to a direct or indirect usefulness for reproduction.[98]

The distinction is important, for if it is true that there is no selection without sorting, it is also true that there can be sorting without selection. In fact, as the levels are connected, selection on one of them is capable of causing sorting on another. This kind of sorting may cause conformations to be propagated that have no connection either to the environment or to any usefulness. Selection that operates on lower levels may lead to sorting on higher levels and vice versa. In the first case, Gould and Vrba speak of an 'ascending causality', and in the other of a 'descending causality'.[99] An asymmetry exists between them: descending causality is inescapable, ascending causality is possible. For example, the propagation or extinction of a species always goes hand in hand with the proliferation or disappearance of the genomes carried by the species, whereas the development of repetitive DNAs may, it seems, have no influence on the phenotypes of the organisms or on what the species become.[100]

Thus the conception of 'communicating levels' separates genesis from usefulness, without, however, entirely abolishing their connection. Certain new characteristics may be propagated thanks to a non-utilitarian sorting, which still remains an effect, albeit an indirect one, of selection, linked with usefulness. It could even be said that the utilitarian reference is thus reinforced: certain genetic mutations, for example, considered random till now and so independent of usefulness, could now be treated as the result of the utilitarian selection taking place at the level of the genome; so those mutations would only be 'random' from the point of view of the higher level, that of the whole organism.[101]

It is none the less true that the conception of 'communicating levels' puts an end to the harmonious coexistence between genesis and

[98] Vrba and Gould 1986: 217.   [99] See examples in Vrba and Gould 1986.
[100] Orgel and Crick 1980; Doolittle and Sapienza 1980.   [101] Vrba and Gould 1986: 225.

usefulness. Natural selection, set in motion on one level, may cause, on other levels, the proliferation of characteristics that do not have to prove their usefulness in a confrontation with the environment. That being so, we can conceive of the existence of conformations that are widespread but lacking in usefulness. The latter thus keeps its status of 'first cause' but the explanations are not necessarily obliged to appeal to it. Nor need the constituting of the human organism, the genesis of which our scenarios are endeavouring to elucidate, inevitably come back to the accumulation of characteristics useful for survival and reproduction. We are equally entitled to envisage it rather as the result of a compromise of several Darwinian effects occurring in parallel on different levels. The fact that we can assign a usefulness to each characteristic does not necessarily mean that we have understood the reason for its genesis: originally, these new characteristics could just as easily be useless and merely constitute a 'raw material' for the secondary uses that made its exaptations.

These remarks on natural selection invite further reflection on explanations by usefulness that are still so often employed in ethnology. Can these alternative formulas explain phenomena of a non-biological order? We might have reason to be wary of this kind of transplantation and its results. The naïve uses of Darwinism applied to culture, which make it an object shaped by natural selection, have a long history and their biases are well known; they are often so serious that the memory of them causes misgivings when we have to remind ourselves that selection processes are nevertheless well and truly at work in the social realm. There is nothing really surprising in that, even so, for the products of culture perfectly fulfil the three conditions necessary for generating a selection process, though not necessarily a natural one. Artefacts, ideas, behaviours also display variation in their characteristics, different propagation rates, and they can be transmitted from one generation to another. So we are justified in conceiving of certain facts of culture as the results of a selection.

Far from wishing to initiate yet another debate on a possible theory of culture, my intention is simply to show that there exist alternative formulas to common-sense explanations of anthropogenesis. The conception of 'communicating levels' as well as the concepts of 'selection' and 'sorting', borrowed from biology, offer just such a possibility. No one will dispute the legitimacy of considering cultural entities as systems of hierarchical levels, comprising strata like the individual, the family, the local group, the regional group, the connubium, the linguistic group, etc. Selection, favouring cultural characteristics because of their usefulness, may operate on each of these strata while leading to a 'non-utilitarian' sorting on others. It is easy to accept that what is useful, for example, for a social group is not necessarily so for the individual and vice versa.

As an exercise in imagination, for example, one could suggest the following explanation of the origin of the sexual division of labour among our ancestors (we shall borrow a few explanatory principles from the hypothesis already alluded to by Alain Testart). Take groups of humans living by hunting and gathering, in which, on the social level, a purely cultural selection of ideas prevails, fostering the propagation of folk theories that comply with certain cultural principles and put at a disadvantage those that do not. Discrimination between the 'good' and 'bad' ideas operates according to social rules that have no direct connection with economic praxis; in other words, selection favours ideas that are acceptable from the point of view of symbolic constraints that do not match economic requirements. Let us assume that among the ideas 'good to think' lurks a principle advocating the separation of women from hunting tools. Let us also assume that our ancestors have worked out symbolic representations of femininity and of hunting that are in perfect accord with this separation. Under those circumstances, social selection would be bound to favour the emergence of a rigid prohibition that would keep women away not only from hunting tools but also from the actual activity of hunting which is possible only when using those tools. So the prohibition selected on the social level leads to a sorting of economic behaviour on the level of the individual, and hunting becomes a masculine activity while gathering is left to women. The selection of ideas will thus have effects not just of an individual order but on the social plane as well, where it will find its secondary expression in the form of an economic phenomenon, the sexual division of labour. Depending on the type of hunter-gathering economy, the consequences in practice will be different: in groups where the roles of hunting and gathering were formerly in equilibrium, the division of labour may increase the efficiency of obtaining food and so acquire a secondary usefulness (exaptation) that is purely economic. In groups where basic food can be obtained through one activity only, either hunting or gathering, the sexual division of labour will prevent the best use being made of the productive potential of one or other of the sexes and so it will become inefficient from an economic point of view (such consequences are known among modern hunter-gatherers, the Chipewyans, for example, where hunting predominates,[102] and the !Kung where gathering is dominant and the men are often idle[103]).

However, let us proclaim it loud and clear: this conjecture, based on a great number of assumptions that are unverifiable in a prehistoric context is, methodologically speaking, as valueless as the unverifiable explanations served up in abundance by our scenarios. The exercise merely serves to show that it is relatively easy to imagine explanations that bring none of the principles of naïve anthropology into play. It contains neither ecological determinism, nor reference to economic usefulness nor to the needs of the individual; we also see the disappearance of the vision of 'stratified man', according to which 'thinking' and 'material activity' constitute two separate layers, requiring different explanations of their functioning. This construction is only a plausible hypothesis, and its sole merit is to demonstrate that the success of the explanations based on schemes of naïve anthropology cannot be due to their being the only ones conceivable.

Other alternative formulas are still being offered to explain the process of hominisation. S. J. Gould, for example, has recalled that the origin of certain morphological characteristics in humans could be elucidated by the mechanism of neotenic retardation[104] (a hypothesis put forward by Bolk as early as 1926[105]). Primatologists emphasise, in fact, that certain differences between apes and humans are uniquely quantitative and that some of them might be the result of a slight chronological discrepancy in the foetal growth of various parts of the body.[106] For example, C. Devilliers and J. Chaline mention a reduction in the iliac bone that transforms the pelvis and makes bipedalism possible; this innovation must have occurred quite abruptly, by a sudden modification in the programme of development of the iliac bone, for it is difficult to imagine a non-functional, intermediate morphological situation, which would have been probably eliminated by natural selection.[107] In the same way, the rounded shape of the cranium in *Homo* could be the effect of a slowing in the rate of growth (neoteny), while the increased cranial volume would be explained by prolongation of the period of growth (hypermorphosis).[108]

Another eventuality which can be taken into account when trying to explain anthropogenesis, is the formation of species by geographical isolation.[109] It is particularly interesting to turn to the model known

---

[102] McGrew 1986.   [103] Lee 1968.   [104] Gould 1977.   [105] See also Montagu 1962.
[106] Schultz 1950: 440–1; Starck 1960: 633–4.   [107] Devilliers and Chaline 1989: 224.
[108] *Ibid.*: 226; see also a critical review of recent works on the subject, Shea 1989.
[109] E.g. Wright 1932; Mayr 1963.

as 'spatial strangulation', in which speciation is envisaged as the consequence of a considerable loss of genetic variability in peripheral populations which, once separated from the ancestral population, retain only a small part of the genetic heritage of the ancestral species (*founder effect*). The stochastic processes that act on the genetic information in these small groups (*genetic drift*), accompanied by a greater facility for propagating mutants in a small population, can bring about real genetic revolutions. The hypothesis of a cladogenesis by geographic isolation is proposed, among others, by Yves Coppens who claims that ancestors common to both hominids and pongids, living in peri-equatorial Africa, found themselves cut into two populations some 10 million years ago, following renewed activity on the fault system of the Rift Valley. This cut-off, tectonic in nature, would soon have become an ecological barrier isolating ancestors of humans from their parent population. The hypothesis finds some support in the absence of pongid fossil remains observed on hominid sites of East or South Africa, as well as by the fact that the East African fauna become endemic from the end of the middle Miocene.[110]

So there are a certain number of explanations that envisage alternative mechanisms, or ones that are complementary to those traditionally favoured by hominisation scenarios. Biologists stress the need to widen still further the scope of conceivable mechanisms, for what has been achieved in that direction in the course of recent decades remains, according to them, very modest in relation to the prospects already opening out today.[111] Modest they may be, but these innovations are enough to convince us that the principles of the explanations called on by commonsense anthropology and its scholarly variants reflect, in their monotony, constraints weighing down our imagination, rather than those that limit the profusion of nature itself.

But will these new hypotheses, appealing to new mechanisms of evolution ignored by naïve anthropology, be better simply from the fact of being new? Better – that is to say reflecting more accurately the reality of the hominisation process? Let us be clear, we have no guarantee of that kind; so we must ask ourselves whether these innovations can bring anything more to the knowledge of anthropogenesis than just the possibility of diversifying the conjectural game. This question leads us directly to the

[110] Coppens 1984: 470–1.   [111] Eldredge 1986: 188.

crucial problem of the validation of the hypotheses, which I have hinted at several times without really dealing with as yet. Let us start by analysing the methods of 'validation' as practised in our palaeoanthropological scenarios. Examination of the way these traditional explanations lay the foundations for their legitimacy is indeed instructive: it will enable us better to understand the importance of alternative explanations, of which we have just reviewed a few, from many examples.

CHAPTER 5

A double game

THE CREDIBILITY OF THE PLAUSIBLE

> And also in the fables of which we were just now speaking, owing to our ignorance of the truth about antiquity, we liken the false to the true as far as we may.
>
> Plato, *The Republic*, 382d

I have repeatedly noted that the causal explanations offered by our scenarios usually took the form of huge generalisations, to which a universal validity was ascribed. 'Tool-making necessitates language', 'life in the savannah implies hunting', 'hunting involves great risks'. Does hunting involve great risks? Where? Everywhere. When? Always. Under what circumstances? Under all circumstances. What hunting? All hunting. The left-hand side of the relations ('if *x*') is thus reduced to the most simple and general formula possible. The right-hand side ('then *y*') appears equally rudimentary and its content can move across in the following 'causal sequence' to the left-hand side, to become the cause of a subsequent element in the causal chain. The paucity of the content decontextualises these statements and in the end they express nothing but relations that are valid *a priori* everywhere and at all times, applied to notions that are virtually abstract because they are too general (society in general, tools in general, hunting in general, etc.).

David Hume advocated explaining all effects by principles that are as general as possible, and always looking for the simplest causes.[1] This precept matches up well with the common-sense view of causality, that displays a constant tendency to select, from a multitude of the necessary antecedents to any effect, one and one only, which is thought to be its cause.[2] Added to this reducing impulse comes the taste for vast generalisations, broadening to infinity the validity of the supposedly causal

---

[1] Hume 1896/1739: xxi.   [2] See for example Hilton 1988.

relations ('Nordic people are more reserved than southerners', 'brunettes are more hot-blooded than blondes').

References to universal laws, or to principles that claim to reduce the diversity of the world to simple equations, are notorious in everyday thinking. It is hardly surprising that the quest for universal laws of history and culture has never lacked its knights errant. The Enlightenment knew these enthusiasms very well. It was one of the dreams of the period to discover rules governing human history, knowledge which would be helpful not only to reconstruct the past, but also to understand the present and to master the future as well. Physics offered then a model of scientific knowledge that had reached a state of definitive achievement, and portraits of Newton decorated the studies of the scholars who all wanted to imitate the great physicist.[3] Reflection on society was not exempt from this aspiration. Of course, in human matters, everything appears to be the subject of chance, fantasy and the free will of individuals. But had not research into 'physical nature' also been formerly faced with a comparable chaos of incomprehensible phenomena? And yet, Immanuel Kant could write with confidence that in the end 'there appeared on the scene a Kepler who, in a quite unforeseen manner, subjected the excentric orbits of the planets to determined laws, and a Newton who explained those laws in accordance with a universal natural cause'.[4] Just as numerous in the eighteenth century were those who shared the hope of similarly discovering the simple principles of 'moral nature', which must surely also be governed by laws 'as fix'd as Fate'.[5]

There were many who cherished the conviction that they had found such laws. Once these laws are set down where formerly everything seemed to be governed by fantasy, individual cases reveal an invisible order they are actually obedient to (so Montesquieu tells us in *L'esprit des lois*).[6]

Illusion was equal to the hopes, and the attempts to build a Newtonian anthropology inevitably fell into the traps of naïve anthropology. Inevitably, since positive knowledge on culture, or 'moral sciences' as it was then called, was exceedingly limited: scholars found themselves constrained, as any good *bricoleur* would be, to make use of such knowledge as was available. So they resorted to the works of ancient authors, to folklore, to common-sense judgements, to introspection, to travel narratives, in short to every kind of source in which imaginary themes

---

[3] Gusdorf 1971: 180.   [4] Kant 1985/1786: 189.   [5] Pope 1993/1733–4: 112. Epistle III.190.
[6] Montesquieu 1979/1748: 115.

were inextricably intertwined with positive observations. Consequently, instead of advancing, knowledge stagnated, bogged down in the ruts of traditional imagery: factual data, which could have corrected these conjectures, were cruelly lacking. Georges Gusdorf makes a very apposite comment on this point:

> In the understanding of the material world, Newton's synthesis is the outcome of prolonged analytical work that had been going on for a good century since Galileo. By contrast, in the human sciences, where research had hardly started, everything happened as if the Newtonian model was proposing a synthesis even before any analysis had been seriously undertaken ... The fascination with Newton acted as a mirage, leading scholars astray by offering them convictions and conclusions before they had mastered the facts.[7]

Indeed, the ambitious attempt at anthropological synthesis, undertaken without waiting for a sufficient empirical basis, ended by reproducing naïve anthropology in a pseudo-scholarly form.

In their approach, the authors of our palaeoanthropological scenarios all display more or less strong affinities with this tradition of the Enlightenment. They accept in good faith a whole treasurehouse of 'universal laws', from which they draw the conclusions they want regarding the existence of our ancestors. So, for example, being certain that hunting always exposes the hunter to great risks, they deduce that the hunting practised by hominids in the Plio-Pleistocene African environment inexorably implied dangers. Is this particular statement subject to empirical assessment when applied to a prehistoric context? Nothing entitles us to assert that it is: the theory is plausible but it is difficult to see what data might disprove it today. Moreover, some of our authors are aware of this problem, because they emphasise more than once the absence of prehistoric vestiges that would allow their conjectures to be tested.[8] But this awareness still does not appear to shake their certainty that the explanations they offer succeed nevertheless in reflecting the reality of prehistoric life.

Indeed, the anthropogenesis scenarios seek confirmation of their validity not in a confrontation with the material vestiges of the past, but principally in the evocation of 'universal laws'. Acquaintance with general principles that would have governed the world 'from eternity' is deemed to provide an adequate basis for the boldest prehistoric reconstructions. This is how the world is made, and not otherwise, for it is unthinkable that it should be made any other way: the rules by which it

---

[7] Gusdorf 1971: 205.
[8] Washburn 1960: 15; Jolly 1970: 16; Tanner and Zihlman 1976: 586; Lovejoy 1980: 343.

functions impose themselves on common-sense thinking with the force and transparency of the first truths. We *know* that animals don't think, that women are weak, men enterprising, hunting dangerous and that it is rash to venture out into the wild savannah alone and unarmed. We *know* that necessity is the mother of invention and that the fundamental reason for things to exist is their usefulness. It is on certainties like these that a good many palaeoanthropological generalisations are built. They seem obvious, indisputable, self-evident, so much so that it occurs to nobody to subject them to empirical examination. This would be nonsensical, one of our authors declares, as absurd as 'looking for archaeological evidence that apples fell to earth 3.5 million years ago'.[9] The 'laws' of biology and of culture would thus be as general as the law of gravity, and, thanks to them, the scientist would be able correctly to reconstruct anthropogenesis simply by means of deduction, even in the absence of prehistoric vestiges. More than a century ago, Clémence Royer was already invoking this argument to justify her theory of human origins: 'Let no one accuse us of gratuitous hypotheses. If these are hypotheses, conjectures, and that is all we can do here, at least they are all resting on ... necessary laws.'[10] There is no shortage of scholars who share that opinion even today:[11] a spontaneous view of the evolutionary mechanisms continues to strengthen them in their conviction that these laws can exist; naïve anthropology offers a whole range of them.

In reality, as we have seen, the useless may also exist, life in the savannah does not necessarily go hand in hand with hunting, women are not always relegated to gathering, certain complex cognitive processes can be realised without articulate language, large canine teeth are not used only for hunting and in defence against predators, bipedalism is not more efficient than quadrupedalism in every situation, etc. The wide range of validity these assertions aspire to is no more than a mirage. It is possible, of course, that at the beginning of human history, life in an open milieu contributed to the development of hunting, that women saw their occupations restricted to gathering because of practical constraints, that articulate language brought with it a growth in our ancestors' mental faculties. Things may have happened that way. But they may equally have happened differently, and we can itemise that 'differently' in a

---

[9] Hill 1982: 529.   [10] Royer 1870: 152.

[11] To give just one example, and what an eloquent one, we can quote C. Coon, who solemnly asserts that 'human history has followed a number of natural laws', while making clear that 'man may be seen to have followed the laws of nature as automatically as inorganic materials, plants and animals' (Coon 1955/1954: 8, 410).

multitude of ways. This reminder will doubtless seem trite, even useless, but it must not be forgotten that there are still many anthropologists, as our scenarios bear witness, who proceed as if they were ignorant of the consequences of this conclusion. If they really understood it, they would be less willing to accept the intellectual game in which the palaeoanthropological scenarios indulge with such happy abandon. Our authors carry on as if their conjectures became credible from the mere fact that they are plausible. Yet one more reason for me to repeat unflaggingly that only in the universe of naïve conceptions, which have no alternatives, can the plausible be identified with the actual. It is only in that *trompe-l'œil* universe that plausibility becomes – as one author affirms – sufficient to accept a hypothesis.[12] In reality, validation based on plausibility can only separate those ideas that fit in with popular common-sense anthropology from those that go beyond it. Thus, the 'plausibility' of a hominisation scenario may guarantee its social success, but it tells us nothing about its value as a representation of historical reality.

BACK TO THE FACTS

That being so, the problem is simple: how do we distinguish, among the hypotheses commonly held to be true, between those that maintain a real link with their referential reality and those that belong entirely to the realm of ideas? The answer, as everyone will have guessed, is as simple as the question: the only way to establish that distinction is by confronting conjectures with empirical reality.

If the precept seems simple, its application is much less so. Statements about our ancestors cannot be directly compared with prehistoric data. The connection can only be made by comparing hypotheses, the fruits of reasoning, with propositions that are themselves the outcome of other reasonings, which this time lead ultimately to the interpretation of fossils and archaeological vestiges. The assertion that hominids hunted is not based on the mere fact that archaeologists have discovered hominids' artefacts mixed up with animal bones; it is put in parallel with an inference that starts from these vestiges and interprets them, relying on the notion that fossil bones accompanied by tools represent the carcasses of animals killed by the makers of the tools. This interpretation, and others of the same type which abound in archaeological publications, seems obvious at first sight, so we should not be surprised at the number of

---

[12] Jolly 1970: 24.

archaeologists who are convinced that an interpretation of prehistoric vestiges is a perfectly natural procedure, requiring no special knowledge. Did we not read, a few years ago, that for archaeological interpretation 'simple common sense is sufficient'?[13]

It is significant that the first to cast doubts on this 'common sense' were specialists in Palaeolithic archaeology. The primitive hunters' way of life, their material culture and its modest traces, still desperately fragmentary, seemed so strange, so far removed from the frame of experience familiar to most people today, that common sense can find few secure landmarks in it and is the more ready to capitulate. Each in his own way, Palaeolithic archaeologists[14] were also among the first to work out a 'dictionary' to translate the enigmatic code of material remains into the language of human behaviour.[15] The only way to construct such a 'dictionary' is through 'actualist' studies – experimental, ethnographic or other – which make it possible to observe cause and effect at the same time, that is both the material trace left by human behaviour and the gesture that produces it. The archaeologist is often compared to the detective; indeed, he has to proceed like Sherlock Holmes, who was not satisfied with examining corpses at the scene of the crime, and so tapped corpses in mortuaries with his cane to improve his ability to interpret bruises.[16]

The development of actualist research, from which we have many results today, provides a good illustration of the difficulties of empirical validation and of the limits it imposes on the production of palaeoanthropological conjectures. I shall give just one example here, found in Glynn Isaac's scenario, where the key role in hominisation is attributed to the emergence of the sexual division of labour and to food-sharing.[17]

Although this conception is based on a fairly classic scheme, Isaac was one of the few authors who attempted to predict how the hypotheses put forward, or at least some of them, might find expression in patterns of archaeological remains. For Isaac, the consumption of both meat and vegetable foods by hominids, inferred from archaeological data, must have implied a sexual division of labour into hunting for men and gathering for women, and this division would lead in turn to food-sharing.

The argument goes as follows: the males, Isaac says, had to venture far afield to hunt, while the women gathered plants near the base sites; consequently, sharing could only take place at these gathering

---

[13] Courbin 1982: 115. [14] Binford and Binford 1966; Binford 1973.
[15] For example 'archaeological theory' (Bayard 1969), 'middle range theory' (Binford 1981), 'science of artefacts' (Dunnell 1971), etc.
[16] Conan Doyle 1992/1890: 64–7, chapter I. [17] Isaac 1976, 1978a, 1978b.

places. The concentrations of animal bones accompanied by stone artefacts should constitute indelible archaeological evidence of these camps and the sharing that went on there. Glynn Isaac thought that certain sites at Olduvai[18] fitted this pattern well, and he saw in these confirmation of his hypothesis of the division of labour, of the transport of food, and of sharing at the base sites. The essential point of this reasoning, passed over in silence in Isaac's early texts, is the assumption that any concentration of bones and stone artefacts is evidence of hunting and of the transport of animal carcasses by hominids.

Since the first publication of this hypothesis, further research has aimed at establishing an actualist data base necessary for the reliable reading of information provided by bone concentrations – research conducted by Isaac's students, among others, and inspired by him. The results have already provided a wealth of clues. It was found that accumulations of animal remains may be formed also by the mere action of various natural forces, such as water transport,[19] or by epidemics and droughts that cause the death of many individuals gathered around a waterhole.[20] On the other hand, while it is true that hunting activities contributed in large measure to creating similar concentrations, we cannot forget that hominids were not the only hunters in the savannah, and that scavenging animals, too, transport and accumulate their prey.[21] Hyenas bring whole carcasses, or parts of them, to their dens; lions have a habit of dragging their prey to the shade of a tree.[22] It has been noted as well that carrying meat to a base site does not necessarily go with food-sharing.[23] As for stone tools mixed up with animal remains, their presence can just as easily be interpreted as traces of a group of hominids who stopped for a while in a place where predators had feasted hundreds of years later or earlier. This plethora of interpretations disturbs the 'natural' logic of the initial argument that identified any concentration of bones and artefacts as a base camp of humans.

With time, Isaac himself accepted these alternatives, clearly mentioning a list of possible readings of this type of vestiges. Here, for the record, is the list:[24]

1. A natural accumulation of bones, accidentally associated with hominids' tools:

---

[18] Isaac 1978b: table 1.1.   [19] Hanson 1980.
[20] Behrensmeyer 1978; Potts 1984; Shipman 1975.   [21] Hill 1972.
[22] Behrensmeyer 1983; Binford 1983: chapter III; Brain 1981; Hill 1979, 1983.   [23] Hill 1983.
[24] From Isaac 1983: 9; Isaac and Crader 1981: 90; completed by Toth and Schick 1986: 46–7.

1a. bones accumulated by water,
   1b. bones accumulated following deaths due to factors other than predation (epidemics, droughts, etc.),
   1c. bones accumulated by animals.
2. A chance juxtaposition of different concentrations of bones accumulated separately by carnivores and by hominids.
3. An accumulation of animal remains by predators or scavengers, reused later by scavenging hominids.
4. Traces of the acquiring of meat by scavenging hominids at a place where animals had died naturally.
5. A base camp with carcasses brought there by hominids (5′: hunters; 5″: scavengers):
   5a. for their individual consumption,
   5b. to feed children,
   5c. for general sharing.

This example shows clearly that even the interpretation of a relatively simple archaeological fact is far from easy, and that common sense is not of much help. The spontaneous reading is inclined to attribute just one meaning, biased in favour of the hypothesis put to the test; in this way it is almost inevitable to produce, no doubt involuntarily, a 'confirmation'.

In order to undertake a genuine validation, it is necessary to establish a system of interpretations founded on the keenest observation of archaeological remains; for a start there must be no more talk of accumulations of bones in general, and we must learn to discriminate between different types, each one recognisable by particular clues, on which the deciphering of the material remains could rest. Research into the principles of interpretation useful in the study of African sites of the Plio-Pleistocene has been going on since the 1970s; C. K. Brain was one of the modern trailblazers,[25] although taphonomy was already being practised early in the nineteenth century: the Reverend William Buckley (1784–1856), holder of the chair of geology at Oxford University, had been engaged at that time in observing hyenas in the Exeter zoological garden, studying how they broke and crushed bones; he used these observations subsequently to interpret fragments of fossil bones from the Kirkdale Cave.[26]

Nowadays the chief task for this kind of research consists in establishing, by means of 'actualist' observations, the catalogue of clues necessary

[25] Brain 1967. [26] Buckland 1823.

to discriminate concentrations of bones left by hominids from those that should rather be attributed to animals or to various natural factors. The major characteristics of the bone assemblages accumulated where animals die naturally are already known.[27] Fairly complete records of the selection of bones by leopards, lions, hyenas and jackals exist.[28] It has been possible to compare this information with knowledge acquired concerning the different ways of treating carcasses by modern hunter-gatherers.[29] In both cases, selective uses of different parts of the carcasses leave their mark on the composition of the bone assemblages that accumulate on the sites.[30] This evidence enables us not only to appreciate the respective roles of animals and hominids in forming the archaeological vestiges found in the same places, but also to infer how the meat was acquired (i.e. hunting versus scavenging).[31] Cut marks that may have been made on the bones by hominids' tools are also being studied, along with striae and cracks left by carnivores teeth.[32] Certain specific alterations on the bone that might have been interpreted as intentional incisions and cracks seem in fact to be either the result of trampling by hoofed animals[33] or marks left by archaeologists' tools in the course of excavations.[34] Lastly, I mention the experiments with artificial assemblages of bone and lithic material, placed in a savannah milieu in order to study the effects of sedimentation and erosion processes that, over the years, transform the inventory of objects left in this type of environment.[35]

The background knowledge thus accumulated forms a factual basis that leads archaeologists to challenge some established interpretations. For example, the assemblage of bones at one of the Olduvai sites, formerly attributed to hominids, matches up well to the characteristics of bone accumulations observed in the dens of hyenas at Amboseli Park in Kenya.[36] Analysis of the incisions and toothmarks on bones from some of the other sites at Olduvai indicates that we are probably dealing

---

[27] Haynes 1988a.
[28] Avery 1984; Avery *et al.* 1984; Binford 1981; Binford, Mills and Stone 1982; Brain 1981; Hill 1972, 1981; Klein 1975; Mills and Mills 1977; Potts 1983; Shipman and Phillips-Conroy 1977; Sutcliffe 1970.
[29] Binford 1979, 1981; Binford and Bertram 1977; Brain 1967; Bunn 1983; Bunn, Bartram and Kroll 1988; O'Connell, Hawkes and Jones 1988.
[30] E.g. Binford 1981; Blumenschine 1986a; Bunn 1986.
[31] 'Consumption sequence model' of Blumenschine 1986b.
[32] Binford 1981; Brain 1981; Bunn 1981; Bunn and Kroll 1986; Haynes 1980, 1983; Shipman 1986a, 1986b.
[33] Behrensheimer *et al.* 1986.   [34] Shipman and Rose 1983.   [35] Schick 1986.
[36] Potts 1984: 343; see also the study of another site by Andrews and Evans 1983.

here with items deposited in the same place by both carnivores and scavenging hominids.[37] These interpretations are sometimes subject to controversy; they are quite obviously provisional and the authors engaged in the polemics are the first to emphasise this. However, what is new and noteworthy is that the discussions are now taking place on the basis of concrete actualist knowledge, that can be tested, may be disproved or, conversely, can be fine tuned through comparison with results of further actualist studies.[38]

Since then, new research perspectives have been modified with respect to previous work. There is much less talk of the rules of social or economic life, and much more about the sedimentation of faunal and lithic material, the marks left by teeth on bones or by bones on teeth, etc. Henceforth, the discussion focuses more on simple principles of mechanics (for example, the study of tooth or lithic traces) than on the formerly so highly valued laws of culture, changes that some researchers still do not really understand, amazed that anyone could 'be fascinated by the way prehistoric humans treated bones'.[39]

What is, or rather what will be, the influence of this new knowledge on further studies of anthropogenesis? Voices are being raised, claiming that the increasing abundance of archaeological data and the progress in methods of interpretation will be able to fill the gaps in our knowledge once and for all. And yet the problem seems more complicated.

Let us return to the example of Isaac's scenario. His interpretation of accumulations of fossil bones and stone products was originally part of the following chain of inferences:

I *If* a combined meat–vegetable diet,
   Then sexual division of labour;
II *If* sexual division of labour,
   Then food-sharing;
III *If* sexual division of labour,
   Then base camps;
IV *If* food-sharing
   and *if* base camps,
   Then transport of food to the base camps;
V *If* transport of food to the base camps,
   and *if* a meat diet,
   Then concentrations of animal bones as vestiges of the base camps.

[37] Shipman 1986a, 1986b.   [38] E.g. Gifford-Gonzales 1989; Shipman 1986b: 704.
[39] Courbin 1982: 117.

The rest of the argument assumed an influence of the division of labour on the development of social life, itself subsequently responsible for the genesis of language. Only sequence v establishes a link between the phenomena that can be inferred from archaeological or palaeontological remains. The other inferences bring into play either an 'observable' element (traces of which may be preserved among the archaeological remains) with a 'non-observable' element (for want of fossil data) (I, III, IV), or else they speak only of 'non-observable' phenomena (II). Now, even if archaeological vestiges become much more abundant than they are today, and even if their interpretation improves still further, it will be possible to validate only one assertion from such a scenario. In this case, we have the means to determine only what our ancestors ate and, occasionally, how they obtained their food and whether they transported it to base camps. We cannot know whether they transported that food in order to share it, nor whether they practised sexual division of labour, and what the consequences were for social life and for the use of speech. The empirical data allow us to test only the lowest stage of the hypotheses; the rest, still based on the mirage of 'general laws', remains unverifiable.

Although new discoveries await us and the methods of analysing them are constantly improving, it is no use hoping that every question will be answered. Our knowledge about anthropogenesis rests on the meagre traces that time has spared, the only clues enabling us to distinguish – to use the good old formula of Buffon – 'between what is real in a subject and what arbitrary element we introduce by pondering on it'. As these traces are rare and fragmentary, only a small part of our conjectures can be submitted to empirical test. Better knowledge of anthropogenesis seems possible, then, if by that we mean better established, but not necessarily much broader knowledge.

We can hardly hope that the majority of the conjectures judged to be reasonable and plausible will eventually be tested, and that we will be one day able to determine the 'causes' of anthropogenesis. One is struck, in this regard, by the constant efforts made by anthropology, which has long been trying to answer questions formerly posed by philosophical, even mythical thought – questions so ill-adapted to the constraints of verification that it is hard to imagine them being treated according to the rules of the scientific game. If anthropology would decide to break away from its naïve tradition, this would only be achieved at the high cost of abandoning a part of its traditional interrogations and retaining exclusively the problems which can be examined through empirical means. The scientific game has its principles, and we must resign ourselves to the idea that, in bowing to them, we lose the comforting illusion that makes us believe that every past event can be known and explained. Unlike myths, science does not aim at explanation at any price. Its main ambition is to establish an empirically testable correspondence between the world and the hypothesis we form of it; so this particular game must be limited to enterprises in which this objective can be attained.

PREHI-STORIES WITH A MORAL

> When a chess player sits down to a game, he must respect a rule which requires him to move his bishops on the diagonal. Nobody will arrest him if he doesn't. But if he refuses to play that way, then he isn't exactly playing chess.
>
> D. H. Fischer, *Historians' fallacies*[40]

If we define the game of science as attempts to construct representations of reality, aiming at a constant improvement of the correspondence between the representations and the phenomena represented, we have to admit that the authors of our scenarios have little hesitation in contravening the rules of the game: correspondence to empirical data does not seem to be their main concern, and archaeological or palaeontological vestiges are often used solely in so far as they can furnish useful accessories to illustrate preconceived ideas, and so help to realise the major ambition, which is to 'explain the causes' of the origin of humankind. ('How did it come into existence? Why did it come into existence?'[41]) Finding the answers to these questions, a task formerly assigned to philosophical speculation, which itself had inherited it from mythology, is taken over by the anthropologists, who, without perhaps always measuring the consequences, cheerfully take on a task that used to be performed under other rules and to other ends than those of scientific inquiry.

The problem of origins has long exercised a surprising fascination on western thought: the hominisation scenarios are, without any doubt, one of its fruits, alongside an abundance of others, as much in the sciences as in philosophy and theology. In all these domains, knowledge of origins was very often identified with knowledge of the causes, and common sense seems to be in perfect agreement with the opinion of the scholars who, like Bacon, proclaimed that true knowledge is knowledge by causes.[42]

---

[40] Fischer 1970: xix.   [41] Lumsden and Wilson 1983: 1.   [42] Bacon *Novum Organum*, II.2.

The human sciences very soon became one of the arenas of a frantic search for 'causes'. Right until today, the 'why' remains more important for them than the 'how', which is only deemed interesting if it gives hope of finding the way to the former ('the most useful part of history is not the dry knowledge of customs and facts; it is the knowledge that shows us the spirit that established those customs and the causes that led to the events', wrote A.-N. Boulanger in the eighteenth century[43]).

In the historical sciences, of which prehistory and palaeontology are part, questions concerning causes are sometimes far from innocent. When philosophical theories referred at the same time to causes and origins, the intention was often to lay down an order for the present. Enlightenment philosophy provides emblematic examples of conjectures on origins, whose prime ambition was to find arguments in support of theories relating to the desirable organisation of society in the present. The conviction that the origin of things determines their nature has very ancient roots, and so has the idea that the essence of things appears in its pure form only in the original state, as yet unadulterated by the vicissitudes of history, the broad outlines of which would already be inscribed in the primordial properties of things ('the essential properties of things', says Vico, 'are the result of the circumstances in which they are born'[44]). Two of our scenarios still assert that the study of the origin of man can teach us about the 'nature of man'.[45] This 'human nature', supposedly formed at the time of anthropogenesis, is thought to determine the whole subsequent course of history, and certain scenarios go so far as to pronounce on the future of civilisation, as if its origin contained an archetype, whose power would control all the vicissitudes of subsequent reality, and as if the knowledge about origin led to knowledge about destiny and the future. So theories of anthropogenesis readily set themselves up as moral tales, wishing not only to describe the 'how' and explain the 'why', but also to reveal the 'direction' of human history, its message, which would be delivered to us as a lesson or a warning.

The most ancient texts in our sample, like that of Clémence Royer, convey an optimistic message about the progress of humanity, generating a state of bliss and dominion over the Earth in a relentless struggle against

---

[43] Boulanger 1766, I: 4.   [44] Vico 1953/1744: 66.
[45] 'In it [the first phase of history] human beings acquired the basic habits of dealing with one another which still guide the behaviour of individuals, communities and nations. These habits are human nature, which can best be understood by learning how it came into being' (Coon 1955/1954: 10). 'The search for understanding of "human nature" leads back in time to a consideration of the process which shaped our physical, social, emotional and cognitive characteristics' (Tanner and Zihlman 1976: 585).

a hostile nature. We recognise here the classic version of the narrative of miserable origins, which, invariably for centuries, has been heaping praise on 'humanity ascending', a panegyric following the formula laconically summed up by Bergson, when he said: 'the humbler our origin, the greater will be our merit in becoming what we are'.

In the eighteenth century, the famous *Second discourse* drew a different morality from its view of origins. Rousseau's primeval men, without being cruel or genuinely bestial, were nevertheless incomplete creatures, lacking many human characteristics. Their nature was not fully realised until the moment when the original mildness found its complement in the benefits of simple culture and in the abundance – quite Spartan, by the way – provided by the hunting and gathering economy. Rousseau's 'noble savage', contrary to what is often believed, is not a purely natural man; he is already a skilled hunter, who has had time to discover the advantages of culture, but he has not yet roused his negative potential, which will mark future civilisation with its unhappy effects. We find the same idea in the conception of the American anthropologist E. E. Ruyle,[46] where our first ancestors' existence provides the image of animal imperfection, from which, in the course of anthropogenesis, human characteristics slowly emerge. The stage of developed hunter-gatherer society represents the climax of that progress; it offers the picture of an organisation based on the communist principles of equality, the just sharing out of property, and reciprocity. Hierarchy, exploitation and competition, all features – in the author's view – of capitalist societies, are unknown. As in Rousseau, decadence creeps in with the transition to an agricultural economy. That is when humanity engaged on the slippery slope of an 'ethical regression',[47] which will lead people to indulge in odious and barbarous practices, like head hunting, scalping, cannibalism, human sacrifice, slavery, all accompanied by the supreme horror of social inequalities.[48] These 'scourges' would be unknown to prehistoric hunter-gatherers, whose way of life would be a direct result of the process of hominisation, guided by the simple rules of biological evolution that creates only what is useful, reasonable and just. Ruyle makes no secret of his Marxist inspirations, and the morality in his anthropogenesis scenario comes down to a trite view of decadent capitalist society, put in parallel with the bucolic picture of Palaeolithic primitive communism.

Ruyle's scenario is intended to be deliberately close, in part at least, to that of Engels, but its general conception of history is also influenced

---

[46] Ruyle 1977.   [47] *Ibid.*: 147.   [48] *Ibid.*; the author refers to a work by Lenski (1970: 23–236).

by some ideas of the counter-culture of the sixties and the seventies, so quick to criticise contemporary society. The Marxist scenarios of Soviet authors, who also refer to Engels, never go as far as that. The axiom of evolutionary progress was one of the cornerstones of Soviet ideology and anthropologists would never have dared challenge it. The texts of M. F. Niestourkh and P. I. Boriskovski appeal to the classic view of the pitiful beginnings of history which in due course ends with the idyllic domination of humanity over nature. However, there is a new element to be added to the traditional explanatory scheme. Engels had written that 'labour created man';[49] Soviet authors returned to this notion and made labour not only the main characteristic of the primordial condition of humanity, but the driving force of progress as well. We should recall that the notion of labour, vague as it might be, occupied pride of place in Soviet propaganda. Here are some of its *leitmotifs*: the 'bourgeoisie', damned as parasitical from the mere fact that it was presented as exempt from labour, so justifying its persecution; the Leninist principle 'if you don't work, you don't eat'; education by 'labour' in Soviet schools; the Stakhanovite cult of 'heroes of labour'; 'resocialisation', as it was called hypocritically, in the 'labour camps' (the edifying designation given to the gulags), etc. The image is clear: labour represents the supreme value, the *raison d'être* of humanity and the guarantee of its dignity. The palaeoanthropologists and prehistorians hastened to add that labour also created man.

But that is not all. Labour could not be individual, carried on in isolation, outside the community; the only labour that counted was within a group baptised by Soviet authors with the name of 'collective'. It is precisely labour in 'collectives', they say, that transformed the ape into man.[50] It is difficult to put forward anything reasonable about the existence of 'collectives' among the early hominids; little doubt remains as to the existence of 'collectives' in the Stalinist totalitarian system, where they were introduced so as to establish a fundamental structure of society, called on to fulfil the objectives of production, indoctrination and control by denunciation.[51]

It is not surprising that the Soviet scenarios should have insisted so strongly on the importance of 'labour' and of the 'collective' in the process of hominisation; the projection of the principles of Soviet society into prehistoric times transforms the conception of origins into a justification of the established political order.

[49] Engels 1971/1896: 55.   [50] Niestourkh 1958: 235–6.   [51] E.g. Zinoviev 1983.

Many are the scenarios that make their accounts parables of humanity's struggle against nature, but others present anthropogenesis as the story of merciless rivalry between humans. Robert Ardrey's book *African genesis* is a typical example. Moreover, its moralising message is not disguised. If our ancestor survived the ecological cataclysms of prehistory, Ardrey asserts, it is because he was able to become 'a predator whose natural instinct is to kill with a weapon',[52] ready to assassinate not only animals but his fellow creatures as well. Humans still carry today the genetic legacy of the primordial killer; we are all the children of Cain.

Ardrey wrote this book when the cold war was at its height, and the awareness of nuclear danger is clearly visible in it. The aim of the narrative, stated several times, is to convince readers that the Rousseauist view of the original goodness of human beings is nothing but a lie, that we are endowed with murderous instincts and that, for the first time, we are equipped with a totally effective weapon, which makes total murder possible. So the narrative of origins is intended as a warning: a mask must be removed, the true face of the human is to be unveiled and we have to understand what this bloodthirsty primate is capable of. An alarm call, certainly, but this message is intended to give hope too, by showing that evolution has also endowed us with, aside from a taste for blood, an efficient brain and free will, which allow the legacy of Cain to be overcome.[53]

We do not know if our earliest ancestors fought each other bitterly, but it is certain that twentieth-century Europeans have done so, no holds barred. Ardrey's scenario, written after two world wars and in dreaded anticipation of the third and definitive one, is a banal transposition of the present into the past. Under the pen of Ardrey – a former playwright – the universe of the early hominids becomes a naïve travesty of modern political life, which seems curiously close to the theatrical reality of *West Side Story*, dominated by the brutal rivalry of enemy gangs.

The notion of original rivalry has lost much of its attraction since the end of the 1960s. The counter-culture once more revived the figure of the noble savage, attributing aggression and war to the decadence of civilisation. In this new view, the earliest humans, quasi flower-children, are no longer fighting against nature, and nature has lost its frightening 'stepmother' characteristics to become a true mother. Struggle is no longer the prime mover of anthropogenesis here, which implies that reference to omnipresent adversaries, whether human or animal, is no longer

[52] Ardrey 1973/1961: 316. [53] *Ibid.*: 301.

indispensable. Human beings are naturally good and distinguished from animals by their faculty of compassion, by altruism, by bursts of fellow-feeling and by their disposition to share everything with others. In the theory of Glynn Isaac, sharing takes the place of combat as the first cause of hominisation, becoming a premise that can explain the origin of everything: bipedalism, sexual division of labour, language, society, etc. This view, which archaeological data have not been able to corroborate despite Isaac's sustained efforts, soon became very popular, matching, as it did, the intellectual climate of the seventies.

Feminists in particular opposed the traditional vision of bloodthirsty combat, for a reason that is easy to guess. The classic theory, which claimed that we became human thanks to the great struggles of prehistoric times, made of males the main heroes of traditional narratives: they alone were supposedly capable of hunting and waging war. What about the females in earliest times? We have seen that their role in the hominisation process was almost non-existent;[54] all they had to do was wait passively for inspiration from their more advanced male companions ('in every shift of occupation of which we know throughout history, women have taken over the jobs formerly held by men, as the men have moved on to something new'[55]). So woman would be a secondary product of hominisation; it was first man who descended from the ape, then woman 'descended' from man.

The absurdity of this view passed oddly unnoticed until feminist anthropology justifiably made it one of its preferred targets. But response to one excess soon became an opposite excess. The hominisation scenario proposed by primatologist Adrienne Zihlman and anthropologist Nancy P. Tanner[56] constructs a kind of inverted misogynist view, being content to reverse the distribution of roles: woman is now the leading actor in hominisation, and it is no longer masculine hunting but rather feminine gathering that is the main source of early subsistence. It was women, too, who were the first to adopt bipedal locomotion, invent tools, share food, practise cooperation and establish durable social bonds. The naturally 'disruptive' males are kept at a distance. If, with time, they hominise, it is again thanks to women, who establish a kind of breeding system: 'Females preferred to associate and have sex with males exhibiting friendly behaviour, rather than those who were comparatively disruptive, a danger to themselves or offspring ... Mothers chose to copulate most frequently with these comparatively sociable, less disruptive, sharing

---

[54] E.g. Isaac 1976, 1978a, 1978b.   [55] Coon 1955/1954: 45.   [56] Tanner and Zihlman 1976.

males – with males more like themselves.'[57] Thanks to this wise and beneficent selection, two results were achieved: on the one hand, the qualities of 'good males' were genetically transmitted to succeeding generations; on the other hand, the genes of males whose crude behaviour did not find favour in the eyes of their more advanced companions were gradually eliminated. The moral of this narrative is not excessively complicated: it amounts to showing the superiority of the female over the male and the dominant role of the fair sex in the emergence of humanity. The whole is served up coated with a very scientific sauce, a skilful blend of sociobiology, primatology and palaeoanthropology.

Another mission adopted by certain hominisation scenarios[58] is to prove the 'unnatural' and 'secondary' character of religious beliefs. The Soviet prehistorian P. I. Boriskovski has devoted special effort to this task.[59] His conception is intended to demonstrate that culture came into being without religion, hence it follows – in the author's logic – that culture can manage without it today. In line with the traditional scheme of conjectural anthropology accepted by Boriskovski, religion appeared at a certain stage in history as a response to the fear felt by the savage when faced with the incomprehensible phenomena of a powerful and hostile nature. The strength of religious beliefs would thus be a function of the weakness of human beings, so that religion would be bound to disappear when civilisation, and in particular science, would give them a reassuring power that could set them free once and for all from fears inherent in the primitive state. This idea, dear to the Enlightenment philosophers, was amalgamated a century and a half later with the Soviet regime doctrine, which declared a veritable war on religion. Boriskovski's scenario is in perfect harmony on this point with the axioms of Soviet propaganda and with the letter of the USSR Communist Party programme, in which the following statement can be found: 'It is necessary to conduct a vast and systematic scientifico-atheist propaganda, to explain patiently the erroneous nature of religious beliefs, born in the past from the oppression felt by man faced with the incomprehensible forces of nature.'[60] Following these instructions, Soviet anthropologists were obliged to engage in 'the struggle against hostile religious ideology'.[61] This struggle continues in the hominisation scenarios.

It is fascinating to observe the multitude of edifying conclusions that the palaeoanthropological conceptions hasten to offer. In reflecting

[57] *Ibid.*: 606. [58] Engels 1971/1896; Ruyle 1977; Boriskovski 1979. [59] Boriskovski 1979.
[60] Quoted from Mongait 1962: 3. [61] Mongait 1962: 3.

on anthropogenesis, our authors easily succumb to the temptation to moralise; it then becomes inevitable that the requirements of the narrative begin to triumph over those of empirical procedure, the rules of which demand, instead of preaching, that its conjectures be not only doubted but also put to the test.

My purpose here is not to gloss on this elementary truth that scientific theories may be conditioned by ideology. I simply aim to illustrate some of the ideological constructions possible with the very simple generative pattern that governs our scenarios. Indeed, all these narratives and their different morals have been made possible by permutations carried out on just one matrix, composed of a list of stereotyped human characteristics that are arranged into reputedly causal chains, in accordance with a catalogue of relations that are themselves held to be plausible and obvious. This conceptual matrix is very efficient and the combinatory game of which it is the instrument, while inadequate for establishing an empirically tested view of anthropogenesis, nevertheless allows many narratives with varying meanings to be constructed. The elements thus made available to anthropologists, accompanied by a few 'universal laws', lend themselves to rearrangements free from any empirical constraint and built under the influence of an intellectual fashion, propaganda principles, an ideological engagement or a particular worldview. Do we play down the role of women? Then our ancestors lived by hunting, and hunting, the driving force of hominisation, was a masculine occupation. Do we rebel against male domination? Then our ancestors lived by gathering, gathering was a feminine occupation and it must be granted prime importance in the causal chain of the hominisation process. Do we admire the progress of civilisation? Then we shall adopt a view of feeble humans with no technical skill; we shall place them in a hostile nature and explain anthropogenesis by the primitive struggle that culminates in access to ever more flourishing culture. Do we doubt the benefits of progress? Then we make primitive nature bountiful, our ancestors altruist, and brotherly sharing becomes the principal antecedent of explanatory sequences.

This game can be played indefinitely, for the generative matrix that makes it possible is as simple as it is accommodating. All that is required in order to proclaim the invention of a new theory of anthropogenesis, or, through it, the advent of 'a New Human Science',[62] is a few rearrangements of old elements found in the treasure house of ideas 'good to think

---

[62] Lumsden and Wilson 1983: 167.

with', that have already stood the test of common sense. And it is logical that the social success of a hominisation scenario so achieved is equalled only by its banality. Here is, for example, what Carleton Coon, the author of a very typical scenario,[63] had to say about the article by Charles F. Hockett and Robert Ascher,[64] which is in its turn a hotchpotch of no less classic clichés:

> In my opinion, the paper by Hockett and Ascher represents a turning point in our thinking about the origins of language and culture, and I congratulate all hands, including the publisher, for its appearance. My own reaction is that the authors' ideas are brilliant, creative and essentially sound...[65]

HOMO COGITANS, HOMO LOQUENS AND HISTORY

> Las imágenes y la letra impresa eran más reales que las cosas.
> José L. Borges, *Utopía de un hombre que está cansado*[66]

'The first storyteller in the tribe began to utter words, not so that the others should return other predictable words to him, but in order to try out how far those words could be combined together and mutually engender others. In order to deduce an explanation of the world from the thread of every possible discourse/narrative, from the arabesque traced by nouns and verbs, subjects and predicates as they intertwined. The characters at the disposal of the storyteller were not numerous: the jaguar, the coyote, the toucan, the piranha fish; or else the father, the son, the brother-in-law, the uncle, the wife, the mother, the sister, the daughter-in-law; the actions these characters could perform were equally limited: to be born, to die, to mate, to sleep, to fish, to hunt, to climb trees, to dig lairs in the ground, to eat, to defecate, to smoke vegetable fibres, to prohibit, to contravene the prohibitions, to give presents or to steal objects and fruits, themselves liable to be classified in a restricted catalogue. The storyteller explored the possibilities contained in his own language, making combinations and permutations of the characters and the actions; and the objects round which these actions revolved. That is how stories came into being.' Such is the origin of the primordial narratives, as imagined by Italo Calvino, himself a notable storyteller.[67]

This entertaining tale lays no claim to be truthful or plausible. It serves simply to illustrate the Lévi-Straussian theory to which Calvino remained attached, whereby traditional narratives, like myths or folk-tales,

---

[63] Coon 1955/1954.   [64] Hockett and Ascher 1964.   [65] Coon 1964: 156.
[66] Borges 1990/1975: 205.   [67] Calvino 1971: 678.

are modelled on pre-existing structures and explore the possibilities for transforming them. The same metaphor could sum up the conclusions of our analysis of the hominisation scenarios. Their authors behave like Calvino's *Narrator* or the *Bricoleur* of Lévi-Strauss; they make use of the elements of a pre-existing conceptual heritage and switch them round, modify and enrich them so as to construct narratives endowed with a 'meaning' or a message or a moral. In the event, the rules of the scientific game may be broken, but the narration triumphs.

For some time now, the human sciences have begun to perceive more clearly the affinities between their writings and the classical narrative procedures. We have even been witnessing a real vogue for comparisons that assimilate scholarly works to literary or, indeed, mythical narratives, often with the explicit aim of proclaiming that the narrative is the only appropriate form of expression for speaking of things human. Palaeoanthropology has not been spared by this tendency: the work of Misia Landau[68] caused a stir by drawing parallels between the structure of six hominisation scenarios and that of the folk-tale, as described by Vladimir Propp.[69] Analogies do exist, of course. The scholarly scenarios of anthropogenesis are rather like folk-tales in that the plot in both begins in a state of equilibrium, which will be first disrupted and then restored by the efforts of a hero, for whom this adventure will become his initiation. It is true that the 'feeble human' of our scenarios calls to mind the character of the 'stupid brother' in fables, and that some of his characteristics would suit a character in a folk-tale. Yet the resemblances remain superficial. We may compare Lucy with Cinderella, hominisation with an initiation rite, but the parallel is not very illuminating, for most of the processes that occur in the real world can be reduced to this mundane plan of an equilibrium disturbed and then restored, in which a Cinderella finds her lucky day. Misia Landau was right to point out that the hominisation scenarios are constructed from prefabricated elements, but these are not provided by folk-tales nor can those tales explain their nature.[70] The old tripartite model, that can be applied to the functioning of a bicycle pump or the flushing of a toilet just as well as to Aristotle's definition of the narrative, is transformed into a hominisation scenario when it takes charge of remarkable conceptual matter, the true source of which – as we have seen – is very often common-sense anthropology, fed as much by philosophers as by ordinary thinking.

[68] Landau 1984, 1991.   [69] Propp 1972/1928.   [70] Stoczkowski 1992c.

Some scholars, while freely acknowledging the place of narrative devices in their texts, nevertheless hope that a difference does exist between the writings of the human sciences and novel writing, as if the narrative had the right to lay claim to truthfulness from the fact of being told by a scholar ('history is a truthful novel', says Paul Veyne[71]). Analysis of the 'narrative' conjectures lavishly handed out by the hominisation scenarios leaves no illusion as to the fanciful nature of the 'truthful novel', for it shows the extent to which the narrative constraints are at loggerheads with the ambition to give a 'truthful' account. Let us forget how unsatisfactory this last, epistemologically rustic adjective is, and note that the 'veracity' of a good many of the hominisation scenarios is – and will probably always remain – uncertain, for want of prehistoric vestiges with which to test their hypotheses. Palaeoathropologists are often content to propose narratives that evolve in a universe of plausibility, in which 'universal laws' evoked by way of justification bear much too close a resemblance to those samples of popular wisdoms assembled so scrupulously by Flaubert in his unrivalled dictionary of received ideas.

A dictionary of anthropological ideas 'good to think with', an anthology of the simplistic but dauntingly 'credible' concepts, still awaits its author. I prefer to emphasise the dangers to which a 'narrative' anthropology is exposed. By avoiding the obligations of empirical validation and preferring instead to unfold in the realm of the plausible, the narrative approach is easily tempted to seek its credibility in the seductive world of naïve imaginary, whose imprimatur bears the stamp of common sense. If the hominisation scenarios seem convincing, this is because their credibility is based on the certitudes of conjectural anthropology, which continues to exercise a powerful influence on western thought. These familiar commonplaces allow a decor to be created that confers an appearance of authenticity on the narrative. As in a movie – to situate the action in the past, for example in the Greco-Roman world, all that is required is a conventional set, which would be credible both for its exoticism and for the familiarity of a vanished civilisation, still present in our imaginary: the obligatory accessories are 'colonnades, peristyles, temples with pediments, monumental stairways, marble statues, triumphal arches, bronze tripods where the fire of the ancient gods burns eternally: an evocative atmosphere rather than an archaeologically accurate reality, always uncertain and inevitably awkward'.[72] Just as the earliest explorers of America presented the exoticism of the Antipodes by resorting to its

[71] Veyne 1971: 10.   [72] Eloy 1988: 259.

mythical attributes codified by Pliny, so the authors of our scenarios depict hominisation by recycling the usual ingredients of an imaginary prehistory, bequeathed to us by naïve anthropology as our heritage; we then marvel at their plausibility, as do Flaubert's Bouvard and Pécuchet who, without knowing the models, found the portraits of ancient kings 'true to life'.

However, we must beware of concluding that archaeological reality is of as little interest to palaeoanthropologists as it was to Flaubert's gullible characters or to the director of *Ben Hur*. Such an assertion would be both unjust and inaccurate. Our scenarios allot a certain amount of space to prehistoric data even if, alas, they do not bring them directly into play in their explanatory reasonings. The fundamental problem of the conjectural procedure on display in the hominisation scenarios is that empirical validation is too often neglected, so that it never carries equal weight with the constraints imposed by rules of the narrative that aims to extract a meaning from the events, or endow them with a moral. And those rules were actually conceived so as to be of use to fiction. Speaking about genesis amounts here to decreeing it, and the account does not inform us how things really happened; it tells how people need to imagine that things happened. The empirical data are appealed to only so long as they do not disturb; their usefulness is that of an illustration, for elements of reality are only evoked to favour the reader's adherence to the unfolding of the fiction.

The constraints of the narrative, like the ambition – inherited from philosophical tradition, which in turn owes it to theology – to know the 'origins' and the 'nature' of things, sit badly with the commitments of science, whose fundamental aspiration is to seek an empirically controlled correspondence between conceptual representations and the phenomena represented. The two genres remain barely compatible, for their principles are at variance: what appears to be a defect in science is often a virtue in narrative and vice versa.

The palaeoanthropological narrative, as conceived by the tradition of western thought, is primarily interested in a total 'explanation' of anthropogenesis, which has to establish an exemplary state of human condition, or its counter-image. The scientific game, for its part, stops short at constructing an image of the world capable of empirical verification.

When the storyteller realises that the information at his disposal is fragmentary and inadequate to satisfy the desire for a complete and absolute understanding, he turns to the *sensus communis* which abounds in fine formulae favourable to moralising interpretations that cannot but be complete and definitive. Scientific knowledge, on the other hand, as its short history shows, is characterised rather by the reverse tendency: it usually obliges us to put aside the familiar opinions, and it disappoints by its semiotic poverty, which precludes the facile grafting on of philosophical extensions loaded with 'meaning'.

So the narrative finds its legitimacy in adjusting to commonly held conceptions, whereas science insists on anchoring itself in empirical data.

This last imperative imposes the working out of precise and unequivocal systems for representing data, in which notions can be calculated, evaluated and measured. Equally clear and unequivocal must be the rules of the inference, freed from the limits of 'natural logic', a few eloquent examples of which we have seen. The storyteller is exempted from these requirements. The labyrinth of natural language is his preferred domain, since precision is no use to him and can even be a drawback when it curbs the polysemy that must 'give food for thought'; and if that polysemy at the same time produces logical incoherences owing to an excess of meanings, the 'woolliness' of language comes to the rescue and mercifully conceals them.

Science builds up knowledge in order to challenge it, whereas the narrative is made to last; the fate of the former is to be demolished, whereas the latter courts admiration. Scientific knowledge contrives to be cumulative, thanks to incessant toings and froings between the general theories and the empirical data, which are being continually enriched. The narrative has a static character, based as it is on a combinatory game that unfolds within the limits of its own generative matrix.

Although everything seems to separate the rules of storytelling from those of science, in the humanities the two genres still live in a very special symbiosis; we may wonder whether it really deserves that name, in that the consequences of the situation are not necessarily of the happiest, especially for knowledge that claims to be empirical: the narrative has its private preserves, where it develops exuberantly and untrammelled, while science suffers from that dual play, loses its identity and betrays its true vocation, its texts becoming yet another means of expression at the service of ordinary thinking. When the story takes a hand in the argument, the original hypotheses soon give way to clichés, for the narrative is like social conversation, of which André Maurois said that it has its strict rules which demand sacrifice of ideas.

'Guessing is always more fun than knowing', W. H. Auden wrote ironically. The poet reserves the right to play with ideas, but the researcher has more than one reason to suspect that knowledge that wants to develop in harmony with this credo may disappoint: founded on a conditioned imagination, it has every chance of getting bogged down in commonplaces and experiencing long periods of stagnation, before, very occasionally, and following a happy combination of circumstances, it succeeds in taking a step forward, which will owe nothing either to the controlled effort of scientists or to deliberate design.

So scientists seem to be faced with an apparently simple choice: either they are content to explore the narrative possibilities offered by the conceptual raw material inherited from the past, or they resolve to explore the external world itself, by confronting hypotheses with empirical data.

But this alternative is deceptive. It would be illusory to hope that scientists might be able to free themselves entirely from the weight of intellectual tradition and look at the world with new eyes, free from any conditioning that culture and their past cannot fail to exert on the thought of the individual. In fact, the real question is to know not whether or not one can be freed from the past, but rather to what extent one is capable of being so freed and in what way.

If the question is rarely asked, it is because scientists think they know the right answer in advance; some believe they have shrugged off history completely, while others are sure they are irremediably its captives. These hasty certainties stem from epistemological ideologies in which too much faith is sometimes placed. It is indeed striking that the problem of the relationship to the past and to tradition lies just below the surface of all epistemological theories, without any of them giving it explicitly the importance it deserves. Yet scientists can never escape the necessity of defining their relationship to the past of their discipline or their culture, and the solutions we are led to adopt in this matter bring in their wake methodological consequences that are by no means negligible.

In our own day, most scientists seem convinced that they are light years away from the attitude of ancient and medieval thinkers, for whom scholarly enquiry was consubstantial with constant reference to their predecessors, whose chronological remoteness could only increase their authority; originality, *novitas*, was considered to be a fatal flaw, and conformity with the ancient *auctoritates* was held to be a legitimate form of epistemological validation.[73] Nowadays we feel closer to the scholars of the eighteenth century, who witnessed the spread of an ideology favouring

---

[73] Mortier 1982: 10–11.

a break with the past and made a new rhetoric fashionable, one destined to glorify originality and present it as the fruit of rejecting tradition. Since then, any self-respecting intellectual activity, and science in particular, has made a point of emphasising its ability to free itself from the past, making rebellion against the established authorities and opinions a cliché, in statements that are the more widespread for being pure form and imposing no practical obligation on their authors. The conviction that one can break with tradition forms part of this new tradition.

In the nineteenth century, Auguste Comte was voicing an opinion that was already largely accepted, when he proclaimed that positive knowledge takes shape not thanks to, but in spite of the past, and that science, the definitive regime of human reason, was built not from the debris but on the debris of ancient systems of thought.[74] Prehistory, a new science that appeared at the same period, immediately made itself the mouthpiece of a similar conviction, announcing that it would extricate itself without delay from the burdensome heritage of beliefs, in order to build a new and positive knowledge based on observation: 'Modern science', wrote Henri du Cleuziou in 1887, in a book devoted to prehistory, 'leaving behind preconceived theories, accepted solutions, the marvellous and the supernatural, now demands facts from its followers, nothing but facts, formally established, strictly tested and utterly irrefutable.'[75]

This ideology of rupture with the past has been joined, almost naturally, by the ideology of empiricism, which saw in factual data an adequate means of salvation, that would be bound to allow science to get away from the past and from its bundle of preconceived ideas: henceforth, scientists wanted to owe everything to new data, nothing to old ideas. This hope is still alive among researchers who cling to modern forms of empiricism; they are by no means rare, despite the repeatedly proclaimed death of positivism. The perennity of these hopes explains, at least in part, the contempt in which the history of science is usually held by practising scientists: so those who study the prehistoric past venerate paradoxically the future, expecting it to provide a rich harvest of data, and believe they can turn their backs for good on the past of their discipline, which promises them no new archaeological vestiges.

But the gradual abandonment of empiricism and orthodox positivism, that we have been witnessing since the 1960s and that accompanies the emergence of epistemologies of a more sociological bent, has nevertheless not challenged the ideology of rupture. The very popular concept

[74] Comte 1963/1844.   [75] Du Cleuziou 1887: 7.

of scientific revolutions has merely extended the notion of the rupture to science as a whole. According to this new epistemological vulgate, deep gulfs separate not only the different types of thought, as Comte would have it, but the different scientific theories as well. Kuhn summed up clearly its view of a history punctuated by catastrophes of change of paradigm, claiming that any scientific revolution empties specialist libraries of the old books and periodicals, now suddenly out-of-date.[76] Kuhn's thesis, reproduced in countless variants by a wide range of authors, has found a logical extension in a fashionable trend of the history of science that openly proclaims its sociological inspiration and asserts that the scientific ideas of each period must be explained by their own 'context' (social, economic, political, intellectual, cultural, etc.). Thus, for example, the emergence of the evolutionist ethnology is supposed to be explained by saying that its creators, being middle-class Victorians, and living in the society in which they lived in their own times, could have only those ideas and no others; this is asserted solely because they did in fact have those ideas and no others; it is a certitude that ideas are a mere reflection of society; all that remains is to find out, whatever the cost, in what way they reflect it.[77]

Even if this assumption may occasionally be heuristically useful, it none the less leads its supporters to think that the history of a science is of no use to the practitioners of that same science today. If, in order to have new ideas about the prehistoric past, for example, it were essential to have a new society in the present, then, instead of excavating or inventing interpretations, it would be better to work towards changing society, so that, by the mysterious laws of the alchemy of 'context', it would then produce a new view of prehistory. It may be no accident that a great many archaeologists who espouse such social determinism in epistemology seem to be strongly attracted by political militancy, often to the detriment of reflection and research, the virtues of which they manifestly do not believe in.[78] In this case, too, the view of history as punctuated by ruptures remains intact and the past of the sciences is carved up into a great many chronological slices, each of which remains separated from the others, being supposedly governed by the rules appropriate to its local 'context'. The slices of the past are reserved for historians (provided, of course, that the nineteenth-century specialist does not encroach on the immeasurably different slice, so it is said, of the eighteenth-century specialist), while practising researchers can be content with the immediate present, dating

[76] Kuhn 1969.   [77] See, for example, Stocking 1987.   [78] See Tilley 1989.

from after the latest revolution, which has kindly swept the libraries clean of 'out-of-date works'.

Orthodox positivism, still surfacing again today where it is least expected, Thomas Kuhn's still popular theory of scientific revolutions, and the sociological approach of today's historians, all agree on at least one point: they all claim that it is the destiny of science to set itself completely free from its own past. Science will achieve this either by following an upward movement along a scale of evolutionary steps, each stage of which marks the transition to a new quality, or by cyclical purification through the regenerating cataclysms of the change of paradigms, or else by moving from one 'context' to another, in so far as each generation would have 'to rethink their view of the world'.[79] Opinions like this, long outworn, have accustomed us to imagining that the history of scientific thought is made up, in the long term, of profound ruptures which periodically free researchers from the pressure that any tradition might exert. In our culture, which idolises change, scholars share with laypeople the belief that the persistence over a long period of elements of the past is an anomaly, and that it is doubly so in the realm of science, conflicting here both with the normal course of history and with the fundamental mechanisms of the metamorphoses of scientific theories.

So it is not surprising that all these epistemological ideologies show very little interest in the problems researchers must confront, faced with the conceptual patrimony bequeathed by the sometimes distant past of their own culture. The persistence in the present of ideas from the past, however little it may be recognised, arouses two types of stereotypical reaction, which, unfortunately, bypass the real question. The first reaction consists in denying the existence of the phenomenon and in insinuating that historical continuities are just an artefact produced by lack of precision in historical research embedded in the study of themes that are too vast, like the *chain of beings* or *primitivism* which used to fascinate Arthur Owen Lovejoy; the perennity of such themes would be only apparent and proportional to their generality. Yet the works of historians of ideas, so discredited for the last thirty years, have been too numerous and too well documented to be refused all credence simply because some of the criticisms levelled at them were pertinent. The second reaction, while acknowledging the existence of persistent ideas, consists in assuming that conceptions that migrate from one historical 'context' to another necessarily belong to the category of the obvious and indisputable facts of

[79] Peter J. Bowler is the recently self-appointed eulogist of the extreme version of this opinion which, in his work, has the advantage of being succinct and explicit: Bowler 2001.

objective knowledge: they would be a matter of 'common sense', as defined by the philosophers of the Enlightenment ('judgements inspired universally by nature in all men' said the d'Alembert *Encyclopédie*[80]). Accepting this naturalist view of common sense amounts to believing that only truisms, which reality itself obliges us to accept as evidence, could remain invariable in the long term, while all other ideas, being arbitrary conventions determined by culture, would inevitably evolve according to historical metamorphoses. Thus, the consensus of epistemological ideologies (otherwise disparate) with regard to the existence of deep ruptures in the history of science leads many researchers to think that long-term conceptual continuities are either misleading artefacts produced by bad historians, or natural facts that escape the movement of history because of their absolute certainty.

Having tried in this book to gather together proofs in support of another view, I can now sum up its arguments in several points. First, we have been able to see that ideas exist that are frankly impervious to historical change and, without being invariable in the absolute sense, change so slowly that a number of epochs, sometimes very remote from each other, are marked by their presence. Second, I have tried to show that the transformation of these ideas follows rules which create the effect of structure: what is genuinely invariable in the long run is not the scenarios, nor the explanatory theories, nor yet the essential ideas in themselves, but the structure underlying all these conceptual constructs. Third, the components of these same conceptual constructs, and the structural rules by which they are organised, constitute an important part of our common-sense knowledge, but this common sense is not a catalogue of certainties stemming from the nature of things; on the contrary, it is a cultural construct, rich in arbitrary ideas that are anything but first truths bereft of prior principles. It must be emphasised, with Clifford Geertz, that this view of common sense as a cultural construct usually gets a hostile reception, because it is inherent in common sense to deny that common sense could be a hotchpotch of received wisdom, accepted by virtue of a social convention masquerading as a natural phenomenon ('anybody in their right mind cannot but accept these natural facts', states common sense as it judges the opinions ... of common sense[81]). Fourth, I have

---

[80] The Article 'Common sense' in the *Encylopédie*; Jaucourt 1969/1751–72, XV: 27–8. This view of common sense is still popular today ('The most important ingredient of common sense, as I intend to use the term and as I believe intuitive use of the term would have it, is now isolated: its objective basis'; Lindenberg 1987: 199).

[81] Geertz 1993/1983: chapter IV.

shown that the certainties of common sense, while being a product of history, are capable of resisting the movements of history, passing with no great modifications from one social context to another and easily surviving changes of paradigms. This persistence, which creates links in time between different 'social contexts', is a fundamental fact of history just as change is, and it is this that creates the continuity of a civilisation.

The theories of anthropogenesis, a sample of which I have analysed, betray, in fact, the influence of a dual determinism: they are tied in, on the one hand, to a succession of earlier conceptions which provide a structured raw material that nurtures innovations; on the other hand, they are subject to the influence of successive historical and cultural contexts, which decide how the heritage of the past is used and amended.[82] Every new act is played here on a stage that is already constructed, prepared by the past. Continuity and discontinuity, innovation and tradition represent two sides of the same coin. Like any social fact, the hominisation scenarios fit into their present without thereby cutting themselves off from the past, and they form the links in a series that crosses the ages. The historiographic mode of the moment urges us to believe that only the 'present', with its empirical data and its context, influences scientific thought, as if the impact of causal factors was measured by their chronological proximity. However, we must not forget that the past, remote as it may be, acts on us with a force no less powerful than that of the present. What would we say, Marc Bloch wondered, about an astronomer who proclaims that the action of the moon on our globe is stronger than that of the sun, because the moon is nearer?[83]

Acknowledging that historical processes can be slow and protracted, that timelags due to the force of inertia are omnipresent, that the ideas of yesterday and the day before weigh on those of the present, does in fact offer a few practical consequences, not only to the historian but also to any scientists who seek a better mastery of their conceptual tools. Fashionable epistemological ideologies insinuate that those tools depend only on the available empirical data and the immediate cultural 'context'. The analysis to which we have subjected the hominisation scenarios suggests that in this particular case the conceptions that the specialists build up cannot be explained in their totality either by the constraints of the chronologically linked 'context', as the sociologising history of

---

[82] Claude Lévi-Strauss, on the basis of his analysis of Amerindian myths, was the first to draw attention to this dual causality, at once structural and historical, which governs the conceptual constructions; Lévi-Strauss 1966: 562.

[83] Bloch 1993/1949: 62.

the sciences would have it, or by the factual data, as empiricism would like. Contrary to what is often thought, scientists do not draw their conclusions from empirical data, any more than they rewrite history in terms of prevailing ideology. In fact, they rather try to organise the heterogeneous conceptual materials that society places at their disposal, and these include new facts and recent ideologies just as much as ancient commonplaces. These various materials are the actual data on which the scientists work; the scientists infer nothing from them; they just put them in order.

And there are two ways of putting them in order: first the one in which speculative ideas predominate and empirical data are subordinate to them, and second, the one where the opposite holds good. Researchers are accustomed to give this second procedure the term 'scientific', but frequently they are content to practise the first. The ignorance of the history of sciences in particular, and of the history of Western thought in general, entails the first procedure, because the lack of historical knowledge favours the transformation of the arbitrary and epistemologically fragile conventions of common sense into 'natural facts', and this shelters them from any attempt at empirical evaluation, whereas the ideas slightly removed from the dogmas of common sense are put aside *a priori*, before their pertinence can be assessed.

In fact, scientists do not have to choose between exploring the combinatory possibilities offered by the conceptual material inherited from the past, and exploring empirical reality. They have to conduct the two operations simultaneously, well aware that the empirical data, interrogated in terms of the interpretative hypotheses, will provide them with answers of an interest proportional to that of the questions asked, and that the questions are not easy to formulate without mastering the conceptual matrices, of which history can reveal all the combinatory possibilities, way beyond those that conditioned imagination enables us to glimpse. It is not a question of some liberation from the past, but rather of learning to make good use of it.

Bibliography

Abercrombie, M., Hickman, C. J. and Johnson, M. L. 1966. *A dictionary of biology*. Aylesbury, Hunt Bernard and Co. Ltd.
Acosta, I. 1598 (first edn 1590). *Histoire naturelle et morale des Indes*. Paris, Marc Orry.
Aeschylus 1976. 'Prometheus bound' (French translation). In *Eschyle, Œuvres*, vol. 1. Paris, Les Belles Lettres (11th edn).
Ainsa, F. 1986. 'De l'Âge d'or à l'Eldorado. Métamorphoses d'un mythe', *Diogène* 133: 23–44.
  1989. 'L'invention de l'Amérique. Signes imaginaires de la découverte et construction de l'utopie', *Diogène* 145: 104–17.
Almquist, A. J. and Cronin, J. E. 1988. 'Fact, fancy, and myth on human evolution', *Current Anthropology* 29: 520–2.
Altman, S. A., ed. 1967. *Social communication among primates*. Chicago, University of Chicago Press.
Andrews, P. and Evans, E. M. N. 1983. 'Small mammal bone accumulations produced by mammalia carnivores', *Paleobiology* 9: 289–307.
Ardrey, R. 1973 (first edn 1961). *African genesis: a personal investigation into the animal origins and nature of man*. New York, Atheneum Publishers.
Aristotle 1968. *Histoire des animaux* (text established and translated by P. Louis). Paris, Les Belles Lettres.
  1990. *Les parties des animaux* (text established and translated by P. Louis). Paris, Les Belles Lettres.
Arnobe 1982. *Contre les Gentils* (text established and translated by R. Le Bonniec). Paris, Les Belles Lettres.
Arnold, A. J. and Fristrup, K. 1982. 'The theory of evolution by natural selection: a hierarchical expansion', *Paleobiology* 8: 113–29.
Avery, G. 1984. 'Sacred cows or jackal kitchens, hyena middens and bird nests: some implications of multi-agent contributions to archaeological accumulations', in Hall, M., Avery, D. M., Wilson, M. L. and Humpreys, A. J. B., eds., *Frontiers: southern African archaeology today*. Oxford, BAR International Series 207, pp. 344–8.
Avery, G., Avery, D. M., Graine, S. G. and Loutit, R. 1984. 'Bone accumulations by hyenas and jackals: a taphonomic study', *South African Journal of Science* 80: 186–7.

Bachelet, M. T. 1885 (first edn 1868). *Histoire ancienne. Grecque et romaine. Classes de 6e, 5e et 4e* (10th edn). Paris, Librairie Classique de A. Courcier.

Bachofen, J. J. 1967 (first edn 1861). 'Mother right', in Marx, R., ed., *Myth, religion and mother right: selected writings of J. J. Bachofen*. Princeton, Princeton University Press.

Baer, K. E. von 1828. *Entwicklungsgeschichte der Thiere*. Königsberg, Bornträger.

Bandini, S. and Baldwin, P. J. 1978. 'An encounter between chimpanzees and a leopard in Senegal', *Carnivore* 1: 107–9.

Barsanti, G. 1990. 'Storia naturalle delle scimmie, 1600–1800', *Nuncius. Annali di Storia della Scienza* 5: 99–165.

Bartholomew, G. A. and Birdsell, J. 1953. 'Ecology and the protohominids', *American Anthropologist* 55: 481–96.

Batten, D. C. 1986. 'Bipedalism revised', *Journal of Anthropological Research* 42: 81–2.

Bayanov, D. and Bourtsev, I. 1976. 'On Neanderthal vs. Paranthropus', *Current Anthropology* 17: 310–14.

Bayard, D. T. 1969. 'Science, theory and reality in the "new archaeology"', *American Antiquity* 34: 376–84.

Bazylevic, K., Bahrushyn, S., Pankratova, A. and Focht, A. 1954 (first Russian edn 1952). *Historia ZSRR [History of the USSR]* (Polish translation). Warsaw, Panstwowy Zaklad Wydawnictw Szkolnych.

Beck, B. 1980. *Animal tool use*. New York, Garland STMP Press.

1982. 'Chimpocentrism: bias in cognitive ethology', *Journal of Human Evolution* 11: 3–17.

Beer, G. 1983. *Darwin's plots: evolutionary narrative in Darwin, George Eliot, and nineteenth century fiction*. London, Routledge and Kegan Paul.

Behrensmeyer, A. K. 1978. 'Taphonomic and ecologic information from bone weathering', *Paleobiology* 4: 150–62.

1983. 'Pattern of natural bone distribution on recent land surfaces: implications for archaeological site formation', in Clutton-Brock, J. and Grigson, C., eds., *Animals and archaeology: hunters and their prey*. Oxford, BAR International Series 163, pp. 93–106.

Behrensmeyer, A. K., Gordon, K. D. and Yanagi, G. T. 1986. 'Trampling as a cause of bone surface damage and pseudo-cutmark', *Nature* 319: 768–71.

Behrensmeyer, A. K. and Hill, A. P., eds. 1980. *Fossils in the making: vertebrate taphonomy and paleoecology*. Chicago, University of Chicago Press.

Bekoff, M. 1972. 'The development of social interactions, play and metacommunication in mammals: an ethological perspective', *Quarterly Review of Biology* 47: 412–34.

Bernheimer, R. 1970. *Wild men in the Middle Ages*. New York, Octagon Books.

Binford, L. R. 1973. 'Interassemblage variability – the Mousterian and "functional" argument', in Renfrew, C., ed., *The explanation of culture change*. London, Duckworth, pp. 227–54.

1979. *Nunamiut ethnoarchaeology*. New York, Academic Press.
1981. *Bones, ancient men and modern myths*. New York, Academic Press.
Binford, L. R. and Bertram, J. B. 1977. 'Bone frequencies and attritional process', in Binford, L. R., ed., *For theory building in archaeology*. New York, Academic Press, pp. 77–153.
Binford, L. R. and Binford, S. 1966. 'A preliminary analysis of functional variability in the Mousterian of Levalloisian facies', *American Antiquity* 68: 238–341.
Binford, L. R., Mills, M. G. L. and Stone, N. M. 1988. 'Hyena scavenging behavior and its implications for interpretation of faunal assemblages from FLK 22 (the Zinj Floor) at Olduvai Gorge', *Journal of Anthropological Archaeology* 7: 1–99.
Blanckaert, C. 1991. 'Premier des singes, dernier des hommes?', *Alliage* 7–8: 113–29.
Bloch, M. 1993 (first edn 1949). *Apologie pour l'histoire, ou métier d'historien*. Paris, Armand Colin.
Blumenschine, R. J. 1986a. *Early hominid scavenging opportunities: implications of carcass availability in the Serengeti and Ngorongoro ecosystems*. Oxford, BAR International Series 283.
1986b. 'Carcass consumption sequences and the archaeological distinction of scavenging and hunting', *Journal of Human Evolution* 15: 639–59.
1987. 'Characteristics of early hominid scavenging niche', *Current Anthropology* 28: 383–407.
Blundell, S. 1986. *The origins of civilisation in Greek and Roman thought*. London, Croom Helm.
Boas, F. 1888. 'The Central Eskimo', *Annual Report of the Bureau of American Ethnology* 6: 399–669.
1940. 'Mythology and folk-tales of the North American Indians' (first edn 1914), in *Race, language and culture*. Chicago, University of Chicago Press, pp. 451–90.
Boas, G. 1948. *Essays on primitivism and related ideas in the Middle Ages*. Baltimore, Johns Hopkins University Press.
Boaz, N. T. 1977. 'Paleoecology of early Hominidae in Africa', *Kroeber Anthropological Society Papers* 50: 37–62.
Bodin, J. 1951 (first edn 1572). 'La méthode de l'histoire', in Mesnard, P., ed., *Corpus général des philosophes français*, vol. v. 3. Paris, PUF, pp. 101–473.
Boesch, C. and Boesch, H. 1983. 'Organisation of nut-cracking with natural hammers by wild chimpanzees', *Behavior* 3: 265–86.
1984. 'Possible causes of sex differences in the use of natural hammers by wild chimpanzees', *Journal of Human Evolution* 13: 415–40.
Bolk, L. 1926. 'On the problem of anthropogenesis', *Proceedings of the Section of Sciences, Kon. Akad. Wetens., Amsterdam* 29: 465–75.

Bondt, J. de 1658. 'Historiae naturalis et medicae Indiae orientalis libri sex', in Piso, G., ed., *De Indiae utriusque re naturali et medica*. Amsterdam, Danielem Elzevirios, pp. 50–86.

Bonnassie, P. 1989. 'Consommation d'aliments immondes et cannibalisme de survie dans l'Occident du haut Moyen Âge', *Annales. Economie, Société, Civilisation* 44: 1035–56.

Bonnefille, R. 1984. 'Palynological research at Olduvai Gorge', *National Geographic Research Reports* 17: 227–43.

  1985. 'Evolution of the continental vegetation: the palaeobotanical records from East Africa', *South African Journal of Science* 81: 267–70.

Bonneville, R. and Vincens, A. 1985. 'Apport de la palynologie à l'environnement des Hominidés d'Afrique Orientale', in Coppens, Y., ed., *L'environnement des hominidés au Plio-Pleistocene*. Paris, Masson, pp. 237–78.

Bordes, F. 1973. 'On the chronology and contemporaneity of different palaeolithic cultures in France', in Renfrew, C., ed., *The explanation of culture change*. London, Duckworth, pp. 217–26.

Borges, J. L. 1975. 'Utopiá de un hombre que está cansado', in *El libro de arena*. Buenos Aires, Emecé Editores.

Boriskovski, P. I. 1979. *Drevneiseie proshloe tchelovechestva* [*Ancient past of man*]. Leningrad, Nauka.

Bory de Saint-Vincent, J.-B.-G.-M. 1825. 'Homme', in Bory de Saint-Vincent, J.-B.-G.-M., ed., *Dictionnaire classique d'histoire naturelle*, vol. VIII. Paris, Rey et Gravier, pp. 269–346.

  1827. 'Orang', in Bory de Saint-Vincent, J.-B.-G.-M., ed., *Dictionnaire classique d'histoire naturelle*, vol. XII. Paris, Rey et Gravier, pp. 261–85.

Bossuet, J.-B. 1722. *Introduction à la philosophie, ou de la connoissance de Dieu et de soi-même*. Paris, Gabriel Amaulry.

  1966 (first edn 1681). *Discours sur l'histoire universelle*. Paris, Garnier-Flammarion.

Boulanger, N.-A. 1766. *L'antiquité dévoilée par ses usages*. Amsterdam, Marc-Michel Rey.

Bowler, P. J. 1986. *Theories of human evolution*. Baltimore, Johns Hopkins University Press.

  2001. 'Myths, narratives and the uses of history', in Roebroeks, W. and Corbey, R., eds., *Studying human origins: the uses of disciplinary history and epistemology*. Amsterdam, Amsterdam University Press, pp. 9–20.

Brace, C. L. 1963. 'Structural reduction in evolution', *American Naturalist*, 97: 39–49.

Brace, C. L. and Montagu, M. F. A. 1965. *Man's evolution: an introduction to physical anthropology*. New York, Macmillan.

Brain, C. K. 1967. 'Hottentot food remains and their meaning in the interpretation of fossil bone assemblages', *Scientific Papers of the Namib Desert Research Station* 32: 1–11.

  1981. *The hunters or the hunted? An introduction to African cave taphonomy*. Chicago, University of Chicago Press.

Breyne, J. P. 1741. 'Observations, and a description of some mammoth's bones dug up in Siberia, proving them to have belonged to elephants', *Philosophical Transactions* 1737, 1738: 124–39.

Britten, R. J. and Davidson, E. H. 1971. 'Repetitive and non repetitive DNA sequences and a speculation on the origin of evolutionary novelty', *Quaternary Review of Biology* 46: 111–31.

Brogniart, M. 1817. 'Cavernes', in Cuvier, F., ed., *Dictionnaire des sciences naturelles*, vol. VII. Paris, Levrault, F. G. Le Normant, pp. 298–309.

Brown, F. H. 1981. 'Environments in the lower Omo basin from one to four million years ago', in Rapp, G. and Vondra, C. F., eds., *Hominid sites: their geologic settings*. Boulder, CO, Westview Press, pp. 149–63.

Brunet, M. *et al.* 1995. 'The first Australopithecine 2,500 kilometres west of the Rift Valley (Chad)', *Nature* 378: 273–5.

Bryson, G. 1945. *Man and society: the Scottish inquiry of the eighteenth century*. Princeton, Princeton University Press.

Buckland, W. 1823. *Reliquiae diluvianae*. London, John Murray.

Buffon, G.-L., comte de 1825a (first edn 1764). 'De la nature. Première vue', in *Histoire naturelle*, vol. I. Paris, Ménard et Desenne, Fils, pp. 150–68.

1825b (first edn 1778). 'Des époques de la nature', in *Histoire naturelle*, vol. II. Paris, Ménard et Desenne, Fils, pp. 1–347.

1825c (first edn 1753). 'Des animaux domestiques', in *Histoire naturelle*, vol. VIII. Paris, Ménard et Desenne, Fils, pp. 1–7.

1825d (first edn 1753). 'De l'âne', in *Histoire naturelle*, vol. VIII. Paris, Ménard et Desenne, Fils, pp. 136–71.

1825e (first edn 1758). 'Des animaux carnassiers', in *Histoire naturelle*, vol. IX. Paris, Ménard et Desenne, Fils, pp. 131–80.

1825f (first edn 1766). 'Nomenclature des singes', in *Histoire naturelle*, vol. XIII. Paris, Ménard et Desenne, Fils, pp. 34–88.

1825g (first edn 1766). 'Les orangs-outangs ou le pongo et le jocko', in *Histoire naturelle*, vol. 13. Paris, Ménard et Desenne, Fils, pp. 89–113.

1831 (first edn 1749). 'Variétés dans l'espèce humaine', in Cuvier, F., ed., *Œuvres complètes de Buffon*, vol. I. Paris, Pillot, pp. 185–441.

1954 (first edn 1749). 'De la nature de l'homme', in *Œuvres complètes de Buffon*, vol. VIII. Paris, PUF.

1984 (first edn 1749). 'De l'âge viril', in *Histoire naturelle* (texts selected by J. Varloot). Paris, Gallimard, pp. 91–7.

Bunn, H. T. 1981. 'Archaeological evidence for meat-eating by Plio-Pleistocene hominids from Koobi-Fora and Olduvai Gorge', *Nature* 291: 574–7.

1983. 'Comparative analysis of modern bone assemblages from San hunter-gatherer camp in the Kalahari Desert, Botswana, and from spotted hyena den near Nairobi, Kenya', in Clutton-Brock, J. and Grigson, C., eds., *Animals and archaeology: hunters and their prey*. Oxford, BAR International Series 163, pp. 143–8.

1986. 'Patterns of skeletal representation and hominid subsistence activities at Olduvai Gorge, Tanzania', *Journal of Human Evolution* 15: 637–90.

Bunn, H. T., Bartram, L. E. and Kroll, E. M. 1988. 'Variability in bone assemblage formations from Hadza hunting, scavenging and carcass processing', *Journal of Anthropological Archaeology* 7: 412–57.

Bunn, H. T. and Kroll, E. M. 1986. 'Systematic butchering by Plio-Pleistocene hominids at Olduvai Gorge, Tanzania', *Current Anthropology* 27: 431–52.

Burnet, J. 1774–92. *Of the origin and progress of language*. Edinburgh, J. Balfour.

Cabanis, P. J. G. 1959 (first edn 1802). 'Rapport du physique et du moral de l'homme', in Cazeneuve, J., ed., *Œuvres philosophiques de Cabanis*. Paris, PUF, pp. 105–631.

Cadman, A. and Rayner, R. 1989. 'Climatic change and the appearance of *Australopithecinae africanus* in the Makapansgat sediments', *Journal of Human Evolution* 18: 107–13.

Calvino, I. 1971. 'La combinatoire et le mythe dans l'art du récit', *Esprit* 402: 678–83.

Capitan, L. 1901. 'La première hache acheuléenne connue', *Revue de l'Ecole d'Anthropologie de Paris* 11: 219–26.

Cartailhac, E. 1889. *La France préhistorique*. Paris, F. Alcan.

Casanova, G. J. 1986 (first edn 1826–38). *Histoire de ma vie* (texts selected by J.-M. Gadair). Paris, Gallimard.

Chambon, A. and Pouliqueu, R., eds. 1986. *Collection Grell*. Paris, Editions Casteilla.

Charnov, E. L. 1986. 'Group selection revisited', *Nature* 321: 23–4.

Chaumeil, J.-P. 1989. 'Du végétal à l'humain', *Annales de la Fondation Fyssen* 4: 15–24.

Chavaillon, J. 1986. 'Premiers outils et vie en société', in Sakka, M., ed., *Définition et origine de l'homme*. Paris, Editions du CNRS, pp. 309–15.

Cioran, E. M. 1960. *Histoire et Utopie*. Paris, Gallimard.

Clark, J. D. 1959. *The Prehistory of Southern Africa*. Baltimore, Penguin.

1964. 'Comment on Hockett and Ascher "The human revolution"', *Current Anthropology* 5: 155–6.

Clébert, J.-P. 1971. *Bestiaire fabuleux*. Paris, Albin Michel.

Clifford, J. and Marcus, G. E. 1986. *Writing culture*. Berkeley, University of California Press.

Clutton-Brock, J. and Grigson, C., eds. 1983. *Animals and archaeology: hunters and their prey*. Oxford, BAR International Series 163.

Cody, M. L. 1974. 'Optimisation in ecology', *Science* 183: 1156–64.

Cohen, C. 1994. *Le destin du mammouth*. Paris, Seuil.

Cole, T. 1967. *Democritus and the sources of Greek anthropology*. Cleveland, Press of Western Reserve University.

Comte, A. 1963 (first edn 1844). *Discours sur l'esprit positif*. Paris, Union Générale d'Editions.

Conan-Doyle, A. 1992 (first edn 1890). 'The sign of four', in *The adventures of Sherlock Holmes*. Ware, Wordsworth Editions, pp. 64–113.

Condillac, E. de 1821 (first edn 1792). *Essai sur l'origine des connaissances humaines*. Paris, Lecointe and Durey.

Condorcet, M.-J.-A. Caritat, marquis de. 1971 (manuscript of 1793). *Esquisse d'un tableau historique des progrès de l'esprit humain.* Paris, Editions Sociales.
Coon, C. S. 1955 (first edn 1954). *The history of man from the first human to primitive culture and beyond.* London, Jonathan Cape.
  1964. 'Comments on Hocket and Ascher "The human evolution"', *Current Anthropology* 5: 156.
Coppens, Y. 1975. 'Évolution des hominidés et de leur environnement au cours du Plio-Pléistocène dans la basse vallée de l'Omo en Ethiopie', *Comptes Rendus de l'Académie des Sciences* 281, series B: 1693–6.
  1984. 'Hominoïdés, hominidés et hommes', *Comptes Rendus de l'Académie des Sciences*, série générale 1: 459–68.
  1985 (ed.). *L'environnement des hominidés au Plio-Pléistocène.* Paris, Masson.
Coppens, Y., Howell, F. C., Isaac, G. L. and Leakey, R. E. F., eds. 1976. *Earliest man and environment in the Lake Rudolf Basin.* Chicago, University of Chicago Press.
Corbey, R. and Theunissen, B., eds. 1995. *Ape, man, apeman: changing views since 1600.* Leiden, Department of Prehistory, Leiden University.
Courbin, P. 1982. *Qu'est-ce que l'archéologie? Essai sur la nature de la recherche archéologique.* Paris, Payot.
Court de Gébelin, A. 1773–82. *Monde primitif analysé et comparé avec le monde moderne.* Paris, L'Auteur.
Cruwys, E. and Foley, R. A. 1986. *Teeth in anthropology.* Oxford, BAR International Series.
Cubitt, G. T. 1989. 'Conspiracy myths and conspiracy theories', *Journal of the Anthropological Society of Oxford* 20: 12–26.
Cuvier, G. 1798. *Tableau élémentaire de l'histoire naturelle des animaux.* Paris, Baudouin.
Daniel, G. 1964. *The idea of prehistory.* London, Penguin Books.
Dart, R. A. 1953. 'The predatory transition from ape to man', *International Anthropological and Linguistic Review* 1: 201–19.
Darwin, C. 1859. *On the origin of species.* London, John Murray.
  1871. *The descent of man, and selection in relation to sex*, 2 vols. London, John Murray.
Daubenton, M. J. L. (undated manuscript, written before 1764). *Discours sur la conformation des singes.* Paris, Bibliothèque du Muséum National d'Histoire Naturelle, Paris, MS 870.
Dawkins, R. 1976. *The selfish gene.* Oxford, Oxford University Press.
Delamétherie, J.-C. 1802. *De l'homme considéré moralement, de ses mœurs et de celles des animaux.* Paris, Maradan.
Delumeau, J. 1978. *La peur en Occident.* Paris, Fayard.
de Waal, F. M. B. 1989. 'Food-sharing and reciprocal obligations among chimpanzees', *Journal of Human Evolution* 18: 433–59.
Diderot, D. 1754 (first edn 1753). *Pensées sur l'interprétation de la nature.* Anonymous publisher.
  1972 (first edn 1773–4). *Supplément au voyage de Bougainville.* Paris, Garnier-Flammarion.

1994 (text written between 1778 and 1780). 'Eléments de physiologie', in Versini, L., ed., *Diderot. Œuvres*, vol. I, *Philosophie*. Paris, Robert Laffont, pp. 1261–317.

1994 (first edn 1782). 'Le rêve d'Alembert', in Versini, L., ed., *Diderot. Œuvres*, vol. I, *Philosophie*. Paris, Robert Laffont, pp. 624–68.

Dike, C. 1985. 'Complexity and closure', in Depew, D. J. and Weber, B. H., eds., *Evolution at the crossroads*. Cambridge, MA, The MIT Press, pp. 97–132.

Diodorus Siculus 1737. *Histoire universelle*. Paris, de Bure.

Doolittle, W. F. and Sapienza, C. 1980. 'Selfish genes, the phenotype paradigm, and genome evolution', *Nature* 284: 601–3.

Driver, H. E. 1961. *Indians of North America*. Chicago, University of Chicago Press.

Duchet, M. 1971. *Anthropologie et histoire au siècle des Lumières*. Paris, Maspero.

Duchin, L. E. 1990. 'The evolution of articulate speech: comparative anatomy of the oral cavity in *Pan* and *Homo*', *Journal of Human Evolution* 19: 687–97.

du Cleuziou, H. 1887. *La création de l'homme et les premiers âges de l'humanité*. Paris, Flammarion.

Dudley, E. and Novak, M. E. 1972. *The wild man within: an image in Western thought from Renaissance to Romanticism*. Pittsburgh, University of Pittsburgh Press.

Dunbar, J. 1780. *Essays on the history of mankind in rude and cultivated ages*. London, W. Strahan.

Dunbar, R. 1989. 'Common ground for thought', *New Scientist* 1646: 48–50.

Dunbar, R. I. M. 1988. *Primate social systems*. London, Croom Helm.

Dunnell, R. C. 1971. *Systematics in prehistory*. New York, Academic Press.

Durkheim, E. 1973 (first edn 1895). *Les règles de la méthode sociologique*. Paris, PUF.

Ehrard, J. 1970. *L'idée de nature en France à l'aube des Lumières*. Paris, Flammarion.

Eldredge, N. 1986. *Time frames: the rethinking of Darwinian evolution and the theory of punctuated equilibria*. London, Heinemann.

Eldredge, N. and Gould, S. J. 1972. 'Punctuated equilibria: an alternative to phyletic gradualism', in Schropf, T. J. M., ed., *Models in paleobiology*. San Francisco, Freeman, Coopen and Co., pp. 82–115.

Eliade, M. 1965. *Le sacré et le profane*. Paris, Gallimard.

1973. *Fragments d'un journal*. Paris, Gallimard.

Eloy, M. 1988. 'Archéologie et décors de cinéma: le forum romain, dans "Cléopâtre" ', in Lequeux, B., ed., *L'archéologie et son image*, VIIIe Rencontres internationales d'archéologie et d'histoire, Antibes, 1987. Juan-les-Pins, Association pour la promotion et la diffusion des connaissances archéologiques, pp. 239–60.

Engels, F. 1945. 'Mowa nad grobem Karola Marksa' [Funeral oration at the burial of K. Marx], in Marx, K. and Engels, F., *Dziela wybrane*. Warsaw, Ksiazka i Wiedza, vol. II, p. 155.

1971 (first edn 1896). 'Le rôle du travail dans la transformation du singe en homme', in Calvet, J.-L., ed., *Marxisme et linguistique*. Paris, Payot, pp. 55–75.

Estioko-Griffin, A. and Griffin, B. P. 1981. ' "Woman the hunter": the Agta', in Dahlberg, F., ed., *Woman the gatherer*. New Haven, Yale University Press, pp. 121–51.

Fagan, R. 1974. 'Selective and evolutionary aspects of animal play', *American Naturalist* 108: 850-8.
Falk, D. 1980. 'A reanalysis of the South African Australopithecinae natural endocast', *American Journal of Physical Anthropology* 53: 525-39.
  1983. 'Cerebral cortices of East African early hominids', *Science* 221: 1072-4.
Ferguson, A. 1767. *An essay on the history of civil society*. London, A. Millar and T. Caddel.
Ferro, M. 1981. *Comment on raconte l'histoire aux enfants*. Paris, Payot.
Fischer, D. H. 1970. *Historians' fallacies*. New York, Harper and Row.
Flannery, R. 1932. 'The position of woman among the Mescalero Apache', *Primitive Man* 5: 26-32.
  1935. 'The position of woman among the Eastern Cree', *Primitive Man* 8: 81-6.
Flaubert, G. 1978 (first edn 1922). *Dictionnaire des idées reçues*. Paris, Aubier Montaigne.
Foley, R. 1983. 'Modeling hunting strategies and inferring predator behavior from prey attributes', in Clutton-Brock, J. K. and Grigson, C., eds., *Animals and archaeology: hunters and their prey*. Oxford: BAR International Series 163, pp. 63-76.
  1994. 'Speciation, extinction and climatic change in hominid evolution', *Journal of Human Evolution* 26: 275-89.
Fourier, C. 1841. *Œuvres complètes*. Paris, Bureaux de la Phalange.
Gaignebet, C. and Lajoux, D. J. 1985. *Art profane et religion populaire au moyen âge*. Paris, PUF.
Galdikas, B. M. F. 1982. 'Orang-utan tool-use at Tanjung Puting Reserve, Central Indonesia Borneo', *Journal of Human Evolution* 11: 19-33.
Galdikas, B. M. F. and Teleki, G. 1981. 'Variations in subsistence activities of female and male pongids: new perspectives on the origins of hominid labor division', *Current Anthropology* 22: 241-56.
Garcilaso de la Vega 1982 (first edn 1603). *Commentaires royaux sur le Pérou des Incas*. Paris, Maspero/La Découverte.
Gardin, J.-C. 1980. *Archaeological constructs: an aspect of archaeological theory*. Cambridge, Cambridge University Press.
  1985. 'Sémiologie et informatique', *Degrés* 42-3: 1-23.
  1992. 'Semiotic trends in archaeology', in Gardin, J.-C. and Peebles, C. S., eds., *Representations in archaeology*. Bloomington, Indiana University Press, pp. 87-104.
Gardin, J.-C. and Lagrange, M.-S. 1975. *Essai d'analyse du discours archéologique*. Paris, Editions du CNRS.
Gardner, H. 1985. *The mind's new science: a history of the cognitive revolution*. New York, Basic Books.
Gardner, R. A. and Gardner, B. 1969. 'Teaching sign-language to a chimpanzee', *Science* 165: 664-72.
Gaudant, J. and Gaudant, M. 1971. *Les théories classiques de l'évolution*. Paris, Dunod.
Geertz, C. 1993 (first edn 1983). *Local knowledge*. London, Fontana Press.

Gifford-Gonzales, D. 1989. 'Shipman's shaky foundations', *American Anthropologist* 91: 180–6.
Gilk, J. B. 1978. 'Patterns of food-sharing among mother and infant chimpanzees at Gombe National Park, Tanzania', *Folia Primatologica* 29: 129–41.
Goethe, J. W. 1890. *Faust* (translated by Bayard Taylor). London, Ward, Lock & Co.
Goguet, A.-Y. 1758. *De l'origine des loix, des arts, et des sciences, et de leurs progrès chez les anciens peuples*. Paris, Desaint and Saillot.
Goodall, J. 1964. 'Tool-using and aimed throwing in a community of free-living chimpanzees', *Nature* 201: 1264–6.
  1986. *The chimpanzees of Gombe: patterns of behavior*. Cambridge, MA, Harvard University Press.
Goodale, J. C. 1971. *Tiwi wives*. Seattle, University of Washington Press.
Gould, S. J. 1977. *Ontogeny and phylogeny*. Cambridge, MA, Belknap Press.
  1982. 'Darwinism and the expansion of evolutionary theory', *Science* 216: 380–7.
  1983. 'The hardening of the modern synthesis', in Grene, M., ed., *Dimensions of Darwinism*. Cambridge, Cambridge University Press, pp. 71–93.
  1991. 'Fall in the house of Ussher', *Natural History* 11: 12–21.
Gould, S. J. and Eldredge, N. 1977. 'Punctuated equilibria: the tempo and mode of evolution reconsidered', *Paleobiology* 3: 115–51.
Gould, S. J. and Lewontin, R. C. 1979. 'The spandrels of San Marco and the Panglossian paradigm: a critique of the adaptationism programme', *Proceedings of the Royal Society of London*, B 205: 581–98.
Gould, S. J. and Pilbeam, D. 1974. 'Size and scaling in human evolution', *Science* 186: 892–901.
Gould, S. J. and Vrba, E. 1982. 'Exaptation: a missing term in the science of form', *Paleobiology* 8: 4–15.
Gouletquer, P. 1988. 'La préhistoire mise en scène', in Lequeux, B., ed., *L'archéologie et son image*, VIIIe Rencontres internationales d'archéologie et d'histoire, Antibes, 1987. Juan-les-Pins, Association pour la promotion et la diffusion des connaissances archéologiques, pp. 165–83.
Gralhon, R. 1975. *Notre pays dans la préhistoire*. Paris, L'Ecole.
  1986. *Histoire de la France, cycle moyen*. Paris, L'Ecole.
Granger, E. 1922. *Nouvelle géographie universelle*. Paris, Hachette.
Grayson, D. K. 1983. *The establishment of human antiquity*. New York, Academic Press.
Greenblatt, S. 1991. *Marvellous possessions: the wonder of the New World*. Oxford, Oxford University Press.
Greene, J. C. 1957. *The death of Adam: evolution and its impact on Western thought*. Ames, Iowa State University Press.
Greenwood, D. J. 1984. *The taming of evolution: the persistence of nonevolutionary views in the study of humans*. Ithaca, NY, Cornell University Press.
Gregory of Nyssa 1944. *La création de l'homme* (translated by J. Laplace). Paris, Editions du Cerf.

Griffin, D. R. 1984. *Animal thinking*. Cambridge, MA, Harvard University Press.
Gusdorf, G. 1971. *Les principes de la pensée au siècle des Lumières*. Paris, Payot.
Guthrie, W. K. C. 1957. *In the beginnings: some Greek views on the origins of life and the early state of man*. London, Methuen.
Haeckel, E. 1868. *Histoire de la création des êtres organisés d'après les lois naturelles*. Paris, Reinwald et Cie.
　　1900. *Etat actuel de nos connaissances sur l'origine de l'homme, Mémoire présenté au 4e Congrès international de zoologie à Cambridge, 1898*. Paris, Reinwald et Cie.
Hale, M. 1677. *The primitive origination of mankind*. London, William Godbid.
Hamilton III, W. J. and Curt, B. 1982. 'Social dominance and predatory behavior of Chacuna Baboon', *Journal of Human Evolution* 11: 567–73.
Hanson, C. B. 1980. 'Fluvial taphonomic processes: models and experiments', in Behrensmeyer, A. K. and Hill, A. P., eds., *Fossils in the making*. Chicago, University of Chicago Press, pp. 156–81.
Haraiwa-Hasegawa, M., Byrne, R. W., Takasaki, H. and Byrne, J. M. E. 1986. 'Aggression towards large carnivores by wild chimpanzees of Mahale Mountains National Park, Tanzania', *Folia Primatologica* 47: 8–13.
Haraucourt, E. 1988 (first edn 1914). *Daâh, le premier homme*. Paris, Arléa.
Harding, R. 1975. 'Meat-eating and hunting in baboons', in Tuttle, R., ed., *Socioecology and psychology of primates*. The Hague, Mouton Publishers, pp. 245–57.
　　1981. 'An order of omnivores: nonhuman primate diets in the wild', in Harding, R. and Teleki, G., eds., *Omnivorous primates: gathering and hunting in human evolution*. New York, Columbia University Press, pp. 191–214.
Hardy, A. 1960. 'Was man more aquatic in the past?', *New Scientist* 7: 642–5.
Harris, J. W. K. 1986. 'Découverte du matériel archéologique oldowayen dans le Rift de l'Afar', *L'Archéologie* 90: 339–57.
Hart, T. and Hart, J. A. 1986. 'The ecological basis of hunter-gatherer subsistence in African rain forest: the Mbuti of eastern Zaïre', *Human Ecology* 14: 29–55.
Hartley, D. 1749. *Observations on Man, his frame, his duty, and his expectations*. London, J. Johnson.
Hastings, H. 1936. *Man and beast in French thought of the eighteenth century*. Baltimore, Johns Hopkins University Press.
Hayden, B. 1981. 'Subsistence and ecological adaptations of modern hunter-gatherers', in Harding, R. and Teleki, G., eds., *Omnivorous primates: gathering and hunting in human evolution*. New York, Columbia University Press, pp. 344–421.
Haynes, G. 1980. 'Evidence of carnivore gnawing on Pleistocene and recent mammalians bones', *Paleobiology* 6: 341–51.
　　1983. 'A guide to differentiating mammalia carnivore taxa responsible for gnawing damage to herbivore limb bones', *Paleobiology* 9: 164–72.
　　1988a. 'Longitudinal studies of African elephant death and bone deposits', *Journal of Archaeological Science* 15: 131–52.

1988b. 'Mass death and serial predation: comparative taphonomic studies of modern large mammal death sites', *Journal of Archaeological Science* 15: 219–35.
Helvétius, C.-A. 1773. *De l'homme, de ses facultés intellectuelles et de son éducation*. London, Société typographique.
1988 (first edn 1758). *De l'esprit*. Paris, Fayard.
Herder, J. G. 1800 (first edn 1784–91). *Outlines of a philosophy of the history of man* (trans. T. Churchill). London.
Hesiod 1960. 'Les travaux et les jours', in *Théogonie, les Travaux et les Jours, le Bouclier* (trans. M. Mazon). Paris, Les Belles Lettres.
Hewes, G. W. 1961. 'Food transport and origins of human bipedalism', *American Anthropologist* 63: 687–710.
1975. *Language origins: a bibliography*. The Hague, Mouton Publishers.
Hildegard of Bingen, 1989. *Le livre des subtilités des créatures divines: physique*. Grenoble, Jérôme Millon.
Hill, A. P. 1972. 'Taphonomy of contemporary and late Cenozoic East African vertebrates', PhD thesis, University of London.
1979. 'Disarticulation and scattering of mammal skeletons', *Paleobiology* 5: 261–74.
1981. 'A modern hyena den in Amboseli National Park, Kenya', *Proceedings of the Pan-African Congress of Prehistoric and Quaternary Studies*. Nairobi.
1983. 'Hyenas and early hominids', in Clutton-Brock, J. and Grigson, C., eds., *Animals and archaeology*. Oxford, BAR International Series 163, pp. 87–92.
1987. 'Causes of perceived faunal change in the later Neogene of East Africa', *Journal of Human Evolution* 16: 583–96.
Hill, K. 1982. 'Hunting and human evolution', *Journal of Human Evolution* 11: 521–44.
Hilton, J. D., ed. 1988. *Contemporary science and natural explanation: commonsense conceptions of causality*. London, Harvester Press.
Hippocrates 1964. 'Des airs, des eaux, des lieux', in Joly, R., ed., *Hippocrate: médecine grecque*. Paris, Gallimard, pp. 74–87.
Ho, M. W. and Sanders, D. T. 1979. 'Beyond neodarwinism. An epigenetic approach to evolution', *Journal of Theoretical Biology* 78: 573–91.
Hobbes, T. 1996 (first edn 1651). *Leviathan*. Oxford, Oxford University Press.
Hockett, C. F. and Ascher, R. 1964. 'The human revolution', *Current Anthropology* 5: 135–68.
Hodder, I. 1986. *Reading the past*. Cambridge, Cambridge University Press.
1989. 'Writing archaeology: site reports in context', *Antiquity* 63: 268–74.
Hodgen, M. T. 1964. *Early anthropology in the sixteenth and seventeenth centuries*. Philadelphia, University of Pennsylvania Press.
Holbach, P.-H., baron de 1786. *De l'état naturel des peuples*. Paris, Veuve Hérissant.
1821 (first edn 1770). *De la nature ou des lois du monde physique et du monde moral*. Paris, Etienne Ledoux.
1822 (first edn 1773). *Système social ou principes naturels de la morale et de la politique avec un examen de l'influence du gouvernement sur les mœurs*. Paris, Noigret.

Holloway, R. L. 1967. 'Tools and teeth: some speculations regarding canine reduction', *American Anthropologist* 69: 63–7.
  1983. 'Cerebral brain endocast pattern of *Australopithecus afarensis* hominids', *Nature* 303: 420–2.
Holloway, R. L. and Coste-Lareymondie, M. C. de la 1982. 'Brain endocast assymetry in pongids and hominids: some preliminary findings on the paleontology of cerebral dominance', *American Journal of Physical Anthropology* 58: 101–10.
Home, H. 1774. *Sketches of the history of mankind*. Edinburgh, W. Creech.
Homer 1946. *The Odyssey* (trans. E. V. Rieu). London, The Folio Society.
Horace 1932. *Satires* (trans. G. Budé). Paris, G. Budé.
Huffman, M. A. 1984. 'Stone play of *Macaca fuscata* in Arashuyama B troop: transmission of a non-adaptive behavior', *Journal of Human Evolution* 13: 725–35.
Hugo, V. 1972 (first edn 1887). *Choses vues, 1830–1846*. Paris, Gallimard.
Hull, D. L. 1980. 'Individuality and selection', *Annual Review of Ecology and Systematics* 11: 311–32.
Hume, D. 1896 (first edn 1739). *Treatise of human nature*. Oxford, Selby-Bigge.
Husband, T. 1980. *The wild man: medieval myth and symbolism*. New York, The Metropolitan Museum of Art.
Innocent III 1855. 'De contemptu mundi', in Migne, J.-P., ed., *Patrologiae cursus completus*, vol. 217. Paris, J.-P. Migne, pp. 702–46.
Isaac, G. L. 1976. 'The African hominids: review of archaeological evidences from time span two and a half to one million years ago', in Isaac, G. L. and McCown, E., eds., *Human origins*. Menlo Park, CA, A Staples Press Book, pp. 489–520.
  1978a. 'The food-sharing behavior of proto-human Hominida', *Scientific American* 238: 90–108.
  1978b. 'Food-sharing and human evolution: archaeological evidence from the Plio-Pleistocene of East Africa', *Journal of Anthropological Research* 34: 311–25.
  1983. 'Bones in contention: competing explanations for the juxtaposition of Early Pleistocene artifacts and faunal remains', in Clutton-Brock, J. and Grigson, C., eds., *Animals and archaeology: hunters and their prey*. Oxford, BAR International Series 163, pp. 3–20.
  1986. 'Foundation stones: early artifacts as indicators of activities and abilities', in Bailey, G. and Callow, R., eds., *Stone Age prehistory*. Cambridge, Cambridge University Press, pp. 221–41.
Isaac, G. L. and Crader, D. 1981. 'To what extent were early hominids carnivorous? An archaeological perspective', in Harding, R. and Teleki, G., eds., *Omnivorous primates: gathering and hunting in human evolution*. New York, Columbia University Press, pp. 37–103.
Jacob, F. 1981. *Le jeu des possibles*. Paris, Fayard.
Jaucourt, le chevalier de 1969 (first edn 1751–72). Article 'Sens commun', vol. XV, pp 27–8, in *Encyclopédie, ou Dictionnaire raisonné des sciences, des arts et des métiers*. New York, Pergamon Press, vol. III, p. 493.

Jennes, D. 1922. 'The life of the Copper Eskimos', *Report of the Canadian Arctic Expedition 1913–1918*, vol. XII. Ottawa, F. A. Acland.
Jerison, H. J. 1973. *The evolution of the brain and intelligence*. New York, Academic Press.
Jolly, C. 1970. 'The seed-eaters: a new model of hominid differentiation based on baboon analogy', *Man* 5: 5–26.
Jones, C. B. and Sabater, P. 1969. 'Sticks used by chimpanzees in Rio Muni, West Africa', *Nature* 223: 100–1.
Jones, T. B. and Kamil, A. C. 1973. 'Tool-making and tool-using in the northern blue jay', *Science* 180: 1076–7.
Jordan, C. 1982. 'Object manipulation and tool-use in captive pygmy chimpanzees (*Pan paniscus*)', *Journal of Human Evolution* 11: 35–9.
Jungers, W. L. 1978. 'On canine reduction in early hominids', *Current Anthropology* 19: 155–6.
Kant, I. 1985 (first edn 1786). 'Conjectures sur le commencement de l'histoire humaine', in Kant, I., *Œuvres complètes*, vol. II. Paris, Gallimard, pp. 502–20.
Kappler, C. 1980. *Monstres, démons et merveilles à la fin du moyen âge*. Paris, Payot.
Kawai, M. 1965. 'Newly acquired pre-cultural behavior of the natural troop of Japanese monkeys on Koshima Island', *Primates* 6: 1–30.
Keeley, L. H. 1980. *Experimental determination of stone tool uses: a microwear analysis*. Chicago, University of Chicago Press.
Keeley, L. H. and Toth, N. 1981. 'Microwear polishes on early stone tools from Koobi Fora, Kenya', *Nature* 293: 464–5.
Keene, A. S. 1983. 'Biology, behavior, and borrowing: a critical examination of optimal foraging theory in archaeology', in Moore, A. J. and Keene, A. S., eds., *Archaeological hammers and theories*. New York, Academic Press, pp. 137–55.
Kelso, J. and Quiatt, D. 1985. 'Household economics and hominid origins', *Current Anthropology* 26: 207–22.
Kingston, J. D., Marino, B. D. and Hill, A. 1994. 'Isotopic evidence for neogene hominid paleoenvironments in the Kenya Rift Valley', *Science* 264: 955–9.
Klahr, D. 1988. 'Dual space search during scientific reasoning', *Cognitive Science* 12: 1–48.
Klayman, J. and Ha, Y. 1987. 'Confirmation, disconfirmation and information in hypothesis testing', *Psychological Review* 94: 211–28.
Klein, R. G. 1975. 'Palaeoanthropological implications of the non-archaeological bone assemblage from Swartklip I, Southwestern Cape Province, South Africa', *Quaternary Research* 5: 275–88.
Köhler, W. 1959. *The mentality of apes*. New York, Vintage Books.
Kondo, S., Kawai, M. and Ehara, A., eds. 1975. *Contemporary primatology*. Basle, Larger.
Korovkin, F. 1974. *Historia starozytna dla klasy V* [*Ancient history, class 5*]. Kaunas, Sviesa.

Kortland, A. 1980. 'How might early hominids have defended themselves against large predators and food competitors', *Journal of Human Evolution* 9: 79-112.
Kortlandt, A. and Holzhaus, E. 1987. 'New data on the use of stone-tools by chimpanzees in Guinea and Liberia', *Primates* 28: 473-96.
Kühme, W. 1965. 'Communal food distribution and division of labour in African hunting dogs', *Nature* 205: 443-4.
Kuhn, T. 1969. 'Comment on the relations of science and art', *Comparative Studies in Science and History* 11: 403-12.
Kummer, H. 1971. *Primate societies*. Chicago, Aldine.
Kurland, J. A. and Beckerman, S. J. 1985. 'Optimal foraging and hominid evolution: labor and reciprocity', *American Anthropologist* 87: 73-93.
Lacépède, B.-G.-E. de la Ville, comte de 1821. 'L'homme', in Cuvier, F., ed., *Dictionnaire des sciences naturelles*, vol. 21. Paris, Levrault, Le Normant, pp. 329-409.
    1830. *Les âges de la nature et Histoire de l'espèce humaine*. Paris, Levrault.
Lactance 1987. *Institutions divines* (trans. P. Monat). Paris, Les Editions du Cerf.
Laitman, J. T. 1986. 'L'origine du langage articulé', *La Recherche* 181: 1164-73.
Lamarck, J.-B. 1809. *Philosophie zoologique*, 2 vols. Paris, Dentu.
    1820. *Système analytique des connaissances positives de l'homme*. Paris, J.-B. Baillère.
    1986 (first edn 1802). *Recherches sur l'organisation des corps vivants*. Paris, Fayard.
Landau, M. 1984. 'Human evolution as narrative', *American Scientist* 72: 262-8.
    1991. *Narratives of human evolution*. New Haven, Yale University Press.
Landes, R. 1938. *The Ojibwa women*. New York, Ams Press.
Latreille, P.-A. 1800. 'Mœurs, ruses, habitation, nourriture et durée des quadrumanes, vulgairement appelés singes', in Sonini, C. S., ed., *Histoire naturelle générale et particulière par Leclerc de Buffon*, vol. XXXVI. Paris, F. Dufart, pp. 247-66.
Laughlin, W. S. 1968. 'Hunting: an integrating behavior system and its evolutionary importance', in Lee, R. B. and DeVore, I., eds., *Man the hunter*. Chicago, Aldine, pp. 304-20.
Lawrence, W. 1849 (first edn 1819). *Lectures on comparative anatomy, physiology, zoology and the natural history of man*. London, Henry G. Bohn.
Leakey, L. S. B. 1967. 'Notes on the mammalian faunas from the Miocene and Pleistocene of East Africa', in Bishop, W. W. and Clark, J. D., eds., *Background to evolution in Africa*. Chicago, University of Chicago Press.
Le Brun, P.-D. (or Ecouchard-Le Brun) 1810 (first edn 1760). 'De la nature', in *Œuvres complètes*, vol. II. Paris, G. Warée.
Lee, R. B. 1979. *The !Kung San*. Cambridge, Cambridge University Press.
Lee, R. B. and DeVore, I., eds. 1968. *Man the hunter*. Chicago, Aldine.
Lefebure, L. 1982. 'Food exchange strategies in an infant chimpanzee', *Journal of Human Evolution* 11: 195-204.
Leffler, P. K. 1976. 'The "histoire raisonnée", 1660-1720: a pre-Enlightenment genre', *Journal of the History of Ideas* 37: 219-40.
Lenoble, R. 1968. *Esquisse d'une histoire de l'idée de nature*. Paris, Albin Michel.

Lenski, G. 1970. *Human societies: a macrolevel introduction to sociology*. New York, McGraw-Hill.
Leonard, W. R. and Hegmon, M. 1987. 'Evolution of P3 morphology in *Australopithecus afarensis*', *American Journal of Physical Anthropology* 73: 41–63.
Leroi-Gourhan, A. 1964. *Le geste et la parole: technique et langage*. Paris, Albin Michel.
Le Roy, C.-G. 1994a (first edn 1764). 'Lettre 3', in Anderson, E., ed., *Lettres sur les animaux*. Oxford, The Voltaire Foundation, pp. 93–101.
 1994b (first edn 1768). 'Lettre du physicien de Nuremberg', in Anderson, E., ed., *Lettres sur les animaux*. Oxford, The Voltaire Foundation, pp. 125–33.
 1994c (first edn 1768). 'Lettre du physicien de Nuremberg sur l'homme. Lettre première', in Anderson, E., ed., *Lettres sur les animaux*. Oxford, The Voltaire Foundation, pp. 144–51.
Leroy, L. 1988 (first edn 1575). *De la vicissitude ou variété des choses de l'Univers*. Paris, Fayard.
Lethmate, J. 1982. 'Tool-using skills of orang-outans', *Journal of Human Evolution* 11: 49–64.
Leutenegger, W. and Shell, B. 1987. 'Variability and sexual dimorphism in canine size of *Australopithecus* and extant hominoids', *Journal of Human Evolution* 16: 359–67.
Levin, H. 1969. *The myth of the Golden Age in the Renaissance*. Bloomington, Indiana University Press.
Lévi-Strauss, C. 1962. *La pensée sauvage*. Paris, Plon.
 1973. 'Race et histoire', in *Anthropologie structurale deux*. Paris, Plon, pp. 377–422.
 1966. *L'homme nu. Mythologiques*, vol. IV. Paris, Plon.
Lévi-Strauss, C. and Éribon, D. 1988. *De près et de loin*. Paris, Odile Jacob.
Lewontin, R. C. 1970. 'The units of selection', *Annual Review of Ecology and Systematics* 1: 1–16.
Lhermitte, F. 'La pensée sans langage', *Diogène* 117: 15–29.
Lindenberg, S. 1987. 'Common sense and social structure: a sociological view', in Holthoon, F. V. and Olson, D. R., eds., *Common sense: the foundations for social science*. Lanham, MD, University Press of America, pp. 199–215.
Livingstone, F. B. 1964. 'Comment on "The human revolution"', by C. F. Hockett and R. Ascher', *Current Anthropology* 5: 150–1.
Lloyd, G. E. R. 1974. *Le début de la science grecque*. Paris, Maspero.
Locke, J. 1947 (first edn 1690). 'An essay concerning the true original, extent and end of civil governement', in Baker, E., ed., *Social contracts: essays by Locke, Hume and Rousseau*. Oxford, Oxford University Press, pp. 1–206.
Lorenz, K. 1973. *Les huit péchés capitaux de notre civilisation*. Paris, Flammarion.
Lovejoy, A. O. 1948. 'The supposed primitivism of Rousseau's "Discourse on inequality"', in *Essays in the history of ideas*. Baltimore, Johns Hopkins University Press, pp. 14–37.
Lovejoy, A. O. and Boas, G. 1965 (first edn 1935). *Primitivism and related ideas in Antiquity*. Baltimore, Johns Hopkins University Press.
Lovejoy, C. O. 1981. 'The origin of man', *Science* 211: 341–50.
Lowie R. 1969 (first American edn 1920). *Traité de sociologie primitive*. Paris, Payot.

Lubbock, J. 1865. *Pre-historic times*. London, Williams and Norgate.
Lucretius 1900. *De rerum natura* (trans. H. A. J. Munro). London, Routledge & Sons.
Lumdsen, C. and Gushurst, A. C. 1985. 'Gene-culture coevolution: humankind in making', in Fetzer, J. H., ed., *Sociobiology and epistemology*. Dordrecht, R. Reidl Publishing Company, pp. 3–30.
Lumdsen, C. and Wilson, O. E. 1983. *Promethean fire: reflections on the origin of mind*. Cambridge, MA, Harvard University Press.
MacArthur, R. H. and Pianka, E. R. 1966. 'On optimal use of a patchy environment', *American Naturalist* 100: 603–9.
McGrew, W. C. 1974. 'Tool use by wild chimpanzees in feeding upon driver ants', *Journal of Human Evolution* 3: 501–8.
　　1975. 'Pattern of plant food-sharing in wild chimpanzees', in Kondo, S., Kawai, M. and Ehara, A., eds., *Contemporary primatology*. Basle, Larger, pp. 304–9.
　　1979. 'Evolutionary implications of sex differences in chimpanzees' predation and tool use', in Hamburg, D. A. and McCown, E. R., eds., *Perspectives on human evolution*, vol. V. Menlo Park, CA, Benjamin/Cummings, pp. 441–63.
　　1987. 'Tools to get food: the subsistences of Tasmania aborigines and Tanzania chimpanzees compared', *Journal of Anthropological Research* 43: 247–58.
　　1992. *Chimpanzee material culture: implications for human evolution*. Cambridge, Cambridge University Press.
Mahn-Lot, M. 1970. *La découverte de l'Amérique*. Paris, Flammarion.
Maillet, B. de 1984 (first edn 1749). *Telliamed*. Paris, Fayard.
Malthus, T. R. 1798. *An essay on the principle of population as it affects the future improvement of society*. London, J. Johnson.
Manly, J. M. 1897. *Specimens of pre-Shakespearian drama*. Boston, Ginn.
Manouvrier, L. 1897. 'On *Pithecanthropus erectus*', *American Journal of Science* 4: 213–34.
Marean, C. W. 1989. 'Sabertooth cats and their relevance for early hominid diet and evolution', *Journal of Human Evolution* 18: 559–82.
Martin, C. 1978. *Keepers of the game: Indian–animal relationship and the fur trade*. Berkeley, University of California Press.
Marshall, F. 1986. 'The implications of bone modification in a Neolithic faunal assemblage for the study of early hominid butchery and subsistence practice', *Journal of Human Evolution* 15: 661–72.
Marx, K. and Engels, F. 1968 (first edn 1846). *L'idéologie allemande*. Paris, Editions Sociales.
Mayr, E. 1963. *Animal species and evolution*. Cambridge, MA, Harvard University Press.
　　1989 (first American edn 1982). *Histoire de la biologie*. Paris, Fayard.
Meek, R. L. 1976. *Social science and the ignoble savage*. Cambridge, Cambridge University Press.

Menzel, E. W. Jr 1972. 'Spontaneous invention of ladders in a group of young chimpanzees', *Folia Primatologica* 17: 87–106.

Meun, J. de 1974. 'Le roman de la rose', in de Lorris, G. and de Meun, J., *Le roman de la rose*. Paris, Garnier-Flammarion, pp. 141–573.

Millar, J. 1979 (first edn 1771). 'The origin and the distinction of rank', in Meek, R. L., ed., *John Millar of Glasgow, 1735–1801*. New York, Arno Press, pp. 175–322.

Mills, M. G. L. and Mills, M. E. J. 1977. 'An analysis of bones collected at hyena breeding dens in the Gemsleak National Park', *Annals of the Transvaal Museum* 30: 145–55.

Milza, P., Bernstein, S. and Gauthier, Y. 1970. *Histoire: classe de 6e*. Paris, Nathan.

Molino, J. 1992. 'Archaeology and symbols', in Gardin, J.-C. and Peebles, C. S., eds., *Representations in archaeology*. Bloomington, Indiana University Press.

Mongait, A. L. 1962. 'Arkheologia i religia' [Archaeology and religion], *Sovietskaia Arkheologia* 2: 3–9.

Montagu, M. F. A. 1962. 'Time morphology and neoteny in the evolution of man', in Montagu, M. F. A., *Culture and the evolution of man*. Oxford, Oxford University Press, pp. 324–42.

Montesquieu, Charles de Secondat, baron de. 1979 (first edn 1748). *De l'esprit des lois*. Paris, Garnier-Flammarion.

Morin, E. 1973. *Le paradigme perdu: la nature humaine*. Paris, Seuil.

Mortier, R. 1982. *L'originalité: une nouvelle catégorie esthétique au siècle des Lumières*. Geneva, Droz.

Mortillet, G. de and Mortillet, A. de 1900. *La préhistoire: origine et antiquité de l'homme*. Paris, Schleicher Frères.

Moscovici, S. 1972. *La société contre nature*. Paris, Union Générale d'Edition.

Murdock, S. P. and Prevost, C. 1973. 'Factors in the division of labor by sex: a cross-cultural analysis', *Ethnology* 12: 203–25.

Myres, J. L. 1908. 'Herodotus and anthropology', in Marett, R. R., ed., *Anthropology and the Classics*. Oxford, Clarendon Press, pp. 121–68.

Nemesius 1844. *De la nature de l'homme* (trans. J.-B. Thibault). Paris, Hachette.

Nieckina, M. and Lejbengrub, P. 1984 (first edn 1982). *Historia ZSRR* [History of the USSR]. Kaunas, Sviesa.

Niestourkh, M. F. 1958. *Proiskhozhdienie tchelovieka* [Origin of man]. Moscow, Izdatielstvo Akademil Nauk SSSR.

Nishida, T. and Hiraiwa, M. 1982. 'Natural history of a tool-using behavior by wild chimpanzees in feeding upon wood-boring ants', *Journal of Human Evolution* 11: 73–99.

Nishida, T., Uehara, S. and Nyundo, R. 1978. 'Predatory behavior among wild chimpanzees of the Mahali Mountains', *Primates* 20: 1–20.

Oakhill, J. V. and Johnson-Laird, P. N. 1985. 'Rationality, memory and the search for counterexamples', *Cognition* 20: 79–94.

Oakley, K. 1957. 'Tools makyth man', *Antiquity* 31: 199–209.

  1968. 'The earliest tool-maker', in Gottfried, K., ed., *Evolution and hominisation*. Stuttgart, Gustav Fisher Verlag, pp. 257–72.

O'Connell, J. F., Hawkes, K. and Jones, N. B. 1988. 'Hadza hunting, butchering and the bone transport and their archaeological implications', *Journal of Anthropological Research* 44: 113–61.
Odum, H. T. 1971. *Fundamentals of ecology*. Philadelphia, Saunders.
Orgel, L. E. and Crick, F. H. C. 1980. 'Shellfish DNA: the ultimate parasite', *Nature* 284: 604–7.
Origen 1968. *Contre Celse* (trans. M. Borret). Paris, Les Editions du Cerf.
Osborn, H. F. 1926. 'Why Central Asia?', *Natural History* 26: 263–9.
Ourman, H., Zwang, A., Pasquier, Y. and Soletchnik, S. 1986. *Histoire: cours élémentaire, 2e année*. Paris, Casteilla.
Ovid 1969. *Metamorphoses* (trans. M. M. Innes). London, Penguin Classics.
Paley, W. 1802. *Natural Theology*. London, R. Faulder and Son.
Patrides, C. 1958. 'Renaissance ideas on man's upright form', *Journal of the History of Ideas* 19: 256–8.
Pausanias 1797. *Voyage historique de la Grèce* (trans. Abbé Geydon). Paris, Deborle.
Perlès, C. 1984. 'La préhistoire dans les manuels de 6e', *Histoire* 4: 90–1.
Perrault, C. 1676. *Suite des mémoires pour servir à l'histoire naturelle des animaux*. Paris, Imprimerie Royale.
Perry, R. J. 1989. 'Matrilineal descent in a hunting context: the Athapascan case', *Ethnology* 28: 33–52.
Petter, G. and Howell, C. F. 1985. 'Diversité des carnivores (*Mammalia, Carnivora*) dans les faunes du Pliocène moyen et supérieur d'Afrique orientale', in Coppens, Y., ed., *L'environnement des hominidés au Plio-Pléistocène*. Paris, Masson, pp. 133–49.
Pianka, E. R. 1974. *Evolutionary ecology*. New York, Harper and Row.
Plato 1871. 'Timaeus', in *The Dialogues of Plato*, vol. III (trans. B. Jowett). Oxford, Oxford University Press.
  1871. 'Protagoras', in *The Dialogues of Plato* (trans. B. Jowett). Oxford, Oxford University Press.
  1871. 'Menexenus', in *The Dialogues of Plato* (trans. B. Jowett). Oxford, Oxford University Press.
Pliny the Elder 1947. *Histoire naturelle*, book XI (trans. A. Ernont). Paris, Les Belles Lettres.
  1977. *Histoire naturelle*, book VII (trans. R. Schilling). Paris, Les Belles Lettres.
Pluche, N.-A. 1746. *Spectacle de la nature*, vol. V. Paris, La Veuve Estienne et Fils.
Plutarch 1770. 'De la fortune', in Plutarque, *Essais de philosophie et de morale* (trans. L. Castilhon). Bouillon, Société Typographique.
Polybius 1921. *Histoire* (trans. P. Waltz), vol. II. Paris, Garnier Frères.
Pope, A. 1993 (first edn 1733–4). *An essay on man* (ed. M. Mack). London, Routledge.
Porphyry 1977. *De l'abstinence* (text established and translated by J. Bouffartigue). Paris, Les Belles Lettres.
Porsniev, B. F. 1974. *O nachale tchelovecheskoi istori* [On the beginnings of human history]. Moscow, Nauka.

Potts, R. 1983. 'Foraging for faunal resources by early hominids at Olduvai, Tanzania', in Clutton-Brock, J. and Grigson, C., eds., *Animals and Archaeology: hunters and their prey*. Oxford, BAR International Series 163, pp. 51–62.
  1984. 'Home bases and early hominids', *American Scientist* 72: 338–47.
Premack, D. 1976. *Intelligence in ape and man*. Hillsdale, NJ, Lawrence Erlbaum.
  1985. 'Comparing mental representation in human and nonhuman animals', *Sociological Research* 51: 985–99.
  1988. 'Minds with and without language', in Weiskrantz, L., ed., *Thought without language*. Oxford, Clarendon Press, pp. 46–65.
Propp, V. 1972 (first Russian edn 1928). *Morphologie du conte*. Paris, Gallimard.
Prudentius 1948. 'Contre Symmaque', in Prudence, *Œuvres* (trans. M. Lavarenne), vol. III. Paris, Les Belles Lettres.
Pufendorf, S. 1706. *Le droit de la nature et des gens ou système général des principes les plus importants de la morale de la jurisprudence, et de la politique*. Amsterdam, Gerard Kuyper.
  1732. *Introduction à l'histoire générale et politique de l'Univers*. Amsterdam, Gerard Kuyper.
Pyke, G. H. 1974. 'Optimal foraging theory: a critical review', *Annual Review of Ecology and Systematics* 15: 523–75.
Pyke, G. H., Pulliam, H. R. and Charnov, E. L. 1977. 'Optimal foraging: a selective review of theory and tests', *The Quarterly Review of Biology* 52: 137–54.
Rabelais, F. 1966. *Le tiers livre*. Paris, Gallimard.
Richards, G. 1986. 'Freed hands or enslaved feet? A note on the behavioral implications of ground-dwelling bipedalism', *Journal of Human Evolution* 15: 143–50.
Robertson, W. 1777. *The history of America*. London, W. Strahan and T. Cadell.
Robinson, J. T. 1972. *Early hominid posture and locomotion*. Chicago, University of Chicago Press.
Roche, H. 1980. *Premiers outils taillés d'Afrique*. Paris, Société d'Ethnographie.
Rodman, P. S. and McHenry, H. 1980. 'Bioenergetics and the origin of hominid bipedalism', *American Journal of Physical Anthropology* 52: 103–6.
Roger, J. 1971. *Les sciences de la vie dans la pensée française du XVIIIe siècle*. Paris, Armand Colin.
Rogers, E. S. 1962. *Round Lake Ojibwa*. Royal Ontario Museum, Division of Art and Archaeology, Occasional Papers 5.
Rosny Aîné, J.-H. 1985. *Romans préhistoriques*. Paris, Robert Laffont.
Rousseau, J.-J. 1973 (first edn 1755). 'Discours sur l'origine de l'inégalité parmi les hommes', in Rousseau, J.-J., *Du contrat social*. Paris, Union Générale d'Editions, pp. 275–438.
Royer, C. 1870. *Origine de l'homme et des sociétés*. Paris, Masson.
Rupke, N. A. 1983. 'The study of fossils in the romantic philosophy of history and nature', *History of Science* 21: 389–413.
Ruse, M. 1982. *Darwinism defended*. London, Adison-Wesley.
Ruyle, E. E. 1977. 'Labor, people and culture: a labor theory of human origins', *Yearbook of Physical Anthropology* 20: 136–63.

Sahlins, M. 1968a. 'La première société d'abondance', *Les Temps Modernes* 268: 641–80.
  1968b. 'Notes on the original affluent society', in Lee, R. B. and DeVore, I., eds., *Man the hunter*. Chicago, Aldine, pp. 85–9.
  1972. *Stone Age economics*. London, Tavistock.
  1976. *Culture and practical reason*. Chicago, University of Chicago Press.
Sainte-Beuve, C. A. 1951 (first edn 1852). *Portraits littéraires*. Paris, Gallimard.
Schea, B. T. 1989. 'Heterochrony in human evolution: the case for neoteny reconsidered', *Yearbook of Physical Anthropology* 32: 69–101.
Schick, K. D. 1986. *Stone Age sites in the making: experiments in the formation and transformation of archaeological occurrences*. Oxford, BAR International Series.
  1987. 'Modeling the formation of early Stone Age artifact concentrations', *Journal of Human Evolution* 16: 789–807.
Schnapp, A. 1997. *Le chasseur et la cité: chasse et érotique dans la Grèce ancienne*. Paris, Albin Michel.
Schultz, A. H. 1950. 'The physical distinctions of man', *Proceedings of the American Philosophical Society* 94: 428–49.
Seneca 1971. *Lettres à Lucilius* (trans. H. Noblot). Paris, Les Belles Lettres.
Service, E. 1962. *Primitive social organisation*. New York, Random House.
Servier, J. 1967. *Histoire de l'utopie*. Paris, Gallimard.
Shipman, P. 1975. 'Implications of drought for vertebrate fossil assemblages', *Nature* 257: 667–8.
  1986a. 'Scavenging or hunting in early Hominids: theoretical framework and tests', *American Anthropologist* 88: 27–43.
  1986b. 'Studies of hominid–faunal interactions at Olduvai Gorge', *Journal of Human Evolution* 15: 691–706.
Shipman, P. and Phillips-Conroy, J. 1977. 'Hominid tool-making versus carnivore scavenging', *American Journal of Physical Anthropology* 46: 77–86.
Shipman, P. and Rose, J. 1985. 'Early hominid hunting, butchering and carcass processing behaviors: approaches to the fossil records', *Journal of Anthropological Archaeology* 2: 57–98.
Simons, E. L. and Pilbeam, D. 1965. 'Preliminary revision of the Dryopithecinae', *Folia Primatologica* 3: 81–152.
Simpson, G. G. 1950. *The meaning of evolution*. Oxford, Oxford University Press.
Smellie, W. 1790. *The philosophy of natural history*, vol. 1. Edinburgh, Charles Elliot.
Smith, E. A. 1983. 'Anthropological applications of Optimal Foraging Theory: a critical review', *Current Anthropology* 24: 625–51.
Smith, G. E. 1912. 'President's address. Anthropological Section', *Report of the British Association for the Advancement of Science* 1912: 575–98.
Smuts, B. B., Cheney, D. L., Seyfarth, R. M., Wrangham, R. W. and Struhsaker, T. T., eds. 1987. *Primate societies*. Chicago, University of Chicago Press.
Sollas, W. J. 1909. 'President's address', *Quarterly Journal of the Geological Society of London* 1909: i–cxxii.
Sophocles 1981. *Sophocle, Œuvres*, vol. 1, *Antigone* (text established by A. Dain and translated by P. Mazon). Paris, Les Belles Lettres.

Spencer, J. 1989. 'Anthropology as a kind of writing', *Man* 24: 145–64.
Stanley, S. M. 1975. 'Clades versus clones in evolution: why we have sex', *Science* 190: 382–3.
Starck, D. 1960. 'Das Cranium eines Schimpansefoetus', *Morphologisches Jahrbuch* 100: 559–647.
Stephens, D. W. and Krebs, J. R. 1986. *Foraging theory*. Princeton, Princeton University Press.
Stewart, D. 1795 (first edn 1793). *Essays on philosophical subject, by the late Adam Smith*. London, T. Cadell Jun., W. Davies; Edinburgh, W. Creech.
Stocking, G. W. 1987. *Victorian anthropology*. New York, The Free Press.
Stoczkowski, W. 1990. 'Modele optymalizacyjne w archeologii, czyli rozwazania o spekulacji metafizycznej [Optimisation models. Some reflections on metaphysical speculation in archaeology]', *Archeologia Polski* 35: 113–33.
  1991. 'Origine de l'homme: entre l'anthropologie naïve et savante'. PhD thesis, Ecole des Hautes Etudes en Sciences Sociales, Paris.
  1992a. 'Préhistoire, ethnologie et approche prédictive: les tentations d'une épistémologie spontanée', in Gallay, A., Audouze, F. and Roux V., eds., *Ethnoarchéologie: justification, problèmes, limites*, XIIe Rencontres internationales d'archéologie et d'histoire, Antibes. Juan-les-Pins, Editions APDCA, pp. 33–44.
  1992b. 'Essai sur la matière première de l'imaginaire anthropologique. Analyse d'un cas', *Revue de Synthèse* 4th series, 113: 439–57.
  1992c. 'Les origines de l'homme. Epistémologie, narration et banalités collectives', *Gradhiva, Revue d'Histoire et d'Archives de l'Anthropologie* 11: 67–80.
  1992d. 'Origines de l'homme: quand la science répète le mythe', *La Recherche* 244: 746–50.
  1993. 'La préhistoire: les origines du concept', *Bulletin de la Société Préhistorique Française* 60: 13–21.
  1995a. 'Le portrait de l'ancêtre en singe. L'hominisation sans évolutionnisme dans la pensée naturaliste du XVIIIe siècle', in Corbey, C. and Theunissen, B., eds., *Ape, man, apeman: changing views since 1600*. Leiden, Department of Prehistory, Leiden University, pp. 141–55.
  1995b. 'Le bipède et sa science. Histoire d'une structure de la pensée naturaliste', *Gradhiva, Revue d'Histoire et d'Archives de l'Anthropologie* 17: 16–43.
  1996. *Aux origines de l'humanité*. Paris, Pocket.
Stomma, L. 1986. 'Géographie mythique. Entre Jules Verne et Gérard de Villiers', *Etudes Rurales*, 103–4: 235–55.
  1988. 'Comptes rendus des conférences de l'année universitaire 1987–1988', *Ecole Pratique des Hautes Etudes, Annuaire* 96: 151–4.
Struhsaker, T. T. and Hunkeler, P. 1971. 'Evidence of tool-using by chimpanzees in the Ivory-Coast', *Folia Primatologica* 15: 212–19.
Strum, S. C. 1981. 'Processes and products of change: baboon predatory behavior at Gilgil, Kenya', in Harding, O. and Teleki, G., eds., *Omnivorous primates*. New York, Columbia University Press, pp. 255–302.

Sugardjito, J. and Nurhadu, N. 1979. 'Meat-eating behavior in orangutans, *Pongo pygmaeus*', *Primates* 20: 513–24.
Sutcliffe, A. 1970. 'Spotted hyena: crusher, gnawer, digester, and collector of bones', *Nature* 227: 1110–3.
Szalay, F. S. 1975. 'Hunting-scavenging protohominids: a model of hominid origins', *Man* 10: 420–9.
Szyfman, L. 1982. *Lamarck et son époque*. Paris, Masson.
Tanner, A. R. 1979. *Bringing home animal: religious ideology and mode of production in the Mistassini Cree hunters*. London, C. Hurts.
Tanner, N. P. and Zihlman, A. L. 1976. 'Women in evolution. Innovation and selection in human origins', *Signs* 1: 585–608.
Teilhard de Chardin, P. 1956. *L'apparition de l'homme*. Paris, Seuil.
Teleki, G. 1973. *The predatory behavior of wild chimpanzees*. Lewisburg, PA, Bucknell University Press.
　1981. 'The omnivorous diet and eclectic habitats of chimpanzees in Gombe National Park, Tanzania', in Harding, O. and Teleki, G., eds., *Omnivorous primates*. New York, Columbia University Press, pp. 303–43.
Testart, A. 1986. *Essai sur les fondements de la division sexuelle du travail chez les chasseurs-cueilleurs*. Paris, Editions de l'EHESS.
Thevet, A. 1982 (first edn 1577–8). *Les singularités de la France antarctique*. Paris, Le Temps.
Tilley, C. 1989. 'Archaeology as socio-political action in the present', in Pinsky, V. and Wylie, A., eds., *Critical traditions in contemporary archaeology*. Cambridge, Cambridge University Press, pp. 104–15.
Tinland, F. 1968. *L'homme sauvage, homo ferus et homo sylvestris*. Paris, Payot.
Tobias, P. V. 1987. 'The brain of *Homo habilis*: a new level of organisation in cerebral evolution', *Journal of Human Evolution* 16: 741–61.
Toth, N. P. 1985. 'The Oldovan reassessed: a close look at early stone artifacts', *Journal of Archaeological Science* 12: 101–20.
　1987. 'Behavioral inferences from early stone artifacts assemblages: an experimental model, *Journal of Human Evolution* 16: 763–87.
Toth, N. and Schick, K. D. 1986. 'The first million years: the archaeology of protohuman culture', in Schiffer, M., ed., *Advances in archaeological method and theory* 9: 1–96. New York, Academic Press.
Toth, N. and Woods, M. 1989. 'Molluscan shell knives and experimental cutmarks on bones', *Journal of Field Archaeology* 16: 250–4.
Toulmin, S. and Goodfield, J. 1969. *The discovery of time*. New York, Harper and Row.
Turgot, A. R. J. 1973 (first French edn 1750). 'On universal history', in Meek, R., ed., *Turgot on progress, sociology and economics*. Cambridge, Cambridge University Press, pp. 61–118.
Tutin, C. E. G., McGrew, W. C. and Baldwin, P. J. 1981. 'Response of wild chimpanzees to potential predators', in Chiarelli, B. and Corruccini, R. S., eds., *Primate behavior and sociobiology*. Berlin, Springer, pp. 136–41.

Tyson, E. 1699. *Orang-outang sive Homo sylvestris: or the anatomy of a pygmie, compared with that of a monkey, an ape and a man.* London, Thomas Bennett.

Varney, N. R. and Vilensky, J. A. 1980. 'Neuropsychological implications for preadaptation and language evolution', *Journal of Human Evolution* 9: 223–6.

Verdier, Y. 1979. *Façon de dire, façon de faire.* Paris, Gallimard.

Veyne, P. 1971. *Comment on écrit l'histoire.* Paris, Seuil.

    1983. *Les Grecs ont-ils cru à leurs mythes? Essai sur l'imagination constituante.* Paris, Seuil.

Vico, G. 1953 (first Italian edn 1744). *La science nouvelle.* Paris, Nagel.

Vigie, B. 1987. 'Essai d'étude méthodologique d'outils sur coquillages de la grotte de Camprafond', *L'Anthropologie* 91: 263–72.

Vilensky, J. A., van Hoesen, G. W. and Damasio, A. R. 1982. 'The limbic system and human evolution', *Journal of Human Evolution* 11: 447–60.

Vincens, A. 1980. 'Interprétation climatique des données palynologiques plio-pléistocène dans la région est du Lac Turcana (Kenya)', *Mémoires du Muséum National d'Histoire Naturelle* 27: 167–75.

Vincent, M., Dupré, J.-P., Lochy, J.-P. and Sémé, N. 1986. *Histoire: la France au fil du temps, de la préhistoire à 1789. Cycle Moyen 1.* Paris, Nathan.

Virey, J.-J. 1801. *Histoire naturelle du genre humain.* Paris, F. Dufrat.

    1824. *Histoire naturelle du genre humain, nouvelle édition, augmentée et entièrement refondue.* Paris, Crochard.

    1827 'Homme', in *Nouveau dictionnaire d'histoire naturelle appliquée aux arts,* vol. XV. Paris, Deterville, pp. 1–270.

    1841. 'Des causes physiologiques de la sociabilité chez les animaux et de la civilisation dans l'homme', *Bulletin de l'Académie Royale de Médecine,* sans numéro, pp. 3–15.

Virgil 1982. *Georgics* (trans. L. P. Wilkinson). London, Penguin Classics.

Vitruvius 1834. *Architecture* (trans. C. Perrault, first edn 1673). Paris, Gucerg.

Voltaire 1879 (first edn 1764). Article 'Homme' (*Dictionnaire philosophique*), in *Œuvres complètes de Voltaire.* Paris, Garnier Frères, vol. XIX, pp. 373–85.

    1963 (first edn 1756). *Essai sur les mœurs.* Paris, Garnier Frères.

    1968 (first edn 1759). *Candide ou l'optimisme.* Geneva, Droz.

Vrba, E. 1980. 'Evolution, species and fossils. How does life evolve?', *South African Journal of Sciences* 76: 61–84.

    1983. 'Macroevolutionary trends: new perspectives on the roles of adaptation and incidental effect', *Science* 22: 387–9.

    1984. 'What is species selection?', *Systematic Zoology* 33: 318–28.

    1985. 'Paleoecology of early Hominidae with special reference to Sterkfontein, Swartkrans and Kromdraai', in Coppens, Y., ed., *L'environnement des hominidés au Plio-Pléistocène.* Paris, Masson, pp. 345–70.

    1988. 'Late Pliocene climatic events and hominid evolution', in Grine, F. E., ed., *The evolutionary history of the robust Australopithecines.* New York, Aldine, pp. 405–26.

Vrba, E., Denton, G. H. and Prentice, M. L. 1989. 'Climatic influences on early hominid behaviour', *Ossa* 14: 127–56.
Vrba, E. and Gould, S. J. 1986. 'The hierarchical expansion of sorting and selection: sorting and selection cannot be equated', *Paleobiology* 12: 217–28.
Wade, M. 1979. 'The evolution of social interactions by family selection', *American Naturalist* 113: 399–417.
Walker, A. 1981. 'Dietary hypothesis and human evolution', *Philosophical Transactions of the Royal Society*, B 292: 57–64.
Walker, S. 1983. *Animal thought*. London, Routledge and Kegan Paul.
Wallace, A. R. 1872 (first edn 1858). 'De la tendance des variétés à s'écarter indéfiniment du type primitif', in *La sélection naturelle: Essais* (trans. L. de Candolle). Paris, pp. 28–44.
Ward, L. F., 1895. 'The relation of sociology to anthropology', *American Anthropologist* 8: 241–56.
Washburn, S. L. 1960. 'Tools and human evolution', *Scientific American* 239, pp. 63–75.
Watson, P. C. 1977. 'On the failure to eliminate hypotheses – a second look', in Johnson-Laird, P. N. and Watson, P. C., eds., *Thinking: readings in cognitive science*. Cambridge, Cambridge University Press, pp. 307–14.
Weiskrantz, L., ed. 1988. *Thought without language*. Oxford, Clarendon Press.
Wells, H. G. 1958 (first edn 1921). 'The Grisly folk', in *H. G. Wells: selected short stories*. Harmondsworth, Penguin, pp. 258–99.
Wescott, R. W. 1967. 'The exhibitionistic origin of human bipedalism', *Man* 2: 630.
White, T. D., Suwa, G. and Asfaw, B. 1994. '*Australopithecus ramidus*, a new species of early hominid from Aramis, Ethiopia', *Nature* 371: 306–12.
Wilcox, T. 1988. 'Hard times for the Cerne Giant: 20th-century attitudes to an ancient monument', *Antiquity* 62: 524–6.
Wilkinson, G. S. 1990. 'Food-sharing in vampire bats', *Scientific American* 262: 64–70.
Williams, G. C. 1966. *Adaptation and natural selection: a critique of some current evolutionary thought*. Princeton, Princeton University Press.
Woldegabriel, G. *et al.* 1994. 'Ecological and temporal placement of early Pliocene hominids at Aramis, Ethiopia', *Nature* 371: 330–3.
Wolpoff, M. H. 1971. 'Competitive exclusion', *Man* 6: 601–14.
Wood, B. A and Stack, C. G. 1980. 'Does allometry explain the difference between gracile and robust Australopithecinae?', *American Journal of Physical Anthropology* 52: 55–62.
Wright, S. 1932. 'The roles of mutation, inbreeding and selection in evolution', *Proceedings of the Sixth International Congress of Genetics* 1: 356–66.
Wynn, T. and McGrew, W. C. 1989. 'An ape's view of the Oldovan', *Man* 24: 383–98.
Wynne-Edwards, V. C. 1962. *Animal dispersion in relation to social behaviour*. Edinburgh, Oliver and Boyd.

1986. *Evolution through group selection*. London, Blackwell Scientific.
Wytteman, J.-P., ed. 1986. *Histoire, géographie. Classe de 6e*. Paris, Armand Colin.
Xenophon 1872. *Entretiens mémorables de Socrate*. Paris, Delagrave.
Zihlman, A. L. 1978. 'Subsistence and social organisation among early hominids', *Signs* 4: 4–20.
 1987. American Association of Physical Anthropologists Annual Luncheon Address, April 1985: 'Sex, sexes, and sexism in human origins', *Yearbook of Physical Anthropology* 30: 1–19.
Zihlman, A. L. and Lowenstein, R. 1983. '*Ramapithecus* and *Pan paniscus*. Significance for human origin', in Ciochon, R. L. and Corruccini, R. S., eds., *New interpretation of ape and human ancestry*. New York, Plenum Press, pp. 677–94.
Zinoviev, A. 1983. *Homo sovieticus*. Paris, Julliard.
Zirkle, C. 1941. 'Natural selection before the "Origin of species" ', *Proceedings of the American Philological Society* 84: 71–123.
 1946. 'The early history of the idea of the inheritance of acquired characters and of pangenesis', *Transactions of the American Philosophical Society*, new series, 25, 2: 91–150.

Index

aboriginal peoples, 3, 81–2, 95
  see also contemporary cultures
actualist research *see* archaeological research
adaptability, 93
adaptation, 151–2, 158–9
  cranium, 156–7
Africa, 58, 65
  East, 56–7, 59, 134, 166
  Plio-Pleistocene period, 175
aggressiveness, 160
  human nature, 182–3
Agta, 115, 118
America (first representations of), 3, 189–90
analysis, logicist, 47–8, 69
anatomy, 105, 159–60
  comparison of apes and humans, 43, 112
  Lamarckism, 148
  neotenic retardation, 165
Anaxagoras, *125*
Anaximander, *125*
ancestors, of humans, 43–4
ancient world *see* Antiquity
animality
  prehuman and early human, 42–3, 45, 77, 128–9
  strata of human nature, 141–3
  Wild Man, 81
animals
  food sharing, 121–2
  fossil remains, 4, 59
  hunting behaviour, 116
  see also predators
Annaud, Jean-Jacques, 11
anthropogenesis *see* hominisation
Antipodes, 81–2, 189–90
Antiquity
  concepts
    bipedalism, 73
    human nature, 120, 142
    human origin, 14–15, 42, 70–2, 84–5, 87, 123

  inheritance of acquired characteristics, 93–4
  nature, 15–16, 20, 63–4, 66
  epistemological principles, 192
  philosophers, 23, 26, 31–2
  portrayal in films, 189
  see also myths
Apache, Mescalero, 116
apes, 61–2, 67, 99
  ancestors of humans, 43–4
  characteristics, 41–2, 112
  chimpanzees, 58, 78, 121
  orang-utans, 81–2
archaeological research, 30–2, 172–7
Ardrey, Robert, *33*–5*n*, *51*, 61, 65, 69–70, 76, 78, 82, 85, 92, 103–4, 106, 113–14, 135, 148, 183
Aristotle, 39, 43, 73, 93–4, *124–5*, 131, 136, 188
art, Palaeolithic, 10
Ascher, Robert, *33*, 44, *51*, 65, 69–70, 82, 85, 87, 89–90, 97, 100, 104, 108–9, 111, 121, 144, 187
Asia, 64–5
assumptions in anthropology *see* naïve anthropology
Athabascans, Northern, 145*n*
Auden, W. H., 191
Australopithecines, 57*n*–8*n*, 65, 160

baboons, 58
Bacon, Sir Francis, 179
Bagford, John, 4
Bahrushyn, S., 9
Bal des Ardents (1392), 79–80
Bartholomew, G. A., 39, *126*
Batten, David C., 76
Bazylevic, K., 9
Beckerman, S. J., *34*, *51*, 121
behaviour, human
  stimuli, 138–40
Bella Coola, 118

225

Bergson, Henri, 181
Bernheimer, Robert, 79
Bernstein, S., 8–10
Bible, the, 20
  Book of Daniel, 74
  Ecclesiastes, 18
  Genesis, 5, 66
  Job, 156
  Leviticus, 119
binary oppositions, *24*–7, 45, 60, 66–7, 127–8
  'human' and animal characteristics, 74–5, 88
  'human' and ape characteristics, 41–2, 44
  strata of human nature, 141–3
  see also inversion
binary sequences, 48
biological determinism, 115
biology, molecular, 94
bipedalism, 40–1, 49, 73–7, 86–91, 111, 129, 158
Birdsell, J., 39, *126*
birthplace, hominisation, 64–5
Bloch, Marc, 197
blood, 118–19
Bock, W., 152
Bohr, Niels, 68
Bolk, L., 165
bone assemblages, 174–7
  see also fossil remains
Borges, José Luis, 187
Boriskovski, Pavel I., *34*, 45, *51*, 65, 69, 87, 102, 106, 108–11, 182, 185
Bory de Saint-Vincent, J.-B.-G.-M., 63
Bossuet, J.-B., 20, 104
Boulanger, Nicolas-Antoine, 12–14, 106, 180
Boulle, Pierre, 44
Bowler, Peter J., 195*n*
Boyle, Robert, 156
Brace, C. L., 94
brain
  and language, 97–8
  size, 40–1, 100–3
  see also cranium
Brain, C. K., 175
Brongniart, A., 31
Buckland, William, 31, 175
Buffon, Georges-Louis Leclerc, Comte de, 12–13, 21–2, 30, 43, 104, 119, 137, 178
Burnet, James (lord Monboddo), 12–13, 43, 106, 112, *124*

Cabanis, P. J. G., 119–20, 146
Calvino, Italo, 187
canine teeth, 91–2, 94–6
carnival, 80
carnivores *see* predators
Cartailhac, Emile, 4

Carvajal, Francisco de, 3
Casanova, Giovanni Giacomo, 2
causal relations, 46–*50*, 52–3, 168, 186
  explanatory mechanisms, 68–9, 132, 134, 147, 150
  first mentions in literature, 123–*4*, 127
  see also causality; hominisation scenarios
causality, 52, 168, 179–80
  cognition, 105–6
  communicating characteristics and levels, 162
  conceptual structures, 197
  explanatory mechanisms, 68–9
  hominisation scenarios, 48–*50*
  ideologies, 186
  see also causal relations
caves, 30–2
Central Eskimo, 117
Cerne Abbas Giant, 80
Cervantes, Miguel de, 79
Chaline, J., 165
characteristics
  animal, 81, 88, 128–9
  ape, 41–4, 61–2, 112
  communicating, 159–64
  explanatory mechanisms, 132, 134, 147, 155
  'human', *36*–46, 67, 88, 123–7, 181, 186
    bipedalism, 74–7, 86–91
    brain size, 100–3
    cognition, 98–9, 102–7
    cooperation, 107–10
    culture, 100–1
    food sharing, 113–14, 121–2
    free hands, 86–91, 101–2
    hunting, 69–72, 107–9, 113–23
    language, 97–100, 110–13
    perfectibility, 104–7
    reduced canine teeth, 91–6
    sexual division of labour, 113–15, 120–1
    social life, 109–11, 121–2
    tool use, 77–9, 82–92, 94–8, 101–2, 122–3
    see also human nature (concepts of)
  see also Lamarckism
Chaumeil, J.-P., 74
child rearing, 115–16
chimpanzees, 58, 62, 78, 99, 112, 121
Chipewyans, 164–5
Christianity
  concept of Paradise, 20
  concepts of human nature, 142
  doctrine on human origin, 5, 16
  see also religion
chronology, 52, 65
Cicero, 15–16, 31, 73
civilisation, industrial, 22–6
Clark, J. D., 39

climate, 56–8n, 134, 137–8
  see also environment
clubs see weapons
cognition, 17, 98–9, 102–7, 138–40
collectives, 182
common-sense anthropology see naïve anthropology
common-sense knowledge (eighteenth-century definition), 196–8
communicating characteristics and levels, 159–64
communication see language
Communist Party of the Soviet Union, 23, 185
Comte, Auguste, 146, 193
conceptual structures, 2, 32, 129–30, 186–7, 191, 196–8
  ethnological research, 139
  explanatory mechanisms, 68–9
  hominisation scenarios, 49–50, 52, 54–6
  longue durée, 27–8, 64, 141
  narrative, 187–8
  see also ideas
Condorcet, Marquis de, 20–1, 106, 120
conflict, 71, 95, 108–9
conjectural anthropology, 42, 130, 171–2, 189–90
  environmental determinism, 136
  sources, 169–70
  struggle for survival, 63
  validation, 178
  see also histoire raisonnée
conjectural history see histoire raisonnée
consensus (of ideas), 130
contemporary cultures, 43, 74, 88, 122, 139, 144–5
  environmental determinism, 137–8
  hunter-gatherers, 26, 164–5
  sexual division of labour, 115–19
  see also aboriginal peoples
context (of ideas), 69, 194–7
continuity (of ideas) see recurrent ideas
Coon, Carleton S., *33*, *51*, 65, 69–70, 78, 85, 87, 92, 104, 106, 110–11, 113–14, 121, *124*, 171n, 180, 184, 187
cooperation, 107–10
Coppens, Yves, 57n, 166
Copper Eskimo, 116–17
correlation of growth see communicating characteristics and levels
Courbin, P., 173, 177
Court de Gébelin, A., 80
cranium
  adaptation, 156–7
  morphology, 160, 165
  see also brain

Cree, Eastern, 116
cultural constructs, 54, 196–7
cultural usefulness, 109–10, 143–4
culture, 100–1, 123n, 138–40, 142, 169
  communicating characteristics and levels, 163–4
  origin, 8–17, 98
  perfectibility, 104–7
Cynics (philosophical movement), 26

Dart, Raymond A., 34
Darwin, Charles, 16, *33*–4, 44, *51*, 62–3, 75, 78, 85, 87, 91–3, 95–6, 100–1, 103, 119, *124*, *126*, 127, 142, 148, 156–9
Darwin, Erasmus, 93
Darwinism, 35, 101–2, 131–*3*, 147–50, 152–8, 163
  adaptation, 151–2
  fitness, 151
  natural selection, 150–1
  sociobiology and optimisation theories, 152–3
  see also evolution
Delamétherie, Jean-Claude, 60, 71–2, 93, 103, 119
Delumeau, J., 119–20
Demosthenes, 40
dentition see teeth
determinism
  biological, 115
  environmental, 16–17, 72, 134–8
Devilliers, C., 165
Dicaearchus, 71
Diderot, D., 22, 93, 141, 148
diet, 57–8, 70–2, 96
  see also food
difference (between human populations), 137–8
dinosaurs, 29–30, 40
Diodorus Siculus, 15, 70–1, 110, *124*, 144
Doctor Pangloss, 155–6
Drake, Sir Francis, 95
dreams, 139
du Cleuziou, Henri, 193
duality see binary oppositions
Dupré, J.-P., 9
Durkheim, Emile, 144, 146

East Africa, 56–7, 59, 134, 166
Eastern Cree, 116
Eco, Umberto, 45
ecological change see environment
economic efficiency, 116–17, 164
eighteenth century, 30, 169–70
  concepts
    adaptability, 93

eighteenth century (cont.)
　bipedalism, 74–5
　common-sense knowledge, 196–8
　human nature, 120, 141–2
　human origin, 43, 70–2, 87, 110, 123
　language, 99
　nature, 60–1, 66
　necessity and innovation, 144
　perfectibility, 104
　prehistory, 4–5, 22–3, 31
　tool use, 77–8
　usefulness, 148
epistemological principles, 192–3
Hippocratic theory, 136
philosophers, 11–18, 20–3, 45, 180, 196
Eloy, M., 189
Empedocles, 19n
empirical data, 1, 5–6, 28–9, 40, 54–6, 129–30, 170, 178–9, 190–2, 197–8
　archaeological research, 30–2, 172–7
　Australopithecines, 160
　environmental change, 56–9, 65–6
　ethnological research, 139, 145
　'human' characteristics, 69–70, 72, 78, 89
　primates, 41
　see also hominisation scenarios
empiricism, 193
Encyclopédie, ou Dictionnaire raisonné des sciences, des arts et des métiers, 196
energy efficiency, bipedalism, 90
Engels, Friedrich, 33–4, 87, 89, 100–2, 104, 124, 138, 140–2, 144, 148, 181–2, 185
Enlightenment see eighteenth century
environment, 51, 61–3
　change, 49, 56–9, 65–70, 72, 75–7, 82–3, 85–6
　see also climate; nature (concepts of)
environmental determinism, 16–17, 72, 134–8
Epicureans (philosophical movement), 23
epistemology, 53–5
　ideologies, 195–7
　principles, 178–9, 190–4
equilibrium, narrative structures, 188
erroneous ideas, 29–30, 91
Eskimo, 116–17
ethnological research, 139, 144–5
Europe
　folklore, 79–81
　　proverbs, 145
　literature, 125–6
evolution, 16, 52, 54–5, 56n, 131–5, 157–8, 182
　historical context, 194
　see also Darwinism; explanatory mechanisms
Ewaipanomas, 3

exaptation, 158–9, 164
excavations see archaeological research
explanatory mechanisms, 68–9, 131–4, 146–7, 158–9, 165–7
　communicating characteristics and levels, 159–65
　Darwinism, 149–58
　environmental determinism, 134–8
　individualism, 146
　Lamarckism, 147–9
　materialism, 138–43
　utilitarianism, 143–5
　see also evolution

Faust, 142
feminism, 86, 184
Fénelon, François de Salignac de la Mothe, 156
Ferguson, Adam, 43, 45
fiction
　Doctor Pangloss, 155–6
　Faust, 142
　portrayal of apes, 44
　portrayal of prehistory, 10–11, 110
　rules of narrative, 190
　Sherlock Holmes, 173
films
　portrayal of Antiquity, 189
　portrayal of apes, 44
　portrayal of prehistory, 11
　westerns, 46
fire, 8–9
Fischer, D. H., 179
fitness, 151–2
Flaubert, Gustave, 189–90
Focht, A., 9
folk tales, 188
folklore
　European, 79–81
　　proverbs, 145
　modern, 156
food, 66, 151, 177–8
　sharing, 113–14, 121–2, 173–4
　shortage, 59, 153
　see also diet; productivity (plants)
forest, 56–9, 61–2, 65–6, 69–70
formulae, explanatory see explanatory mechanisms
Fort Ternan site, 65
fossil remains, 166, 172
　animals, 4, 59
　see also bone assemblages
　dinosaurs, 30
　hominids, 66, 70
Fourier, Charles, 23
France, schoolbooks, 7–11, 27

Galen, 136
Gardin, Jean-Claude, 47
Gardner, R. A. and Gardner, B., 99
gathering, 114–16, 164–5, 173–4
  see also hunter-gatherers
Gauthier, Y., 8–10
Geertz, Clifford, 196
gender, 121
  roles, 184–5
generalisations, 168–9, 171
genetic change, 166
genomes, 161
geographical isolation, 165–6
Goethe, Johann Wolfgang von, 80, 142
Goguet, A.-Y., 78, 109–10, 144
Golden Age see nature (concepts of)
Gould, Stephen Jay, 155–6, 158–60, 162, 165
Gralhon, R., 9–10
Greco-Roman period see Antiquity
Gregory of Nyssa, 15, 73, 85, 91, *126*
Gusdorf, Georges, 170

Hadar Kada Gona site, 89
Haeckel, E., 88, 107
hands, free, 86–91, 101–2, 158–9
Haraucourt, Edmond, 11, 79, 110
Hardy, A., 76
Hart, T. and Hart, J. A., 58
Helvétius, Claude-Adrien, 13, 19, 21–2, *126*
Hercules, 80
Herder, J. G., 62, 71, 99, *124*
heredity see communicating characteristics and levels
Hesiod, 19n
Hildebert, the Venerable, 20
Hill, Andrew, 65
Hill, Kim, *34*, 44, *51*, 66–7, 69, 72, 92, 100, 102, 113–15, *126*, 150–1, 171
Hippocrates, 136
Hippocratic theory, 136–7
histoire raisonnée
  binary oppositions, 45
  cognition, 103
  conceptual structures, 27–8
  cooperation, 109
  hominisation scenarios, 32, 34
  human nature, 141–2
  prehistory, 28–32
  progress, 23
  struggle for survival, 106
  Voltaire, 156
  see also conjectural anthropology
historical context (of ideas), 69, 194–7
history
  and human nature, 180
  in schoolbooks, 6
  of science, 5, 54, 192–8
Hobbes, Thomas, 144
Hockett, Charles F., *33*, 44, *51*, 65, 69–70, 82, 85, 87, 89–90, 97, 100, 104, 108–9, 111, 121, 144, 187
Holbach, Paul Henri Thiry, Baron d', 13–14, 21, 136
Holmes, Sherlock, 173
Home, Henry, *124*
Homer, 3, 31
hominids, *51*, 56–9, 64–6, 70, 78, 160, 166, 172, 174
  cognition, 139–40
  fitness, 151
  Neanderthals, 31
  sexual dimorphism, 96
  sexual division of labour, 121
hominisation, 6–8, 60, 67, 105–7, 134–5, 140
  apes as ancestors, 43–4
  birthplace, 64–5
  environment, 61–3
  and human nature, 180
  ideologies, 180–7
  see also prehistory
hominisation scenarios
  environmental change, 56–9, 69–70, 72–3, 75–7, 82–3, 85–6
  explanatory mechanisms, 131–3, 143–4, 148–50, 152–4
  'human' characteristics, 69–72, 75–9, 82–123
  morphology, 45–56
  narrative, 187–90
  selection, 32–8
  validation, 166–7, 170–3, 177–9
  see also causal relations; empirical data
homo sapiens, 64
Horace, 26, 70–1
Huffman, M. A., 83
Hugo, Victor, 119
human behaviour see behaviour, human
'human' characteristics see characteristics
human nature (concepts of), 141–3, 180–4
  see also characteristics
human origin see origin (concepts of)
human populations (difference between), 137–8
human sciences, 32, 180, 188–9, 191
Hume, David, 168
hunter-gatherers, 23–6, 145n, 164–5, 181
  see also gathering; hunting
hunting, 49, 71–2, 111, 170, 172–4
  cooperation, 107–9
  environmental change, 68–70
  sexual division of labour, 68, 113–21, 164–5
  tool use, 122–3
  see also hunter-gatherers

idealism, 140–1
ideas, 1, 69, 194–8
  consensus, 130
  erroneous, 29–30, 91
  and exaptation, 164
  of hominisation, 38
  preconceived, 179
  recurrent, 3–4, 53–6, 147, 186–90
  see also conceptual structures
ideologies, 26–7, 35, 54–5, 180–7, 198
  epistemological, 195–7
  scientific, 193–4
imagination, 1–2, 130, 139
individualism, 17, 146
industrial civilisation, 22–6
infancy *see* reproductive functions
inheritance of acquired characteristics
  see Lamarckism
innovation, and necessity, 62, 143–5
intellectual tradition, 192
  rejection of the past, 193–6
interpretation (of empirical data), 172–7
Inuit *see* Eskimo
inversion, 43–4, 86, 91, 129, 184
  concepts of nature, 19–20, 22–3
  see also binary oppositions
Isaac, Glynn L., *33*, 56n, 113–15, 121–2, 150, 173–5, 177–8, 184
isolation, geographical, 165–6

Jacob, François, 29, 135
Job, 156
Jolly, Clifford, *33, 51*, 65, 69, 82, 96, 108, 111, 113–15, 122, 158–9, 170, 172

Kanapoi site, 75
Kandyaus, 43
Kant, Immanuel, 146–8, 169
Kappler, Claude, 4
Keene, Arthur S., 153
Kelso, J., *34, 51*, 66, 113–15
Kenyapithecus, 65
knowledge
  common-sense (eighteenth-century definition), 196–8
  scientific, 191–2
Köhler, W., 76
Korovkin, F., 8–10
Kortland, Adrian, 58
Kuhn, Thomas S., 194–5
!Kung, 116, 164–5
Kurland, J. A., *34, 51*, 121
Kwakiutl, 118

labour
  concept, 182

sexual division, 68, 113–18, 120–1, 139, 164–5, 173–4
Laetoli site, 75, 89
Lamarck, Jean-Baptiste de, *33*–4, 44, 73, 85, 87, 92–3, 101, 131, 148–9
Lamarckism, 92–4, 101–3, 127, 129, 131–3, 147–9
  see also characteristics
Landau, Misia, 188
language, 97–100, 110–13
  exaptation, 159
Latreille, Pierre-André, 41
Laughlin, W. S., *33, 51*, 69–70, 100, 104, 113–14, 122
Lawrence, W., *125*
laws, universal, 169–71, 177, 189, 196
Le Brun, P.-D., 81
Le Mere, 95
Leibengrub, P., 8–10
Lenin, V. I., 23
Leonardo da Vinci, 95–6
Leroi-Gourhan, André, *33*, 44, 87, 97–8, 113–15, 160
Leroy, L., 78
levels, communicating, 160–4
Lévi-Strauss, Claude, 43, 91, 118, 187–8, 197n
Lewontin, R., 155–6
Lhermite, F., 98–9
Linnaeus, Carolus, 43
literature
  concepts of human nature, 142
  'human' characteristics mentioned, 123–7
  popular, 79
    environmental determinism, 137–8
  Romantic, 26
Lochy, J.-P., 9
locomotion, free hands, 89
logic, 54–6
logicist analysis, 47–8, 69
longue durée structures, 27–8, 64, 141
Lovejoy, Arthur Owen, 195
Lovejoy, C. O., *34, 51*, 87, 96, 170
Lowenstein, R., 5
Lowie, Robert, 117
Lubbock, John, 16, 43
Lucretius, 14–15, 31–2, 70–1, 78–9, 95, 104, 110, *124–6*
Lumdsen, C., *34*, 44, *51*, 75, 87, 113–15, 121
Lysenko, T. D., 94

macaques, 83
McLennan, J. F., 16
Macrobius, 70–1
magic *see* religion
Malthus, Thomas R., 62
Manouvrier, Léonce, 64

Marx, Karl, 138, 142, 144
Marxism, 102, 181–2
materialism, 17, 138–44
matrices, conceptual *see* conceptual structures
Maurois, André, 191
Medawar, Peter, 157
menstruation, 118–19
mental faculties *see* cognition
Mescalero Apache, 116
Metternich, Prince Klemens von, 145
Middle Ages
  epistemological principles, 192
  folklore, 79–80
  portrayal of apes, 44
Millar, J., 106
Milza, P., 8–10
Miocene period 57n, 61, 166
'missing link', 81–2
modern folklore, 156
molecular biology, 94
Montagu, M. F. A., 94
Montesquieu, Charles de, 13, 169
moralisation, 180–3, 186
Morgan, L. H., 16
morphology
  anatomy, 105, 148, 160, 165
  comparison of apes and humans, 43, 112
  of hominisation scenarios, 45–56
Morris, Desmond, 142–3
Mortillet, Adrien and Gabriel de, 64
Moses, 20
myths, 71–2, 189–90
  Hercules, 80
  of origin, 18–19
  Prometheus, 84
  see also Antiquity

naïve anthropology, 2, 32, 69, 129–30, 171–3, 188–90
  concepts of nature, 66–7
  eighteenth century, 30, 169–70
  explanatory mechanisms, 131–2, 146–7, 153–4, 163, 165–7
  hominisation scenarios, 53–6, 123, 127
    cognition, 107
    hunting and diet, 70–2
    language, 99–100
    religion, 185
    sexual division of labour, 120
    struggle for survival, 82–5, 109
    tool use, 95, 102
narrative, 46, 187–92
natural causes (bone assemblages), 174–5
natural selection, 63, 94–5, 150–4, 159–64
  bipedalism, 90
naturalists, 61, 66

nature, human *see* human nature (concepts of)
nature (concepts of), *51*, 107, 120
  benevolent, 19–26
  hostile, 7–10, 12–18, 56–7, 59, 180–1, 185
  transitional, 60–1, 63–7, 71–2, 103, 127–9
  see also environment
Neanderthals, 31, 64
Nebuchadnezzar, King, 74
necessity, and innovation, 62, 143–5
Nemesius, 15
neotenic retardation, 165
Newton, Sir Isaac, 169–70
Nieckina, M., 8–10
Niestourkh, M. F., *33*, *51*, 75, 78, 85, 87, 108–9, 182
nineteenth century
  concepts
    animality, 43
    human nature, 141–2
    human origin, 70–2, 87–8, 123
    nature, 66
    prehistory, 31
    progress, 23
  Hippocratic theory, 136–7
Northern Athabascans, 145n

Oakley, Kenneth P., *33*, 39, 75, 85, 89–90, 97, 100, *124*
Ojibwa, Northern, 116–17
Olduvai sites, 174, 176–7
Omo Shungura site, 89
opposing pairs (of attributes)
  see binary oppositions
optimisation theories, 67, 152–4
orang-utans, 81–2
Origen, 85, *126*, 144–5, 156
origin (concepts of), 8–17, 70–2, 87, 123, 179–81
  culture, 98, 100, 106–7
  human
    Antiquity, 42, 84–5
    Christian doctrine, 5
    eighteenth century, 43, 60, 110, 120
    nineteenth century, 87–8
    myths of, 18–19
Osborn, Henry F., 64–5
Ourman, H., 8
Ovid, 19n, 70–1, 73, *125*

palaeoanthropological scenarios
  see hominisation scenarios
palaeoanthropology *see* conjectural anthropology; hominisation
Palaeolithic period, 7–8, 52
  archaeological research, 173
  art, 10

Palaeolithic period (*cont.*)
  in schoolbooks, 27
  see also Plio-Pleistocene period
Pangloss, Doctor, 155–6
Pankratova, A., 9
Paradise *see* Christianity; nature (concepts of)
Pasquier, Y., 8
past, the
  rejection of (intellectual tradition), 193–6
  relationship to
    hominisation scenarios, 197–8
    scientists, 192–3
Pausanias, 70–1
perfectibility, 104–7
perishable materials, tools, 90
Perry, R. J., 145*n*
philosophers
  Antiquity, 26, 31–2
  eighteenth century, 11–18, 20–3, 45, 61, 180, 196
  sixteenth century, 78
Pianka, E. R., 58
Pilbeam, D., 160
Pithecanthropus, 64
plant foods *see* diet; food; productivity (plants)
Plato, 73, 84, 91, 93, 120, *125–6*, 168
plausibility, 189–90
  conjectural anthropology, 172
play, 83–4
Pliny the Elder, 3, 73, 119, *126*, 189–90
Plio-Pleistocene period, 52, 57, 59, 61, 72, 134
  Africa, 175
  see also Palaeolithic period
Pluche, Abbé, *126*, 156
Polybius, 15
pongids, 166
Pope, Alexander, 71, 146, 169
popular literature, 79
  environmental determinism, 137–8
populations, human (difference between), 137–8
Porphyry, 71, *125*
Porsniev, B. F., 45
positivism, 193–5
posture, morphology, 160
preadaptation *see* exaptation
preconceived ideas, 179
predators, 7–9, 57–9, 66, 108–9
  creation of bone assemblages, 174–7
  see also animals
prehistory
  eighteenth-century concepts, 4–5, 22–3
  empirical data *versus* conjecture, 28–32
  and epistemological principles, 193
  in fiction, 110

and philosophers, 11–16
in schoolbooks, 6–11, 14
see also hominisation
primates, 41, 58–9, 70, 82–95
  apes *see* apes
  sexual dimorphism, 96
  tool use, 77–8
principles, epistemological, 178–9, 190–4
productivity (plants), 58
  see also food
progress, 21–3, 63, 180–2
prohibitions, 117–19, 164
  see also religion
Prometheus, 84
propaganda, 185
Propp, Vladimir, 188
Prudentius, 31, 73
Pseudo-Plutarch, *125*

Quiatt, D., *34*, *51*, 66, 113–15

rabbits, brain size, 101
Raleigh, Sir Walter, 3
received wisdom *see* common-sense knowledge; ideas; naïve anthropology
reciprocity *see* food; sharing
recurrent ideas, 3–4, 53–6, 147, 186–90, 195–7
rejection of the past (intellectual tradition), 193–6
relationship to the past
  hominisation scenarios, 197–8
  scientists, 192–3
religion, 9–10, 13–15, 48, 185
  see also Christianity; prohibitions
Renaissance period, Hippocratic theory, 136
reproductive functions, 115–16
residence, hunter-gatherers, 145*n*
revolutions, scientific, 193–5
Romantic literature, 26
Rosny Aîné, J.-H., 11
Rousseau, Jean-Jacques, 3, 12, 21, 39, 43, 76, 104, 107, 112, 120, *124–5*, 181
Royer, Clémence, 23, *33–4*, *51*, 61, 78, 80, 85, 108–9, *124*, 171, 180–1
Russia *see* Soviet Union
Ruyle, Eugene E., *33*, *51*, 62, 65, 69, 85, 87, 89–90, 92, 97, 108, 122, 146, 181, 185

Sahlins, Marshall D., 23–7
Sainte-Beuve, C. A., 1
savannah, 56–9, 61–2, 65, 69–70
scavenging, 39, 174–7
scenarios of hominisation *see* hominisation scenarios

schoolbooks, 6–11, 14
  France, 27
science, 1, 190–4
  concepts of human nature, 142–3
  history of, 5, 54, 195–8
  human sciences, 32, 180, 188–9
  principles, 178–9
  universal laws, 169
scientists, relationship to the past, 192–3
seated position, free hands, 88
selection *see* natural selection
sequences, binary, 48
seventeenth-century concepts
  necessity and innovation, 144
sexual dimorphism, 96
sexual division of labour, 68, 113–21, 139, 164–5, 173–4
sharing, 183–4
  see also food
shell tools, 90*n*
Sherlock Holmes, 173
Shipman, P., *34*, *51*
shortage, food, 59, 153
Siberia, 118
sixteenth century, philosophers, 78
Smith, S. E., 140
social life, 9, 13, 103, 109–11, 121–2, 138, 145*n*, 146
  primates, 83–4
sociobiology, 152–4, 161
sociology (of ideas), 194–6
solitary life, 110, 112
Sollas, W. J., 140
Sophocles, *125*
sorting, 162
Soviet Union
  and anthropology, 182, 185
  Communist Party, 23
  schoolbooks, 7–11
spatial strangulation, 165–6
speciation, 165–6
Spencer, Herbert, 16, 109
Spenser, Edmund, 79
Stewart, Dugald, 18
stimuli (affecting human behaviour), 138–40
Stoczkowski, Wiktor, *133*
stone tools, 174–5, 177
storytelling *see* narrative
strata (of human nature), 141–3
stratigraphy of functions *see* exaptation
structures
  conceptual *see* conceptual structures
  narrative *see* narrative

struggle for survival, 60–4, 82–5, 103, 106–7, 109, 135, 141–3, 153–4
symbolism, 74, 136, 164

taboos *see* prohibitions
Tanner, Nancy P., *33*, *51*, 65, 76, 82, 86–7, 96, 109, *126*, 170, 180, 184–5
taphonomy, bone assemblages, 175–6
teeth, 39–40, 150
  Australopithecines, 160
  canine, 91–2, 94–6
  size reduction, 158–9
Tertiary period, 52
Testart, Alain, 116–18, 164
Thacker, C., 156
Tiwi, 116
tools, 8, 49
  exaptation, 158–9
  hominisation scenarios, 77–8, 85–91, 101–2
  environmental change, 82–3
  hunting, 122–3
  origin of language, 97–8
  play, 83–4
  reduced canine teeth, 92, 94–6
  stone, 174–5, 177
  see also weapons
traditional explanations of hominisation
  see explanatory mechanisms
truthfulness, 189
Tylor, E. B., 16
Tyson, Edward, 112
Tzetzes, Johannes, 15

universal laws, 169–71, 177, 189, 196
usefulness, 76–7, 123, 147, 154–7
  anatomical, 148–9
  and communicating characteristics and levels, 159
  cultural, 109–10, 143–4
  language, 98
  and natural selection, 150–2, 160–4
utilitarianism, 10, 17, 112, 143–5
utopias *see* nature (concepts of); progress

validation, hominisation scenarios, 166–7, 170–3, 177–9
validity, universal laws, 171
variation *see* communicating characteristics and levels
Varro, 70–1
Verne, Jules, 138
Veyne, Paul, 2, 189
Vico, Giambattista, 142, 180
Villiers, Gérard de, 137–8
Vincent, M., 9

Vinci, Leonardo da, 95–6
Virey, J.-J., 39, 72–3, 88, 93, 103, 106–7, 109, 112, *124*, *126*, 141, 144
Virgil, 63–4, 66, *124*
Vitruvius, 15, 31, 73
Voltaire, 12–14, 78, 80–1, 106, 156
von Baer, K. E., 140
Vrba, Elisabeth, 158–9, 162

Wallace, A. R., 16
Ward, L. F., 140
Washburn, Sherwood L., *33*, *51*, 65, 78, 87, 89–90, 92, 100–1, 104, 110–11, *126*, 160, 170
weakness, 82–5
　women, 119–20
weapons, 13, 78–80, 82–3
　hunting, 117–18
　teeth and nails, 95–6
　see also tools
Weiskrantz, L., 99

Weismann, August, 94
Wells, H. G., 11
Westcott, R. W., 76
westerns, 46
Wild Man, 79–82, 129
Williams, W. G., 152
Wilson, O. E., *34*, 44, *51*, 75, 87, 113–15, 121
Wolpoff, M. H., *33*, *51*, 65, 78, 82, 85, 87, 89–90
women, 86, 113, 115–20, 129, 184–5
　and hunting, 164

Xenophon, 73, 76, *125*

Yagua, 74

Zihlman, Adrienne L., 5, *33*, *51*, 65, 76, 82, 86–7, 96, 109, *126*, 138–9, 170, 180, 184–5
Zola, Emile, 1–2
Zwang, A., 8